MASTERS OF NOTHING

MATTHEW HANCOCK & NADHIM ZAHAWI

MASTERS

OF

NOTHING

HOW THE CRASH WILL HAPPEN AGAIN UNLESS WE UNDERSTAND HUMAN NATURE

Biteback Publishing

First published in Great Britain in 2011 by
Biteback Publishing Ltd
Westminster Tower
3 Albert Embankment
London
SE1 7SP
Copyright © Matthew Hancock and Nadhim Zahawi 2011

ISBN 978-1-84954-143-5

10 9 8 7 6 5 4 3 2

A CIP catalogue record for this book is available from the British Library.

Set in Garamond and Opificio by Namkwan Cho
Cover design by Namkwan Cho

Printed and bound in Great Britain by
CPI Group (UK) Ltd, Croydon, CR0 4YY

CONTENTS

To Martha, my inspiration
To Lana, Doody and Fali

ACKNOWLEDGEMENTS

We both owe our thanks to our staff at Westminster. We could not have written the book without our team of researchers, William Hensher, Jennifer Donnellan, Simon Smethurst-McIntyre, and Luke Maynard, who worked on this book on top of their day-to-day responsibilities, and Helen Thomas, who gave up her own time. We are, as ever, grateful to Helyn Dudley and Marie Sallergard, who kept our lives in order while we wrote it. We are very grateful to Nick Boles, Janan Ganesh, Michael Hart, Peter Kellner, Adam Levinson, Jesse Norman, Stephan Shakespeare and Nick Walmsley, who read and commented on early drafts, whose comments improved the book immeasurably, and who kept us going. We are grateful to Iain Dale, Sam Carter and their team at Biteback publications, who were a pleasure to work with and taught us how publishing works. We are very grateful to Lord Adonis, Peter Riddell, Loren Austin, and Zoe Grun at the Institute for Government, for organising the launch, and to the Chancellor and his team at 11 Downing Street for allowing us to launch it there.

We conducted a wide range of interviews, including with some who prefer to remain anonymous. All were fascinating, many were passionate and some deliciously indiscrete. Among others, we are very grateful to: Henry Angest, Mark Bathgate, Meyrick Chapman, George Cooper, Nigel Doughty, Charlie Dunstone, Patrick Evershed, Lord Flight, David Halpern, Greg Hands, Sajid Javid, Stephen King, Sir Andrew Large, Andrew Law, Ruth Lea, Jonathan Martin, Jon Moulton, Ben Page, Neil Record, Vincent Reinhart,

Rohan Silva, Seamus Smith, Lord Turner, Simon Walker, Robin Wight and David Wright.

YouGov helped us explore aspects of human behaviour by carrying out interviews and polls, and we are especially grateful to Carole Stone, Stephan Shakespeare and Joe Twyman. Sponsorship to fund the research was provided by Johan Christofferson and Killik & Co, and we are specifically grateful to the Partners at Killik & Co. Finally, we are both grateful to our wives and families who put up with us when we added months spent writing a book to our already busy lives.

AUTHOR BIOGRAPHIES

Matthew Hancock is an economist and politician. He has been MP for West Suffolk since 2010, and is a member of the Public Accounts Committee and the Standard and Privileges Committee. Before entering Parliament he worked for his small family company, as an economist at the Bank of England, and as Chief of Staff to George Osborne. He once held the world record for the most northerly game of cricket ever played.

Nadhim Zahawi is an entrepreneur and politician. He has been the Member of Parliament for Stratford-on-Avon since 2010 and is a member of the Business, Innovation and Skills Select Committee. Prior to entering Parliament he started the market research and polling organisation YouGov, taking it public in 2005 and continuing as Chief Executive until his selection as a Parliamentary Candidate. He is also a non-executive Director of FTSE 250 recruitment business SThree Plc. He is a keen horse rider and used to be a useful show jumper many decades ago.

INTRODUCTION

This book is about how people behave.

Not how we think we behave, or how we'd like to behave, but how we really do.

It is a story of how failure to understand how we really behave helped cause one of the biggest crises in the history of capitalism. It's a story of the extraordinary extremes of human behaviour we witnessed by the so-called Masters of the Universe, of their greed, recklessness, and irrationality. Of how failure to understand that behaviour led to policy mistakes that magnified the crisis. And of how the crisis will happen again unless we do.

In short, this is a book that looks at the world as it is, not as we would wish it to be, and tries to draw lessons from what we see.

Some time ago, economists started to make an assumption that people were always rational. Treating everyone as a pure *homo economicus* helped make it easier for economists to build up models of how the world works. It helped explain things, and at first gave new insights. But over time, this assumption was used not just to explain the world, but to run it. It came to underpin our whole framework in business, in banks and in government for how the economy was run.

But we are not always rational. We all know that from every day of our lives. We may be rational some of the time. But when did someone last behave irrationally towards you? Was it this morning, or yesterday? Or perhaps last week? When did you last snap at someone without good reason? Today in the rush hour? From road rage to falling in love, we are surrounded by irrational behaviour. As new polling research for this book reveals, people are often irrational: they buy things they do not need and cannot afford, they fly off the handle at the smallest question, and they get carried away. Our hearts and our heads are often in conflict; the outcome is usually influenced by both.

Try as we might, individuals' actions cannot be accurately modelled. The average brain is around a million times more complex than a desktop computer. Modelling group behaviour is harder still. And we should be grateful we can't model everything accurately. Wouldn't life be dull?

These quirks of behaviour matter. The rules written for paragons of rationality had unintended consequences that overwhelmed the whole system. A combination of perverse rational incentives and raw human impulses led to group behaviour which was self-reinforcing and dangerous. Yet the growing storm went unnoticed by the authorities, because of their belief in the system they had created.

To stop another crash on this scale happening again, we need to understand how people really behave, and apply those lessons to how we run our economy.

For all the extraordinary development in our understanding of how the natural world works, and for all the amazing new technology that surrounds our lives, we know precious little about how and why human beings behave as we do. Worse, we apply almost nothing of what we do know to critical questions about how we manage our economy.

Pioneering thinkers and centuries of effort have expanded the perimeters of scientific knowledge past the wildest dreams of our forefathers. The scientific method of rigorous empiricism building a body of knowledge has improved the condition of man, and has made the modern world of widespread comfort in which we live possible for many.

When it comes to the empirical question of understanding

human behaviour, of the balance between rationality and irrationality, of nature versus nurture, our thinking has hardly advanced. It's all there in Aristotle: the battle between the rational and irrational; our need to develop self-control; the danger of wayward emotions; the pull of physical desires on the mind. The ancient descriptions of behaviour are as telling today as when written over two thousand years ago.

Individual strands have developed, but until recently there has been little attempt to undertake systematic, quantitative, empirical work to synthesise different academic disciplines. Basic empirical questions about group behaviour, or the extent to which we are driven by logic, greed, our loss aversion or reciprocity, have moved on little.

Fortunately, after such a drought, our understanding of how we behave has recently begun to make rapid strides. Fascinating new studies are starting to bring together the links between how we think – neuroscience and psychology – how our bodies react to how we think – physiology – and how those thoughts lead us to organise ourselves as groups – sociology, politics, and economics. Rich seams of collaboration are opening up.

This new research is being applied to policy too. Paying people to recycle is significantly more effective than fining them if they don't. Simply changing the way letters from the taxman are written increases tax yield enormously.

These new steps are important, but alone are not enough. For policies themselves are part of the system we all live in. So while it is necessary to base policy on observations of how we behave, it is not sufficient. We must also understand the dynamics: how people will react to policy, both alone and in groups. In some of the most important areas of policy, like managing the economy, this is very hard to predict. But it is safer to base policy on a recognition of how little we know than on a false assumption that we know far more. The implications are profound.

In the real world of our jobs, our savings and our homes, the financial crisis that started in 2007 has dealt an almighty shock to how we thought the economy worked. For too long, policymaking made assumptions about how people *ought* to behave, without stopping to observe how we actually *do*. Assumption was taken as observation.

On this mistake whole structures of economic theory and policy were built. So it was taken as read that if people took on debt it must be because they were sure they could pay it back. If banks made loans, it must have been because they had assessed the likelihood that the borrowers could pay them back. And the regulators believed that with inflation targeting they had solved the age-old problem of how to manage the broader economy. These theories and policies that used flawed assumptions of all-pervasive rationality contributed to the creation and bursting of one of the largest economic bubbles in history.

This book attempts to bring the latest insights of human behaviour into the debates of our times. With real stories and emerging academic evidence we try to explain human behaviour. Drawing on a rich and growing field of research from a wide variety of disciplines, we find lessons for how we can try to run our economy in future.

Polling was undertaken for this book to shed light on the question of how rational people think they are and how they actually behave. The very first part of this polling brings out the colourful way in which we humans see ourselves. Forty-three per cent of people claim they are always rational. But only 34 per cent claim their friends are always rational.

Yet we find confidence in the fact that just because behaviour is often irrational does not mean that it is unpredictable. After all, history shows that in economic life, ups and downs, cycles and bubbles are inevitable. These are not caused by capitalism. Indeed the free-market economy has powerfully proved to be the best way to sustain and enrich well-being. For markets to be free, and to retain widespread trust and support, they require a strong framework.

In the recent past, we have learned the hard way what happens if that framework is wrong: if we assume people are always rational, that groups of people are rational too, and that if anything does go wrong, a rational government can step in to sort it out.

This attitude came at a time when the soft, cultural constraints on behaviour were being questioned. Long gone were the days captured in *Mary Poppins*, when the boss punched through Mr Banks's bowler hat as a symbol of shame after his son caused a run on the bank. There is no longer the strict social code that governed society. That social hierarchy was rightly challenged, to the advantage of many who had been excluded, and the unspoken rules that dominated society withered away. In their place came the thrilling combination of amazing new technology and rapid globalisation, as two billion people – a third of the world's population – joined the global economy for the first time.

Like dreams, all bubbles need a kernel of truth for the story to take hold. In the bubble that led to the financial crisis, a combination of new technology and globalisation told an intoxicating tale about how the rise of the East had improved the world's prospects, and how advanced technology had allowed this new global economy to be managed better than ever before. People everywhere bought into the story, because it was true.

The sequence of events is well documented. The rise of the East had a benign effect on our lives. With so many people trying to compete in the global market, empowered by a new ability to communicate, the cost of goods and services in the West was driven down. The success of the newly-connected societies led to a rapid rise in middle classes and entrepreneurs, who saved a high proportion of their income.

They needed somewhere safe to put their new savings, and after the shock of the Asian crisis of 1998, largely through their governments, they invested it in the West. These events should have been a triple bonus for the West: cheaper goods, new markets, and plenty of cash-rich investors.

At the same time, the promise of the dot-com bubble had burst, and in the face of recession, interest rates were cut sharply. The rapid drop in the cost of everyday items, like televisions, computers and cars, meant that inflation, as measured, stayed low. In the UK, within the narrow inflation-targeting regime, interest rates were held low to keep inflation positive. But not all prices stayed low. Asset prices, like housing, rose. Yet in the UK, the inflation target itself was changed to remove the rapidly rising cost of housing. So interest rates were held down.

So what was the problem?

The easy supply of credit and its artificially low cost combined to create a vast debt bubble. We enjoyed it. Borrowing against the rising price of your house (mortgage equity withdrawal) became the rage. New homeowners were offered 125 per cent of the value of their house in mortgages. More credit card offers than you could ever use flew in through the door. The Royal Bank of Scotland even sent an application for a credit card with a £10,000 limit and the chance to buy air miles to one Monty Slater. Monty Slater was a dog.

This uncontrolled expansion of debt might have been containable but for the fact that the banks that supplied the credit were affected by a combination of powerful new technology and a radical new attitude from regulators. The good news story gave everyone – banks, consumers, and the authorities – a justification for believing the hype. Anyone arguing that it was unsustainable had to confront this good news.

New technology gave financiers confidence that they had

found a brand new way to lend more at a lower risk. By packaging up loans into bundles and renaming the debts in smart new language, like alchemists they thought they had converted risky loans into risk-free assets. Because they sold most of the loans on, they cared little about the quality of the loans, only the quantity. The new technology gave financiers false confidence that they could handle the lending, and a culture of growth without restraint meant they pushed ever expanding boundaries.

Armed with this good news story of the rise of the East and the dispersal of risk, we were told boom and bust had been abolished. Many believed it. Arguing against this new paradigm was unpleasant, costly, and ineffective. Responding to small crises of the past, like the collapse of BCCI and Barings banks in the UK and the Savings and Loans institutions in America, regulators hid behind the apparent new objectivity of rules and models. Many of these rules and models assumed that humans behave rationally and the good times would never end.

But psychology tells us that much of human behaviour is irrational, and history tells us the good times always end.

To understand why behaviour matters, it is telling to look at the financial crash from the perspective of those who saw it coming. There weren't many. But there were some who spoke out. Their problem was that no one wanted to listen.

Their testimony is that anyone who stood in the way of the dream was brushed aside. Like fools in the corner, they were ignored. The louder they shouted, the more deafening the silence in response. Leading bankers tried to make the case, among them Sir Andrew Large, then Deputy Governor of the Bank of England. Professional economists like Raghuram Rajan spoke out about their worries, but to no avail. They and others like them were consistently ignored.

It is astonishing that even as events tested prevailing assumptions and found them wanting, no one listened. From the collapse of hedge fund Long Term Capital Management to the default of Russia in 1998 and the dot-com crash, a series of bubbles should have raised questions. As each collapse happened, governments stepped in to clear up the mess, not stopping to consider the underlying problems that caused each crisis. Of course, the urge to prevent economic misery was understandable, but the failure to recognise and deal with the underlying problems was mistaken.

So the almighty debt bubble grew, all the more quickly because it was effectively condoned by governments. In the United States, Alan Greenspan, the Chairman of the Federal Reserve, in charge of US monetary policy for five terms from 1987 to 2006, had a simple approach: he would not act against a growing bubble, but would instead deal with the consequences when it burst. The growth and bursting of a series of small bubbles strengthened his belief in this approach. In each case, by cutting interest rates quickly, the Western economy recovered.

Greenspan even went so far as to tell the world that he would rescue the US economy from any crisis. Such a promise built up the boom still further. In the UK, Gordon Brown made exactly the same mistake, claiming he had abolished boom and bust, and encouraging companies, banks, and households to borrow even more. This implicit government support meant that instead of dealing with the underlying problems, each time the bubble burst, it was simply being pumped back up. It was a failure of leadership and of political economy of grand proportions.

Meanwhile, in the everyday life of the big banks, natural human behaviour was exerting its power. It has been observed that the patterns of group behaviour look just like the flocking of wild animals. With the story of global opportunities, rapidly rising personal pay, and explicit government support all urging it on, the financial herd stampeded into the boom with unprecedented energy and aggression.

When a herd stampedes, individual animals may peel off, able to sense a danger looming in the distance, but few follow. These were the fools in the corner, the Cassandras of the crisis. Back with the herd, one more peels off, then a few more. They can see the danger ahead but the majority still haven't noticed. Then suddenly, without warning, the mass of the herd turns. These were the majority. They did not peel off early, and their eyes were opened only as the crash became real. Finally, left behind, are the animals that carried on regardless, now separated from the herd. They are the sorry few who couldn't face up to the severity of the crisis, who hoped against hope and reason that it would just be a blip.

Looking at the turning point in this way helps understand how bubbles burst: unpredictably, and with uncertain timing, but in a recognisable pattern that has happened many times before. Elegant histories have been written of past bubbles, from the collapse of the moneylenders of fifteenth-century Florence to the Dutch tulip bubble in the 1630s and the British railway mania of the 1840s. Our goal is to recognise the patterns in human behaviour behind the bubbles. They are intrinsic to how we behave in groups, and can no more be abolished than society itself. Bubbles are appearing, growing, and bursting all the time. Our job is not to abolish them but to mitigate the harm they can do, before, during and after.

A study of bubbles of the past also shows how different their impact can be. Many bubbles, for example in an individual stock price or an individual commodity, can deflate relatively harmlessly. Some can have distorting effects. Yet others can bring down whole economies: nearly always when the bubble is financed through debt. As history shows, recessions caused by the bursting of debt bubbles are deeper, longer lasting, and have more dramatic consequences.

The growth of a bubble is usually driven not only by how people behave but by who is driving that behaviour. As a bubble grows, research shows that the most bullish optimists tend to be promoted, and promote like-minded others, gaining power over the cautious and careful. Psychological studies show that groups reinforce each other in playing down anxiety or risk. The body's physical response to imagining a great prize is physiologically the same as winning the prize. So we shun those who try to break the mould, and who challenge the group's imagination that they will win the prize. The same is true among regulators, who suffer cognitive capture by poachers turned gamekeepers. That way, during a long boom, not only are people driven by the irrational refusal to acknowledge risk, but the people most likely to acknowledge risk are shunned, while those least likely to worry are promoted. So the bubble inflates.

Furthermore, sex determines human behaviour more than any other single factor. Our sex affects how we grow, think, and behave. Does it matter, then, that the senior echelons of finance are almost exclusively male?

Some say that because finance requires aggressive, risk-loving, typically male characteristics, it's naturally dominated by men. Let's set aside the immorality and incivility of much trading floor behaviour. Physiological research into trading room performance shows that irresponsible risks are reduced when more women are around, but that people tend to hire, reward and promote people similar to themselves. Evidence from City traders bears this out. But crucially, new analysis shows that companies with more women on their boards tend to perform better compared to those with boards dominated by men. So rather than being male-dominated because finance is by nature aggressive and risk-loving, the evidence suggests that the culture of finance is aggressive and risk-loving *because* it is dominated by men.

Around the world, very clear interventions have successfully broken the male-dominated culture in finance. The evidence shows that once women reach around a third of any group, the culture tends to change and the male bias is replaced with a meritocracy. Because the problem is of culture obstructing merit, changes are needed to benefit fully from the capabilities of half of our population.

Many people react with horror at the thought of quotas on boards. Since it is in a company's interest to promote on merit, surely, they ask, the best thing to do is to leave it in the hands of the company? But this argument falls foul of the central insight of this book: that in the design of policy, we need to recognise how people actually behave, not how we might wish them to.

The argument also applies to pay. If banks acted in their shareholders' best interest, it is clear their pay would not be so extraordinarily high, or would have risen so fast over recent years. Compared to most organisations, banks pay a huge proportion of their profits to senior management rather than their owners, the shareholders. Worse still, they entered into contracts with employees which reward failure. So-called incentivisation packages can be both financially dangerous, by encouraging higher risk-taking, and morally outrageous, by rewarding performance which, whether implicit or explicit, relies on taxpayer subsidy. Given the extremes that such rewards for failure reached, there are both economic and moral imperatives to act. In a world short of capital, banks need to keep cash as capital to support the economy and make their balance sheets safer.

The widespread assumption that a self-interested decision must always be the right one also wrongly implies that business activity can be amoral and separated from ethics. Yet businesses do not act in a moral vacuum. They are made up of human beings who all play their role in society. Like any other group of people, business leaders need to take responsibility for their actions – right or wrong. Whether legal or not, immoral actions within businesses should not be ignored just because there's a logo on the door. So people who behave immorally, like the senior bankers who pay themselves huge sums of taxpayers' money, should not just be addressed within the economic framework, but, like anyone acting immorally, should be socially shunned.

We must recognise here the diversity of the financial industry. A very small number of very big banks pose risks to the whole economy should they fail. They should be distinguished from the thousands of smaller finance companies that pose no such risk, can claim no taxpayer support, and contribute enormously to Britain's economy. While people in smaller companies also have a responsibility to behave ethically, their behaviour was more distant from the causes of the crash.

The failure in the past to base policy on how people really behave is not a narrow problem. It spreads across vast swathes of the academic economics profession. Whole careers have been built in modern economics by creating mathematical models based on assumptions known to be flawed. Models can, of course, be helpful, and bring insight to unexplained problems. But the march of the model through economic academia has come to displace the search for understanding of how economies really work. The consequence has been both to infuse policymaking with impractical models, and to take resources away from the crucial task of understanding better how people really behave.

With modern technology, such empirical study can be very powerful. Modern companies use detailed information to understand better than their customers what their customers are likely to want. They design their businesses by observing their millions of customers.

Large companies now use this sort of empirical understanding of human behaviour. Our ability to understand it is set to make huge new advances. We should also harness its power to design an economic framework that is more robust, stable, and prosperous.

Nevertheless, our understanding will never be complete.

Even if we can predict, on average, large amounts of individual behaviour, predicting the precise dynamics of a herd – whether human or animal – is impossible. A group of humans is moulded by experience, reacts to events and has infinite detail. When it comes to designing policy, we have to recognise this fact, not pretend otherwise.

So we should be cautious about an approach based on increasingly complicated rules. People adapt to rules, so the discretion of policymakers in reacting to circumstances and adapting to fit the changing world is necessary and valuable.

Such discretion involves subjective judgements. Of course it is important to choose carefully who should exercise the discretion. Let us recognise that we are all flawed, but that purely objective policy is not possible. So discretion must be exercised carefully, within a clear framework, and embedded in accountable institutions that give it legitimacy and promote good decision-making. At least then when judgements don't come right, most can agree we at least made the best judgement we could.

Applied to the financial crisis, this points to giving strong institutions more discretion to run the financial system. Trying to run complex systems with complex rules leads in an infinite loop of complication to the point where no one understands either the system or the rules, including those who have devised them. Instead, complex systems should be run with fairly simple rules that can be applied intelligently, so that while no one can predict the precise future of the system, everyone knows where they stand within it.

Embedding discretion to adapt the rules in strong, respected institutions helps legitimise subjective judgements. Crucially, the institutions should also be able to change, to be challenged, and to themselves adapt.

This culture must change in Britain to stop another financial crisis. Designing policy to change culture is difficult, because the outcome is hard to measure. But again, research into human behaviour can help guide us. Behaviour is heavily dependent upon social norms – what is deemed normal by people directly affected. Behaviour that violates a social norm tends to be deemed unacceptable and so is punished. By changing social norms – for example, making reckless risk-taking an embarrassment to colleagues or ensuring sexism is socially unacceptable – so culture can be changed both to encourage and reward behaviour that has positive side effects, and to discourage behaviour that is damaging.

In a culture in which limits of behaviour were dictated by the need to abide by detailed, rigid rules, the social norm was to get around the rules to maximise personal advantage. As no one had the discretion to adapt them, those rules were widely gamed and so failed in their broader purpose. After all, the FSA investigation into the biggest bank failure in the history of the world, the Royal Bank of Scotland, found the bank did not break a single rule.

The proposed reforms in Britain move clearly in the right direction, as they give clear discretion to the authorities. Such discretion should be used to engender a culture of responsibility, where the social norm is to behave responsibly. Of course, regulators fail too, so the system must be able to withstand regulatory failure as well.

The changes already put in place in Britain are vital. But to stop the crisis happening again, they are only a first step. To do that we need to understand that bubbles will grow and will burst, and we need to change our whole philosophy of economic policy, and with it the culture and morality of finance, to be based not on how we'd like people to behave, but on how we really do, warts and all.

Chapter 1

FOOLS IN THE CORNER

When a true genius appears in the world you may know him by this infallible sign, that the dunces are all in confederacy against him. Jonathan Swift

On a dark January night in 2004, the Deputy Governor of the Bank of England took the short trip from Threadneedle Street to the Strand in central London.

As he wrapped himself up in his coat and skipped up the steps to the newly refurbished lecture theatre, an audience of economics students waited patiently.

Sir Andrew Large stood to deliver a speech that, with hindsight, was one of the most powerful and eloquent warnings about the coming crash.

A full three years before the freezing of the money markets and the first run on a British bank since 1866 and four years before the biggest financial crisis in the history of capitalism, a man at the top of one of the most respected institutions in the world laid out what was happening, and the risks that it posed to us all.

If the financial crisis were a Shakespeare play it would be *King Lear*. Like the economists of our own time, Lear is a rationalist who insists, against all reason, that a person's inner life can be reduced to a neat little formula. In the opening scene he asks his three daughters: 'Which of you shall we say doth love us most?'[1] When Cordelia, his youngest, challenges this grotesque attempt to quantify the unquantifiable, she is disinherited. Satisfied nonetheless with the rehearsed answers offered by the other two, Lear abandons his formal powers and cedes them to his children, believing they can be trusted to behave in the kingdom's best interests. He's wrong. During the course of the play we see the collapse of traditional authority, unrestrained greed in the ascendant, and the livid exposure of a series of flawed assumptions about human nature.

This chapter is about Lear's fool.

In the play, the loyal court fool repeatedly warns Lear of impending catastrophe. First he's laughed at, then ignored. Lear won't listen because do so would mean accepting that he's made a mistake – and that there will be a terrible price to pay. It's far easier to dismiss the fool in the corner as a mad contrarian.

In November 2008, the Queen famously asked economists at the LSE: 'Why did no one see it coming?' In doing so she crystallised the mood of a nation, aghast at the near collapse of its financial system, the onset of the deepest recession in living memory, and the loss of public trust in the financial establishment.

But the Queen was wrong. Some did see 'it' coming. Each piece of the jigsaw that together built the banking crisis was identified, and some people even put the pieces together. Speeches were given, and presentations delivered.

In the years before the crisis a small number of economists, regulators and financiers discovered they had been inadvertently cast in the role of the Fool. They saw what others chose not to see and they spoke of what they saw. But they found that no one with the power to act wanted to listen.

❧

What Sir Andrew had to say in his LSE speech questioned a central assumption on which the explosion in finance had been based. His argument rested on a simple distinction between two concepts: technical sophistication and progress. According to Sir Andrew they might be related but they were emphatically not the same thing.

Since the late 1980s, bankers, economists, regulators and politicians had generally assumed that increased technical sophistication in the financial system would translate into greater stability across the economy. Computer technology, which allowed financial assets to be whizzed across the globe at the touch of a button, supposedly ensured that the riskiest assets would always find their way into the hands of those most able to bear the risk. Financial crises, it was assumed, occurred because risk was too concentrated. Recent financial innovation meant it would be safely diffused across the system, like chlorine molecules in a swimming pool.

In 2005 Larry Summers, the former US Treasury Secretary, produced one of the most definitive statements of the view that technical sophistication and progress were one and the same. Summers drew an analogy between financial innovation and the history of transport. He pointed out that people once supplied their own power. Then they started using modes of transport which they personally owned, like horses. Then they increasingly relied on vehicles which other people owned, provided by intermediaries, like planes. Summers concluded that this drive towards innovation and complexity was 'overwhelmingly positive'. Just so in finance: 'The best single way to think about the process of financial innovation is as representing a similar process of movement across spaces, spanned not by physical space, but by different states of nature. It seems to me that the overwhelming preponderance of what has taken place has been positive.'

In the US, this belief in the financial system's majestic advance towards self-regulatory perfection became known as the Greenspan doctrine, after its most powerful proponent, Alan Greenspan. The doctrine's most influential convert on this side of Atlantic was Gordon Brown, who considered the venerable Greenspan a personal friend. When 'the Maestro' (as he is known by his admirers) finally retired in 2006, Brown wrote in *The Times* calling him 'the greatest economist of his generation' and arguing that his doctrine had equipped us 'for the fast-changing global economy of the future'.[2]

But according to Sir Andrew, all these heroic arguments about efficiency and risk dispersion hinged on a big 'If'. The system was only safer *if* everyone knew what they were doing – that is, if they properly understood the risks they were dealing with. And yet the modern financial system itself conspired against such an understanding. In spite of 'steps forward through enhanced disclosure and improved accounting standards, there [had] been other steps back towards opacity: the result of the sheer complexity, speed of movement of risks, and in some cases obfuscation through Special Purpose Vehicles, or other off-balance sheet devices'.[3] He noticed that for many firms, cultivating complexity had become an end in itself. After all, the more complicated a product or institution became, the harder it was for investors and regulators alike to track the underlying risks. And the less risky an institution appeared to the outside world, the more easily it could borrow to take on even more risk.

Sir Andrew's insight was that financial institutions were not only gaming the regulators but also eroding trust in one another. Financial liberalisation and increased savings flowing from the rapidly developing world meant that the West was awash with cheap money, so much so that it had become more difficult for banks to make any through traditional means. In response, financial institutions had developed ever more ingenious ways of doing business: the age of securitisation, credit derivatives, monoline insurance and shadow banking had arrived. 'The existence of new concentrations of risk might not matter if their new holders are fully aware of the risk,' said Sir Andrew. 'But new holders of such risk may not have the same understandings of what the risks consist of, as those who generate them. And accordingly they may behave in unexpected ways when shocks arise.'[4] No one knew if all parties would, or could, honour their obligations in the event of a market shock. This could lead to financial hysteria and a 'one-way' market at the very moment when calm was most needed.

The speech was warmly received by its undergraduate audience; questions were dutifully asked and answered. The text was published on the Bank's website.

No one noticed.

When Sir Andrew returned to the Bank the next morning, the explosive speech was not the subject of heated debate. There were no seminars called. No research was commissioned. In the newspapers over the following days, there was no reference made to Sir Andrew or the speech.

Sir Andrew was a banker by trade. In policy circles, he told us, '[he] was considered a bit of a maverick, which was not particularly comfortable'. This isolation went right down to the level of language. He told us the economists would talk of:

> The concept of cycles ... and the concept of cyclical smoothing and all these soothing words that are used, which are rather foreign to me when thinking about financial stability, because financial stability has got nothing to do with smoothing at all. It's all to do with spikes and discontinuities. And also it's to do with uncertainty as to whether and when such discontinuities might arise.

Sir Andrew continued to make similar speeches, and argue the system was unsustainable for another two years. Then, in January 2006, he quietly retired early, before his term was up.

His speeches infuriated the then Chancellor because they warned of the dangers of excessive borrowing. But he felt compelled to make them. He told us:

The reason I did so was because I said to myself, look, the one thing I can do is at least to point out that if all this carries on it's all going to end in tears. I can't tell you how, no one can say how – but if you have a combination of ever-rising indebtedness and unknown events that will test your system one way or another, then sooner or later all these things will come together and it *will* end in tears.

The fact that a Deputy Governor of the Bank of England, with an acute sense of where the risks lay, felt that all he could do was make speeches is a serious indictment of the regulatory regime, of which more later.

So here was a man with an impeccable track record, who after a career in banking, had become Chairman of the Securities and Investments Board, the forerunner of the FSA. As Deputy Governor of the Bank of England he occupied a position of weight, and he spoke with great clarity about the problems that we faced. He was ignored.

Why were these warnings ignored? What is it about human behaviour that meant those with most to lose turned a blind eye to the growing storm? Why were those who warned of the risks treated as the fool in the corner? And what can we learn, to help ensure they get a better hearing next time?

For Sir Andrew Large was not alone.

ↄ

Since 1982, central bankers and the world's most distinguished economists have gathered each spring at the small town of Jackson Hole, Wyoming. Here they exchange frank views on the latest economic theories, try, then fail, to agree on international policy frameworks and swap stories about the personal oddities of their respective finance ministers back home. The conference is set against a melodramatic backdrop of mountains, lakes and pine forests, giving members of the world's most urban profession a chance to play at being American frontier folk for a week. Seminars and formal discussions are interspersed with whitewater rafting sessions and long hikes through rough terrain, where the latest growth figures are breathlessly discussed while the party stops to admire the view.

In 2005, Raghuram Rajan, the IMF's talented young Chief Economist, had been invited to deliver a paper at Jackson Hole. His subject: 'Has Financial Innovation Made the World Safer?' His conclusion: no. It was a daring and iconoclastic argument, for in the audience looking up at Rajan through his huge trademark spectacles was the central banker of central bankers, the most powerful man in finance: Alan Greenspan, 'the Maestro'.

A popular legend about Greenspan claims that when he needed to think he would sit in his bath, poring over sheaves of economic data, looking for tell-tale patterns about the future in the raw numbers. A hard-line free marketeer, he had overseen and advised on a great era of deregulation in the financial sector. Having safely steered the American economy through the 1987 stock market bust, the global panic of 1998 and the bursting of the dot-com bubble in 2000–2001, he felt under no obligation to justify his legacy.

Rajan stepped up to the lectern, took a deep breath, and politely told his audience that they had made the world a more dangerous place.

Originally, Rajan had been asked to the conference to argue, like Larry Summers, who was also present, that Alan Greenspan's eighteen-year tenure at the Fed had made the financial system safer. But the more he considered the evidence, the less convinced he had become of his own argument.

Instead he argued that technical change, institutional change and deregulation meant that instead of being incentivised to protect depositors' money, those working in finance were encouraged to take higher risks, and to follow everyone else in finance in herding behaviour. Stewardship and prudence were downgraded.

Rajan explained that because pay was tied to short-term returns, financial managers would want to take so-called 'tail risks': risks that almost always paid off with higher returns, but when they went wrong would be catastrophic. That way, most of the time the managers would take home a higher pay packet. If the risk did materialise, they might be fired: a small cost compared to the super-sized bonuses they got while the going was good.

Similarly, because these managers' pay was set relative to their peers, financial managers were incentivised to follow the herd. We will explore in later chapters how the natural human instinct anyway is to follow the herd. These incentives reinforced natural human behaviour.

Rajan did not pursue his argument to its logical conclusion. What he overlooked was that, when combined, these two behaviours multiplied. Herding on its own causes groups of people to move or act in fits and starts, so that the behaviour of the group is unpredictable and irrational. Taking tail risks increases the fragility of the system when a gamble goes wrong. When a herd takes a tail risk that goes wrong, the results are spectacular.

Nevertheless it was a brilliant analysis of what Rajan would later term the 'fault lines' which ran through the global financial system, and there was somewhat daring about addressing the taboo subject of pay in front of some of the best-paid people in finance.

The speech did not go down well.

One of the first members of the audience to respond was Larry Summers. He said he found 'the basic, slightly lead-eyed premise' of the paper 'to be largely misguided' and cited the Swedish and Japanese banking crises of the 1990s as evidence that systemic risk was caused by irresponsible lending from plain old retail banks, or 'vanilla banking' rather than the financial alchemy practised by the high-rollers on Wall Street. He also said that in a rational world, had new forms of insurance like credit default swaps been available to investors back in the 1980s, then the situation following the 1987 stock market bust would have been a lot more stable.

But Summers missed one of Rajan's central points, which was essentially the same as Sir Andrew's. The imagined impregnability of the modern financial system depended on assumptions that had not been tested; indeed, that were seemingly unfalsifiable. The past twenty-five years of market behaviour were no guide at all to the next ten. Gesturing back to the three major market shocks which occurred on Greenspan's watch, Rajan asked, 'Can we be confident that the shocks were large enough and in the right place to fully test the system?... Perhaps we can sleep better at night if we pray "Lord, let there be shocks, let them be varied and preferably moderate so we can test our systems".'

This point about scepticism is important. Rajan and Sir Andrew were right to argue that while financial innovation had dramatically increased what it was possible to *do* in financial markets, it had seriously undermined our ability to *know* what it was those markets were doing. Their focus on the essential *novelty* of the financial system confounds the argument that they were backward-looking Luddites. On the contrary, it was their critics who were too fixed on the past, convinced that they could use it to peer into the future, like Alan Greenspan sitting in the bath with his tables and charts.

This was a misuse of history, which cannot possibly tell us which way the markets are headed. But when we look back beyond our own lifetimes it can tell us something more important – about how adept people are at explaining away risk. We will see more of this in Chapter 5 when we come to think about bubbles, but first let's imagine if Summers would have thought differently if he had considered the historical precedent for ignoring the warnings of impending catastrophe.

People living in the early 1900s who argued that war between Britain and Germany was impossible deployed now-familiar arguments. Technology had made the world a safer place: Britain's vast fleet and state-of-the-art dreadnoughts supposedly meant no European power would dare provoke a general conflagration. No general or politician would be so irresponsible; the world's economies were too well integrated. Rational self-interest would prevent an immensely destructive war between the great powers. And where was the precedent? Britain hadn't been involved in a European conflict since the Crimea sixty years before. Why would it suddenly abandon its long-term strategy of non-interference in European affairs?

The symmetry is eerie. The lesson is that people in all ages dangerously overestimate their ability to remain in control of events, when all too often it's the mad internal logic of the system they've created which is really in control. Far from making the system safer, technical development actually augments this effect. The historian John Keegan writes that in the years before the First World War the generals of the great European powers had been told to draw up detailed war plans in anticipation of an event no one wanted to, or believed could, happen. Their guiding philosophy was to prepare assiduously for the worst-case scenario. The war plans were enormously complex documents designed to mobilise millions of men rapidly. They operated on a 'use it or lose it' principle whereby the first army to call up its troops and speed them towards the front would be able to smash the enemy while he was still asleep in the barracks. On the continent, generals harassed politicians to give the order to mobilise as soon as possible, convinced that delay would have meant losing the crucial early advantage. As a result, cold logistics fatally undermined diplomacy during the summer of 1914. And so events assumed their own lethal momentum at the very point when measured reflection was most needed.

Sir Andrew Large and Raghuram Rajan saw that a similar dynamic was lurking in the global financial system. Perverse inner mechanics could easily hijack people's best intentions. The modern financial equivalent of the generals' war plans were the computer models which told traders what to buy and what to sell in times of market stress. Gerald Ashley, a former bullion trader at the Bank of International Settlements, explained to us what happened during the crisis: 'When markets fall the only thing that goes up is correlation. If everyone is using the same model and all the models are saying "sell" then who else is buying?' What the generals found in August 1914 is that because everyone was working on the same 'use it or lose it' principle, nobody captured the advantage it was supposed to bring. France and Britain mobilised quickly enough to intercept the German Army on its way to Paris. In the same way, because every bank was working on the same assumption that it suddenly had to sell its junk mortgage-backed securities, nobody wanted to buy them. Their value collapsed and hundreds of billions of pounds were wiped off the books. Panic had been unwittingly hard-wired into an ostensibly risk-free system.

Dr Doom

In 2006, a year after Rajan's speech at Jackson Hole, another man took to the stage, this time at the IMF in New York.

He had an unreadable stare and an utterly unplaceable accent. His name was Nouriel Roubini and he was about to deliver the speech that would make him famous.

In early 2007, he announced, America would fall into recession. And it would hurt.

He cited several causes: an oil price shock, declining consumer confidence, a once-in-a-lifetime housing bust and higher interest rates from the Fed. But that wasn't all.

Even armed with Roubini's predictions, the Fed would still be powerless to prevent a recession. Lowering interest rates would have no effect on growth because America had acquired a glut of housing and consumer goods. The only place for banks and firms to invest their money would be in an economically unproductive share buy-back 'bonanza'.

Savouring the audience's dismay at this gloomy prognosis, Roubini proceeded with his argument. The oil shock was safely assured by constraints on supply and rising political instability abroad. Meanwhile the housing bust would be devastating because American consumer spending had become so dependent on mortgage equity withdrawal. He also drew the vital link between the housing sector and financial markets, noting that the banking system was highly exposed to the risks associated with mortgage debt and that this risk was dispersed elsewhere through the system via other financial institutions which had purchased mortgage-related assets from the banks. Or as he put it: 'You could not rule out some systemic effects if one of those institutions goes belly-up.' Finally, he noted that a recession in America might have a knock-on effect given that so much of the rest of the world moved to the rhythm of the US economy.

Roubini concluded his speech. As he stepped down from the lectern, the IMF moderator moved in to thank him, remarking, 'Perhaps we will need a stiff drink after that.' The audience laughed and perhaps they were laughing at Roubini too. After all, he was a professional pessimist. He had built an entire career at New York University prophesying doom. This was exactly the kind of Nostradamus act they had expected to see that night.

In support of his argument Roubini provided several historical analogies featuring identical economic conditions – an oil shock, monetary tightening and the bursting of a bubble – which had tipped the US into recession. He focused particularly on the stock market crash of 1987. But as another economist, Anirvan Banerji, pointed out, for every analogy Roubini dealt, it was possible to counter with a different one in which America had weathered the storm:

> In the fall of 1998 in the wake of the Russian default and the LTCM crisis, many predicted a recession. As Nouriel might recall, President Clinton himself called it the worst financial crisis in fifty years, and *Time* magazine had Alan Greenspan, Robert Rubin, and Larry Summers on its cover as the 'Committee to Save the World'. But, once again, a recession was averted. Using our retrospectoscopes we can explain why there was or was not a recession in each case, why some shocks were that potent and not others, but that is not so easy before the fact.

According to Banerji, there was something too subjective and 'non-rigorous' about Roubini's approach. What was needed instead was an 'objective stable framework', featuring a wide range of closely monitored economic indicators. Naturally this was the method which Banerji himself practised. But as we shall see throughout this book, this faith in objectivity – and it was a faith – proved fatal.

Michael Mandel, writing in Bloomberg Businessweek, was equally dismissive: 'I'm far less worried about the possibility of a steep recession than Roubini is. Economists don't know much, but they do know how to cushion downturns through sharp cuts in interest rates and injections of liquidity into the financial system.' The central bankers knew what they were doing. Even if all the events Roubini predicted came to pass, the Fed would pump enough money into the system to avert disaster.

In many ways Roubini was vindicated. Belatedly, the world did sit up and pay attention. An article published in the *New York Times* in August 2008 while the subprime crisis was in full swing, showered praise on his IMF speech, even though the same newspaper had ignored it two years before. Roubini was suddenly cast in the role of America's grim oracle. The paper called him 'Dr Doom', the man who had seen a financial nightmare coalescing in the margins and tried to warn the world. Unlike Sir Andrew Large, Roubini was catapulted to fame. He was invited onto primetime news programmes to dispense his wisdom to reverential journalists, his online consultancy business made millions counselling shaken bankers and his book, *Crisis Economics,* became a bestseller. Most ironically of all, he became a confidant of central bankers and finance ministers, those who had helped guide the system into the recession that he had predicted. New York University's dismal sage was always a phone call or an email away when advice was needed about which bank or market would go under next.

This last point is important. Roubini now occupies an immensely powerful position because he was noticed by the media. Given this fact, it is important to be clear about exactly what he did and did not predict and why, of the handful of economists who saw imminent catastrophe, he was the one who became famous.

Roubini predicted a recession in the US which he thought might spread to the rest of the world. What he did not predict was a global financial crisis so severe that only a multi-trillion dollar rescue package from governments across the world could prevent the destruction of free-market capitalism. He did not see that the financial system had become hopelessly addicted to cheap credit, that it had become impossibly complex and dangerously opaque. He made no mention of the rise of the shadow banking system – the invisible network of unregulated or lightly-regulated entities where banks hid their riskiest assets from regulators, investors and each other. Nor did he cite rabid short-term speculation fuelled by utterly skewed pay incentives. In short, like a general practitioner, he had noticed some impaired cognitive function, some erratic behaviour – but missed the monstrous tumour behind it.

So why Roubini? We would argue that there was something oddly reassuring about the way Roubini predicted the recession. He couched his argument in the language of traditional economics, citing huge impersonal forces – oil, housing, the Fed – rather than excessive risk-taking and the opacity of the financial system as causes. These forces could be seen and measured, their movements could be tracked and predicted by the experts.

In other words, Roubini became a celebrity because his analysis of the crisis was in the language of the 'objective' economic framework which dominated thinking before the crash, even though he predicted a recession and not a global financial crisis. While accused of being 'non-rigorous' for using subjective analysis, Roubini dealt in bullet-points and spoke the language of the times. In a sense he was telling a different version of the same old story.

Like Large and Rajan before him, Roubini questioned the assumptions made by the economics profession. They were rejected by the economic consensus of the time.

Sir Andrew Large told us of the intellectual vanity which characterised the pre-crisis policymaking community: 'It was a rather funny sort of time, everyone felt they knew everything.' Monetary policy was the key policy area and had tended to crowd out the financial stability agenda. People seemed to think that price stability would lead to financial stability; they had forgotten that ever-increasing indebtedness would one day lead to crisis.

Unfortunately the pervading sense of objectivity associated with inflation targeting was transferred into the more complex realm of financial stability. For example, in the models used to predict inflation, banks' balance sheets were assumed to be sustainable, imagining that they would always drift back to a sustainable level. Sir Andrew, by contrast, made one the best pre-crisis analyses of the risks inherent in the system because he made the least number of assumptions and was modest about what he knew. Finance was doing too many new things on an unprecedented scale to make any sound predictions about how people would respond when things went wrong.

Accepting this argument, however, requires economists and policymakers to reconcile themselves with gaps in their knowledge. Recent work in psychology has confirmed the inability of experts to admit their own ignorance.

In 2010, two cognitive psychologists, Son and Kornell, devised a study to show how expertise might lead to over-confidence. Experts in two fields – mathematics and history – were provided with a list of names divided into three different categories. The task was to say whether a given name belonged to a particular category. For example, when given the following information: 'Mathematician – Johannes de Groot', participants had to decide whether Johannes de Groot was a famous mathematician and could answer 'Yes', 'No', or 'Don't know'. The three categories were mathematicians, historians and athletes. Within each category a third of the names actually belonged to the category, i.e. were real mathematicians, historians or athletes; a third belonged to a different category – 'Mathematician – Mohammed Ali'; the final third were made-up names – 'Mathematician – Benoit Thoron'.

During the trial, Son and Kornell found that the experts were less likely to answer 'Don't know' in a category featuring their area of expertise. More interestingly they were more likely to say 'Yes' to made-up names attached to their specialist subjects. Mathematicians answered 'Yes' nineteen times to made-up mathematicians but only seven times to fictional historians; historians said 'Yes' eight times to made-up historians but only four times to invented mathematicians. In the words of Son and Kornell: 'Experts were fooled into endorsing falsehoods because they failed to admit that they did not know.'

As a commentary on the calibre of economic analysis in the years leading up to 2007, this is pretty hard to beat. But there were other reasons relating to the way economists think and work which resulted in the dismissal of Sir Andrew's and other's views.

During the twentieth century, academic economists came to regard their subject as something akin to a hard science and adopted many of the conventions of the scientific community. Modern science works by establishing a consensus, hence its huge emphasis on peer-reviewed research. Modern economics has followed suit, even though as a discipline it's far more dependent on assumed first principles and educated guesswork than the controlled experiments which form the mainstay of the scientific method.

The rejection of Roubini's 2006 prediction that the United States faced a 70 per cent chance of recession was a stark illustration of this. Where did the figure come from? As Roubini himself admitted, he pulled it out of his nose:

> I think if you had said '50 per cent' you look like a wimp: it means you are not sure. So if you have the guts of believing there is going to be a recession, you should say something higher than that – and that is where the '70 per cent' comes from.[5]

In spite of the necessary imprecision of the field, taking on the economic consensus came to be seen as tantamount to challenging the scientific consensus: absurd.

Beneath the ideological surface of a group consensus, there is a more fundamental emotional need for a shared vision. After all, the human capacity for group co-operation has played a huge role in our evolutionary success story. Professor Jared Diamond has argued that the major turning point in the fortunes of *homo sapiens* was not the rise of higher cognitive functions in the brain, but the perfection of the human larynx, allowing for the take-off of language which brought the exchange of ideas and unprecedented social organisation.

Our desire to conform, rooted in the deep structures of the human psyche, is profound enough to subordinate more rational considerations. In the 1950s, Solomon Asch conducted a famous experiment into the nature of conformity. He showed his test subjects three different lines of obviously different length. Then he surrounded them with a group of people who were in on the experiment, whose job it was to insist that the lines were all of the same length. Confronted with the pressure to abide by group expectations, over 70 per cent of the subjects misreported the length of lines at least once.

This is not something restricted to experimental laboratories. In 1995, three teams of climbers combined and attempted to climb K2, the second-highest mountain in the world after Everest, on the border of Pakistan and China. The group persevered despite worsening weather conditions. Tragically, six of the group died on the mountain. In a study by Searle,[6] the impact of groupthink is identified in the desire to press ahead. As one of the survivors is reported to have said: 'The most dangerous thing about groups is that everyone hands over responsibility for themselves to someone else.' You lose a sense of personal responsibility, and feel less able to express dissent.

The phenomenon has been repeated. Mountaineering groups of four of more are more likely to suffer fatalities. This is because once the weather turns no one in the group wants to be the spoilsport who suggests they turn back. A set of shared theoretical assumptions can foster a real sense of camaraderie. This is our evolutionary reward for helping to define group identity. Soldiers have described the sense of 'pervasive well-being'[7] which they experience when performing military drill. Sharing a professional consensus is perhaps the intellectual equivalent of this.

In this case, the professional consensus was to build economic policy on the assumption of perfect rationality. Banks were allowed to operate with no limit to the amount of debts they built up, and were asked to decide for themselves if their business models were sustainable. We know that this was a false assumption. And we have seen how some people questioned it.

Crucially, regulators felt these pressures too. As Adair Turner, who became Chairman of the FSA in September 2008, said: 'Regulators are also taken in by an intellectual framework that explains the bubble as rational, because humans have a bias to optimism, to believe the world has improved for the better.'[8]

An example of the prevailing attitudes that had taken over the FSA is the way it dealt with Northern Rock as late as 2007. Northern Rock had reported a capital ratio of 9.74 per cent at the end of March 2007, which was in breach of capital requirements. They informed the FSA of this in April 2007. While the FSA normally regards capital shortfalls as extremely serious, it continued to allow Northern Rock to waive the standard Risk Mitigation Programme required of almost every other bank.

The FSA now admits it failed to take heed of a further eight warning signs that should have showed them the weaknesses in Northern Rock. The main reason this occurred is claimed to be that supervisors were so indoctrinated with the confidence of the market that they dismissed anomalies and warning signs as mere blips.[9]

Why did no one with the power to act do so?

The Power of Stories
Answering that question explains why one economic theory and not another is allowed to become the consensus. In

science, a given hypothesis gains influence because it provides the best possible explanation for the existing evidence; in economics the most popular theories are those which provide us with the most compelling stories.

Every culture tells itself stories. A narrative imposes form and causality on what would otherwise be the random chaos of experience. Stories provide us with the reassurance that we, and not the universe, are in control. The crime novelist P. D. James once said that 'what the detective story is about is not murder but the restoration of order'.[10] Not only is it aesthetically important that the serial killer gets caught, but the killer's motive must be explicable – it has to proceed from some formative psychological experience and semi-forensic investigation of motives which the detective unravels, clue by clue, as the narrative progresses. By the end, it's not only the crime that gets solved, but the criminal.

Economic narratives perform a similar function. Consider the astounding popularity of Marxism, which formed the official ideology of half the world's governments at the height of the Cold War. The Marxist view of the world triumphed not because it provided the best analysis of the facts, but because it proposed both to identify and solve the fundamental cause of social injustice: private property. This narrative was compelling because it moved the most intractable problems of human nature out of the subjective realm of ethics and the democratic process and turned them into a simple question of technical administration. It followed that Utopia was around the corner; we no longer had to change ourselves, merely the laws surrounding property ownership and access to power.

Before the financial crisis, economists and governments in the West were telling a different story, albeit one that was no less seductive in its simplicity. According to this narrative, for the first time in history, deficit spending would lead to sustainable long-term growth. Debt 'smoothed consumption', allowing banks and individuals to buy today what they could pay for tomorrow. Even though neither experienced a rise in real income this was possible because, for reasons discussed in the previous chapter, the value of the asset purchased, whether a house or another bank, would inevitably rise in value, allowing the debt to be paid off over time. Debt financing ensured that there need never again be a slump in demand, which is why the Chancellor was able to insist there would be 'no return to boom and bust'. This turned the nation's debt managers, the banks, into both the brains and beating heart of the economy. In the UK it meant we no longer had to feel insecure about being out-exported by Germany and Japan, or out-competed by the Far East – we had a new way of creating wealth, and it was just as good. The link between this story and Marxism was that both laid emphasis on private property, in one case a source of 'evil', in the other a source of aspiration and a means of 'good'.

In the two countries worst affected by the financial crisis, Iceland and Ireland, the nationalistic appeal of this narrative was even more overt. Iceland, whose banks held assets worth an eye-watering 1,000 per cent of GDP on the eve of the crisis, appeared to have transformed itself from a small, economically-negligible fishing nation, into a frozen Hong Kong of the North Atlantic, while the Republic of Ireland, which styled itself the 'Celtic Tiger' economy, was finally able to end seventy years of humiliating comparisons with its former colonial ruler, thanks to a booming financial sector.

Where there were questions of national pride or political prestige involved, challenging the financial mythology was difficult. Once personal profit was introduced into the mix it became all but impossible. This is what Patrick Evershed discovered in the years before the boom.

Evershed was a veteran asset manager who had been following business and economic cycles for over fifty years. He told us how he had come to learn that 'people are backward looking when making investment decisions. You can only sell things that have been going up. But it is wrong to sell shares which are good value simply because the share price has crashed'. In contrast to consumer goods, 'when people see the price of an asset rising, they don't reduce their demand for it, they want to join in'. This meant he came under intense pressure from his clients to buy financial assets during the boom. Evershed was convinced, however, that the debt financing which had driven the price of assets up could not go on forever. Debt had made the system so fragile, that the tiniest market tremor could send the entire economy spiralling into recession.

But just like Lear's fool, when he stated the nature of the problem, he found that 'people thought [he] was mad'. The more convinced Evershed became that the economy was headed for disaster, the more urgently he felt that the public needed to be warned. He spent £100,000, including £50,000 in the run-up to the 2005 election, on newspaper advertisements warning of the problem, 'but the consequence was people thought I was madder than they'd thought before'.

Lord Flight, like Evershed, was a City old hand with an acute sense that something, sometime had to give. As Shadow Chief Secretary to the Treasury, he argued for the need to be positioned right for when it did. But Flight came up against a problem: 'When the public don't want to hear it, there's no use in peddling economic bad news.' He continued: 'We did all sound like the dog that had barked too often. I was banging on down this line from 2002. The problem was the boom went on much longer than would usually have been the case because we imported deflation.'

This view also permeated the banks. The testimonies of whistleblowers from the period are a key example of this and often, due to the closed nature of the financial sector, the only way to back up this commonly accepted point. Paul Moore, head of group regulatory risk at HBOS in 2002–05, stated in 2009 that he had been threatened and eventually fired for stating in internal reports that the bank was 'going too fast', 'had a cultural indisposition to challenge' and 'was a serious risk to financial stability ... and consumer protection'.[11] He explained further:

> They said exactly what I expected them to say. The way ... Andy Hornby presented the case was as a completely unexpected drying up of the wholesale money markets, and they seemed to distinguish this from an over-eager sales team. But the reality is there is a direct connection between an over-eager sales team and their requirement for substantial wholesale funding.

Moore described the bank culture and bank bosses as being 'in an environment like a fast-moving river'. The social norm was to ignore the naysayers:

> They were not inclined to listen to a different view... I was one person speaking out with experience who did see, in a generic sense, the writing on the wall. Even non-bankers with no credit risk management expertise would have known that there must have been a very high risk if you lend money to people who have no jobs, no provable income and no assets. You simply don't need to be an economic rocket scientist or mathematical financial risk management specialist to know this; you just need common sense.

The case of Tony Dye formed another instructive example to politicians and financiers alike that no one could afford to be wrong for long. Dye had worked as a pension fund portfolio manager at the Phillips and Drew fund. During the late 1990s he had refused to invest in American equities, convinced that they were massively over-valued. For several years his fund languished at the bottom of performance charts as more bullish rivals cashed in on the US stock market. Dye intended to bide his time and reap the rewards of the inevitable bust, but the managers of his parent firm, UBS, eventually lost patience and fired him in 2000. Dye's successors scrabbled to reverse his contrarian investment strategy. A month later the dot-com bubble burst and the US stock market plunged. Phillips and Drew hadn't had enough time to load up on as many US equities as their competitors and quite unwittingly found themselves catapulted to the top of the league, all thanks to Tony Dye.

Dye can be seen as a high-profile victim of the sector's refusal to accept what it saw as pessimists. This is despite the fact that men like Dye were shown to be on the right track by the markets' behaviour in the lead-up to the crash. The Asian Tigers crisis in 1997 and the collapse of LTCM in 1998 both should have sent shock waves around the market. However on both occasions central banks merely slashed interest rates and delayed the inevitable, leaving Dye to wait until 2000 for his vindication.

Dye continued to call problems with the market in the years after the crash. Towards the end of 2002, in a letter to the *Financial Times*, he predicted an imminent housing crash in the UK on a similar scale to the house-price slump of the early 1990s.[12] Up until his death in late 2007, Dye was warning that the boom was unsustainable. No firm would rehire him, so he started his own fund. Although posthumously proved correct, the economics were against him. Dye was right at the wrong time, and his fund was not a success.

Most bubbles take time to develop. Indeed the biggest, most dangerous bubbles gestate for years. These long bubbles are exacerbated not only by the behaviour of decision takers, but by a change in who is taking the decisions. To understand the crash, we need to look at who was on the up, and what kind of people were increasingly put in positions of responsibility.

The answer is worrying. With only a few admirable exceptions, in the boom years the bulls of the financial world made strides up the corporate ladder. The evidence shows that in the financial crisis, those with the riskiest attitudes, in the riskiest businesses, with the most aggressive manner were most likely to be promoted. The cautious tended to be left behind, grounded at the bottom rungs of the ladder. So a bitter irony of the crash is that as the system took on more dangerous risks, those predisposed to see it coming were marginalised in favour of the more aggressive, in turn exacerbating the cycle.

The phenomenon is by no means new. Roger Babson was described by J. K. Galbraith in his book on the Great Crash as an 'educator, philosopher, theologian, statistician, forecaster and friend of gravity'. He was also a fool in the corner. He used intuition and common sense in his approach to the markets. His 'ten commandments' included instruction not to be fooled by a name, and to keep speculation and investment separate. He forecast the Great Crash but thanks to his less orthodox approach, he was largely dismissed. As Galbraith writes, 'in these matters, as so often in our culture, it is far, far better to be wrong in a respectable way than to be right for the wrong reasons. Wall St was not at a loss as what to do about Babson. It promptly and soundly denounced him'.[13]

Galbraith wrote of the period before the Great Crash of 1929: 'Never before or since have so many become so wondrously, so effortlessly or so quickly rich.'[14] This fantasy of wealth without work combined with the rags to riches narrative of the American Dream to create the toxic speculative frenzy which led to the Wall Street Crash. Then, as now, economic theory is what gave the story its shape, but it was the profit motive which lent it irrational emotive momentum, that led to the promotion of the bulls, and the rejection of those who sounded caution but were wrong for too long.

This mindset is demonstrated by the people who piled their

money into Madoff Investment Securities. In total, $36 billion were invested, since the average 10 per cent returns Madoff's company offered were well above those offered by any others. Even in 2008, one of his S&P 500 funds reported a return of 5.6 per cent, when the average return on the index was minus 38 per cent. Of course as we now know the returns were entirely fictional, even as far back as 1999. Harry Markopolos, a financial analyst, repeatedly alerted the Securities and Exchange Commission (SEC), after he took just four hours to prove that they were statistically and mathematically impossible to achieve in the way Madoff said he achieved them.[15] Yet he struggled to be heard, and although many insiders suspected Madoff of wrongdoing, people still piled their money in.

And it was not just investors. Charlie Dunstone, CEO and co-founder of Carphone Warehouse, described how when he was invited onto the board of HBOS, his initial reaction was slight confusion: he remembers thinking that as he was in retail and sold mobile phones, being on the board of Halifax made sense. But he should have known something had gone wrong when he was invited onto the board of HBOS. What did he know about the inner workings of banking? But at the time he was flattered, and thought they must have known what they were doing. The promise of the dream was irresistible.

It was too tempting a story to let facts get in the way. As the psychologist David Tuckett has said: 'Even though intelligent investors knew that the returns were basically impossible, they thought he was a superman. In the pursuit of returns all rationality was lost'.[16]

UBS' head of mortgage research wrote an article about the 2006 American mortgage crop, entitled 'Is this the worst vintage ever?' This was not a new theme. In 2003 she had written 'Is the US Housing Market a Bubble?' But as a former colleague related: 'She went to the board and said, "This is crazy. As soon as rates go up, these will default." Meanwhile the rollover was getting bigger and bigger. The board said, "Thanks very much," and bought more subprime assets. In the end, she resigned out of disgust.'

It is extremely hard to tell people something they do not want to hear. If a friend is infatuated with someone, the awkward conversation where you try to tell them their beloved is absolutely wrong for them is inevitably ineffective. They have bought into the story of romance wholeheartedly. Your intervention doesn't stand a chance.

Deep psychological processes subliminally reinforce our faith in the stories we tell ourselves. One of these has been recently identified as the 'backfire effect'. When we confront a threat to our worldview – that complex network of belief, story, prejudice and habit which we use both to define ourselves and to make sense of our experience – the backfire effect snaps into action. It is an unconscious defence reflex – helping to shield our preconceptions against incoming hostile ideas, working as an information filter to confirm our prejudices and soothe our doubts. The tragicomic consequence of the effect is that the more we learn about the things which are important to us, the less we know. In his wide-ranging study of self-delusion, *You Are Not So Smart,* David McRaney describes several studies which observe the backfire effect in action.

In 1997, Geoffrey Munro and Peter Ditto devised a study in which people were divided into two groups depending on their attitude towards homosexuality. The group who said they were pro-gay were given a spurious scientific study (devised by Munro and Ditto) which employed cutting-edge research to show that homosexuality was in fact a form of mental illness. The anti-gay group were given an equally fake study which suggested that homosexuality was an entirely natural form of human behaviour with a solid biological basis. McRaney reports the backfire effect: 'On either side of the issue, after reading studies which did not support their beliefs, most people didn't report an epiphany, a realisation they've been wrong all these years. Instead, they said the issue was something science couldn't understand.' When asked about other contentious topics later on, both groups said 'they no longer trusted research to determine the truth'. Rather than allow core ethical beliefs about what it meant to be human come into question, the backfire effect dismissed the very validity of the scientific method.

In 2006, Brendan Nyhan and Jason Riefler produced a series of fictitious newspaper articles on controversial issues in American politics. The articles were designed to chime with people's political prejudices and deliberately misrepresented certain key facts. Subjects in the study were given the pretend articles to read and then immediately handed a genuine news report with the correct version of events. For example, one article made the claim that the United States found weapons of mass destruction in Iraq, the next accurately reported that WMDs were never found. Those who supported the war and tended towards the conservative end of the political spectrum unsurprisingly tended to agree with the first article and dismiss the second. Crucially the conservatives reported that not only did the genuine news article fail to dilute their belief in the discovery of Iraqi WMDs but they actually found that the second article positively enforced that belief. Nyhan and Riefler repeated the study with other emotive issues like stem cell research and abortion. Once again they found that if the second correct article contradicted a participant's ideological convictions, then their belief in the initial fictitious report was only strengthened. This held true all the way along the political spectrum.

When we look back at the raw numbers, it is difficult to see how policymakers were not more suspicious of the boom. Sir Andrew told us that even though we couldn't know how the system would react to a market shock, the one thing we did know was that debt was growing faster than the economy. Startling statistics leer out of tables and graphs. By 2008 UK financial services held debts worth more than the annual output of the entire British economy. Including international companies with significant operations in London, the figure rises to more than double. The American financial sector, by contrast, held debts worth around half of annual US output. Reflecting the high bank debts, UK household debts were higher, as a proportion of household incomes, than any major economy ever in history. Surely this couldn't go on?

Then factor in the backfire effect. The more the evidence mounted, the more strongly people clung to their cherished worldview: the belief that complexity meant progress, that in the modern age high indebtedness was not only normal but necessary and that self-interest, if nothing else, would ensure the stability of financial markets. As Gordon Brown told an appreciative crowd of City aristocracy in his 2007 Chancellor's Mansion House speech, 'a new world order' had been created and we were witnessing the dawn of 'a new golden age for the City of London'. The backfire effect also explains people's preference for short-term historic analogies to make the case both for and against the crisis. One of its effects is to heighten our belief in evidence we have already acquired while at the same time making us sceptical of new evidence. When challenged, we look to our past for reassurance.

In laboratory conditions it is ethically impossible to demonstrate what the psychological effects of abandoning a worldview might be – to force an override of the backfire effect in other words. But we can infer it will be devastating. The extreme emotional distress that results when the veil is torn and the true nature of things revealed, forms the dramatic climax of *King Lear*. This ultimately is why so few people could bring themselves to believe what they were told by those who saw it coming.

Even as the evidence mounted, people found it hard to accept the coming storm. This was the tension most eloquently expressed by Chuck Prince, CEO of Citigroup, America's largest bank, who saw the early tremors in the markets in July 2007 but said, 'When the music stops, in terms of liquidity, things will be complicated. But as long as the music is playing, you've got to get up and dance. We're still dancing.'

Just a few weeks later, the music stopped and the fools were vindicated.

There is something of Lear in Alan Greenspan's famous testimony to a congressional hearing on the banking crisis in October 2008. He can see the fault lines and fissures in his worldview but the backfire effect cannot repair them:

> I made a mistake in presuming that the self-interests of organisations, specifically banks and others, were such as that they were best capable of protecting their own share-holders and their equity in the firms... I have found a flaw. I don't know how significant or permanent it is. But I have been *very distressed* by that fact... *I was shocked*, because I have been going for forty years or more with very consider-able evidence that it was working exceptionally well.

Greenspan could not, however, claim that he had not been warned. Like others, he had not listened. The bubble had been allowed to grow unchecked, and the bursting was upon us.

Chapter 2

TIPPING THE BANDWAGON

A network which, like the little girl with the curl, when the going was good was very, very good – but when it turned bad was horrid. Andrew Haldane, 2009

'Even the most diehard bear among us is thinking of ways to improve his personal lot, even if it is only to buy more gold and guns.'[17] John Mauldin, writing flippantly in 2009, was not exaggerating. Bankers were out stocking up on pistols, anticipating anarchy on the streets.[18] One trader was instructed curtly by a colleague: 'I couldn't afford a bunker, but I looked at it... You can get bunkers made, or buy an ex-MOD one. Best toilets, blast doors and air supply come from Switzerland. Best bunkers are made in the US. Store water and some tinned food. Vitamins are good to have.'

This visceral fear came from the same world that ignored Sir Andrew Large, dismissed Roubini, and criticised Rajan. How did we get from the lampooning of anyone who struck a note of caution, to this? The dynamics of a crash – the herd behaviour and the tipping point – are as much determined by human behaviour as the build-up of the bubble.

In this chapter we look at how people behaved as the world tipped from an unsustainable boom to a dramatic bust. The timing and exact nature of this sudden, extreme reaction could not be predicted, but its shape is common. We see it throughout history: bubble after bubble with the same tipping dynamic. We see it in nature: when a herd suddenly turns or a flock takes off as one. Every time, it is a combination of rational and irrational behaviour that is at once inevitable and near-impossible to predict with precision.

The dynamics of behaviour in the last year of the boom, and the shift from boom to bust, are vital to understanding how finance works. They reveal important truths about the way people will naturally act. And if we are to design a policy framework that is more successful in mitigating the effects of the economic cycle, we must understand these truths.

With hindsight, the most often cited point of no return is the fall of Lehman Brothers on 15 September 2008. For everyone, both those inside and outside the financial world, this was the game-changer: the bank was left to fail. The inaction of the US government tipped the system over the edge. For those looking on from outside, what had been a series of market jitters and a credit crunch became an international obsession. For those on the inside, their confidence was shattered and their faith in the system undermined.

Yet this simple analysis of the tipping point overlooks the fact that the market collapse was first revealed well over a year before, in the early summer of 2007. First, in June, amid a raft of shocked headlines, the investment banking powerhouse Bear Stearns was forced to bail out one of its hedge funds because of exposure investments in subprime mortgages, which had been given a top AAA rating by all three major rating agencies. Meanwhile, with less fanfare but equal importance, in July the lesser-known German bank, IKB, collapsed when two of its funds faced a severe funding crisis after investor confidence drained away. As we will see, these two events between them foreshadowed the financial crisis, yet it didn't strike with its full force for another fourteen months.

Herding and What It's All About
Like the animals that we are, groups of humans behave like herds.

Imagine the sun beating down relentlessly on the African plain. A herd of wildebeest graze peacefully together. All is calm. Suddenly, one animal senses a threat. It instinctively moves closer to the herd for protection, fearful of being isolated from the herd. Then a couple more notice, and jostle for protection, looking for safety in numbers. Then some more realise, and others, until suddenly, fear rips through the whole herd. As one body, with each individual looking to shield itself among the others, the herd stampedes. As the herd gathers momentum, it takes on a collective character.

Now imagine when the herd turns. As they stampede, from time to time one animal will turn away from the herd, but no others follow. These are the fools in the corner. Then, entirely unpredictably, one more turns and this time the herd follows, almost all following the new route. This is the tipping point when the herd turns. All but a few stragglers set off in the new direction.

In Britain, each winter, we witness the beauty of the starling murmurations as these migrating birds prepare to fly south. Their flocking, like herding, has repeated and recognisable patterns. The behaviour of each bird is fairly simple, yet the movement of the flock is unpredictable, as the birds twist and flow.

You see the same thing if you disturb a herd of sheep, albeit less dramatically. Surprise one and she will start towards the others for safety. A couple may notice, and likewise beat a retreat. Then some more. A ripple of movement spreads through the whole group. And then you take just one more step and they all, together, as if with one mind, trot away to a safe distance.

People behave in herds too. In fashion, for example, very few of us choose to stray too far from the herd. But a few extroverts leave the pack with outlandish new ideas. Most of the time, while we may enjoy the sight, no one takes their lead. But occasionally, they catch on and people imitate them, until we reach a tipping point of respectability, and the herd of mainstream shoppers follows.

After the incidents in June and July 2007, the crisis was clear to see for those actually watching. They saw loss pile on top of loss and the finance sector gradually break down. They saw confidence turn to doubt, they watched feelings of unease grow more intense. The final failure of Lehman was the denouement, the moment that doubt became despair and the truth was unavoidable. The herd tipped. And we are now beginning to look back with fascination at how long the crisis took to work its way through the system.

Why did the system tip when it did? How can we explain the timing? The answer can be found in the combination of natural human behaviour in an unsustainable system, which together perpetuated the boom, heightened the tipping point, and accelerated the bust.

What Happened

To get to the root of the tipping point, we need to rewind to early 2007, when the true flaw of subprime mortgages began to emerge. The concept of 'subprime' meant mortgage companies were explicitly lending to people who were deemed risky. The loans were marketed attractively to encourage people to take them out, but they masked hidden fees and a higher future rate of interest than traditional prime mortgages.

Subprime lenders, keen to maintain the high volume of sales, started to offer mortgages with 'teaser rates': a lower interest rate that would only last for a limited period. These were snapped up, even though the interest rate would be jacked up to a much higher level once the period had ended. People who would not previously have been able to get a mortgage signed up in droves. They were persuaded to pay the up-front fee and take the teaser rate in the expectation they could always re-mortgage on another teaser rate. This process is similar to the 'o per cent on balance transfers for six months' that credit card companies offer, where people can rack up their credit card debt, but pay no interest on it by immediately transferring it to a new card – until the offers run out.

Home ownership became seen as an ethical imperative. Those uncomfortable with lax access to mortgages faced a clear moral argument from the government. In the United States, Bill Clinton, in a resonant speech delivered with his customary rhetoric from the White House in 1995, told the American people:

> You want to reinforce family values in America, encour-age two-parent households, get people to stay home? Make it easy for people to own their own homes and enjoy the rewards of family life and see their work rewarded. This is a big deal. This is about more than money and sticks and boards and windows. This is about the way we live as a people and what kind of society we're going to have.

Questioning the credit that made home ownership possible was pitched directly against this ideology. The irony is that unsafe lending to people who have no hope of paying for it is unethical too.

It is part of the job of a bank to make a loan on risky projects, when they are not entirely sure the money will be paid back. Indeed, a modern economy could not function without banks putting savings to use by financing valued activities of enterprise and home ownership. But banks had always been cautious about who they lent to, and who would bear the first loss if things went wrong.

Now, not only were banks being encouraged to make

loans that might not be paid back, but they used new technology to pass on the loans. So the people making the original decision to lend were not the ones that ended up being owed the money. The idea was to improve the efficiency of finance, and ensure that risk was more effectively distributed throughout the system, enhancing stability.

Alongside the new technology, a new language was born to describe the new financial products. This new language was shorthand for those who knew what was going on. But it also obstructed scrutiny of the new developments. Many people, including senior management, did not want to admit to not knowing what the alphabet soup of new acronyms stood for, as use of the new language implied confidence that you knew what you were talking about. It is abundantly clear now that the new technology merely meant different ways of doing the same old things: lending and investing money for a fee or interest. In effect, the new technology and language that went with it made the system more complex, avoided regulatory and tax rules, and made prudent management of banks yet more difficult. The emperor had no clothes.

It is not necessary to be bamboozled by the language.

The first piece of new technology used by banks was the mortgage-backed security, known as an MBS. Its purpose was simple. The bank would package up a group of loans, and sell them to an investor – or even another bank – as an MBS. The investor might want to purchase one of these securities to get a higher return than that offered by less risky securities, like government bonds. The bank might want to sell them in order to move them off its own balance sheet, thus freeing up capital, and enabling it to earn new fees by using the money to make more loans.

An MBS did not consist of just one person's mortgage. Banks took individual mortgages, and bundled them together. They then separated them into different tranches by level of risk, and a credit rating agency was approached to give a top

AAA rating to the least risky tranche, which would be paid back first in the event of a default. Middle tranches, called 'mezzanine' in the new language, were given lower ratings like BB, and the most risky, called an equity tranche, would be paid back last, so investors would lose out first if any of the borrowers defaulted. By chopping up bundles of mortgages in this way, investors could pick and choose the level of risk they wanted: they could take the risk on the lowest tranche, where homeowners might not pay their mortgages each month, but gain a higher yield than that offered by the AAA assets. From 1997 to 2007 new issuance of these so-called MBSs almost quadrupled from $600 billion to over $2 trillion. An efficient market was thought to have been developed: those willing to bear the risk would snap up the riskier tranches, while those who wanted to play it safe would buy the higher-rated tranches. Everyone was a winner.

In older language, an MBS was a loan book that could be bought and sold at a market price.

Clearly not all of the loans could be rated AAA. So banks started grouping the lower-rated tranches of MBS into new securities, known as a Collateralised Debt Obligations, or CDOs. This allowed some of the riskier parts of MBSs to be given the gold-plated AAA rating. The idea was simple: surely even all the riskiest homeowners wouldn't stop paying their mortgages at once? Complicated mathematical models were created to gauge the likelihood of this happening, backing up the conclusion of the banks that someone, somewhere would still be paying their mortgage, even if interest rates moved higher. Once again, the CDOs were divided into tranches, and once again, investors could select the level of risk they wanted to own. By creating layers of different debts structured by different levels of risk it was believed that risk was then in some way averaged out. Risk had been diversified by spreading it out through the system, so that it sat with those most willing to bear it.

Again in the old language, a CDO was a combination of the weakest parts of several loan books, in which it was harder to calculate what was at risk.

Next, the banks set up special investment vehicles (SIVs), or their closely related special purpose vehicles (SPVs), to hold the CDOs. This took the whole process off their balance sheet, meaning they could sit back and reap the rewards without worrying about where the risks were, or allocating any capital in case things were to go wrong.

An SIV sounds clever, but in layman's terms it is simply a part of a set of loans the bank didn't want to admit to having in their accounts. The technique was not restricted to the private sector. The UK Treasury used off-balance-sheet accounting to hide increased spending through the Private Finance Initiative (PFI) and increased promises of future public sector pension payments, worsening the subsequent fiscal crisis.

Finally, the banks created a further clever twist. Enter the Credit Default Swaps (CDS). These are a form of insurance to protect the lender in the case of a debt defaulting. When investors bought CDSs, they made protection payments to insurers, like American International Group (AIG). In exchange, should there be defaults, the insurers must deliver the original value of the bond in full. The owner of the CDS is effectively paying an insurance premium to cover for a fall in the bond's value in the event of a default. CDSs were therefore used by investors to hedge against a fall in the value of MBSs – even if all homeowners did stop paying their mortgages, you could still rest easy as you would receive a payout from owning a CDS. The issuers paid the credit rating agencies to give the insured bonds the AAA rating. Once again, banks made money from the sales of CDSs, and also used them to hedge risks on their own balance sheets. AIG became hugely profitable from selling this insurance cheaply, so capturing a massive market share in the sale of CDSs.

The problem was that all the packaging up, the slicing and

dicing, had obscured where the real risk was in the system. What if homeowners started to default more quickly than expected? What if vast swathes of homeowners all defaulted at once? Would the insurers be able to pay out? Wouldn't the supposed AAA tranches suddenly be exposed to a greater risk than the models had suggested? Even worse, would the legal structures be solid? Who would know what each tranche was really worth?

At the time, though, the financial sector was seduced by innovation, not realising that the new technology of MBSs, CDOs, SIVs and CDSs had obscured where the risks really lay.

To put it in context, it was so complicated that when PricewaterhouseCoopers (PwC) went into Lehman after it fell, it took teams of ten about ten days just to start to understand the products they were dealing with, let alone the deals that had been done.[19] Or think of it this way. The Bank of England's Executive Director for Financial Stability, Andrew Haldane, who sits on the new Financial Policy Committee, has calculated how much a diligent investor would need to read for the various products on offer. Staggeringly, your standard CDO investor on average would have to read over 30,000 pages to understand the product. This is nothing compared to the CDO-squared investor, who ought to be looking at about 1,125 million pages. As a point of comparison, War and Peace is a mere 1,358 pages. The complexity of the system cannot be overemphasised.

The new language that shrouded the system confused not only those looking on from outside, but those actually working in the organisations that built it up. Stephen King, Chief Economist of HSBC, put it boldly: 'The city has created its own language. This bamboozles the public and to be honest even many in the industry… People tend to go along with it because they do not want to be the one who says they do not understand it.'[20] There was a fast-paced City language that comforted those inside its sphere and excluded those without. Greg Hands, now Parliamentary Private Secretary to the Chancellor, worked as a derivatives trader and marketer for eight years. He pointed out this internal manipulation of sales people by traders.

As an example, he described a sales person who would tell a trader that a client needed an updated price on a structure they were looking at yesterday. The trader would know there was a strong chance the client wanted to deal, or they wouldn't have come back to ask for an updated price. So he would decide to increase the price to the client, even though it hadn't really changed, because that would net him more money. At first, the sales person would be confused, but if he questioned it would get a dismissive reply like 'Oh, it's because of the theta.' The sales person would hesitate: 'Oh … what is that again?' The trader would reply: 'It's the time decay.' At this point, still confused, the sales person would become too embarrassed to ask any more questions, and retreat back to the client to explain the price change.

Amid the confusion of the new language, the central justification for the changes was that those willing to bear risk were being matched with those willing to offload it. Again, this was meant to help spread the risk in the system to those who could best bear it. This principle was based on the attitude and preference of the investors. If investors rationally knew how much risk they could absorb, only those able to bear the potential losses would take on the most risky debts. But this of course overlooks two fundamental flaws. First, that thanks to the recent explosion in complexity, it was unlikely investors would have full information and understanding. Second is the fact that investors are not paragons of rationality, capable of exerting flawless judgement. They are swayed by human emotions and desires as much, if not more, than the rest of us. As John Kay wrote in August 2007, a full year before the balance tipped, 'if trading was motivated not by differences in attitudes and preferences but by differences in information and understanding, risk would gravitate not to those best able to bear it but to those least able to comprehend it'.[21] His observation would be revealed as painfully prophetic.

In turn, authorities let their fears be allayed by a false sense of security. When they looked at the total exposure to subprime mortgages, they saw the net exposure was relatively small. What they did not see, or want to see, was that because bets had been laid on the back of the subprime mortgage market, the gross exposure was huge. With the network of CDSs on the back of CDOs, you would only need a few CDOs to go bust to bring major institutions to the brink of bankruptcy.

The consequence of this complicated new system was close to financial alchemy: it was to turn a risky mortgage into an AAA-rated bond, a gilt-edged security. It meant that the balance sheets of banks still stood up to scrutiny, which meant they could borrow still more money, to fund still more of these money-making tricks.

Of course, at the bottom of all of this were the proud new owners of houses across America. But as long as interest rates stayed low, house prices didn't fall and people kept paying their instalments, everyone benefitted.

Between 2004 and 2006, US interest rates rose by over 4 percentage points, from 1 per cent in June 2004 to a high of 5.25 per cent in June 2006. On a variable rate mortgage, this of course increased the cost of repayments. This also coincided with many mortgages coming to the end of the initial low-interest period, which prompted a huge jump in monthly payments. In July 2006, US house prices began to fall.[22]

You may not know that in the US, mortgages are tied to the property, not the person. Astonishingly, Chuck Prince didn't know either. It has big implications. If you can't meet your payments, or your house is worth less than your debts, you can simply walk away. If you relinquish it to the original owner, in this case the bank, you can avoid the foreclosure process. Sure enough, thousands of US homeowners began to send back their title deeds. The early morning post in mortgage banks across America became known as the 'jingle mail' – as keys were physically and metaphorically sent back to the bank. As rates rose and prices fell, more homes were abandoned. The impotent sets of keys came in a steady flow into the mail of the banks. As entire streets of newly-built housing were abandoned, prices fell still further. Banks across America became the unintentional owners of more and more houses, almost all worth less than they paid.

There was going to come a point of no return. As 2006 turned into 2007, it came.

The impact on the banks at first seemed to come out of nowhere. HSBC started the ball rolling when it wrote down $10.5 billion in goodwill and fired its US Head of Mortgages in February. More dramatically, on 2 April, New Century Financial, one of the biggest subprime mortgage lenders in the US, filed for bankruptcy after a month of difficulties. In response to worry in the market, government-backed firms Fannie Mae and Freddie Mac offered new long-term fixed-rate mortgages designed to let typical subprime owners switch and divert the potential crisis. Meanwhile, UBS closed its new hedge fund arm after it was hit by subprime losses.

These incidents weren't isolated, but few thought they were systemic. By June, the warning sign flashed brighter from one of Wall Street's most infamous institutions: Bear Stearns. The fifth-largest securities firm on Wall Street announced it had spent $3.2 billion bailing out two of its funds that had been exposed to the subprime market. The so-called Timberwolf CDOs, packaged by Goldman Sachs, were only launched in March 2007. By the end of June, $100 worth of investment was worth $83, and by the end of July just $15. ABN Amro, then about to be purchased by RBS, was another significant buyer of the flawed Timberwolf CDOs.

Like HSBC, Bear Stearns too fired its head of asset management and launched an inquiry into the failure of the funds. The collapse of the Bear Stearns funds sent shockwaves throughout the finance sector. It called into question the value of the CDOs that flooded the system, which had been bought and sold on the basis of their supposedly secure AAA rating. Bear Stearns funds had invested in securities it thought were safe. But thanks to the dramatic rise in subprime mortgage defaults, the value of these securities dissolved.

A source at the time who was close to Jimmy Cayne, the bridge-loving Chairman and CEO of Bear Stearns, stripped it down to the essentials: 'This stuff wasn't triple A. There's going to be a big debate about this.'[23] He was right with the first part but seriously understated the second.

The realisation that the AAA assets could be almost worthless caused alarm in all corners of the financial sector. As Brad Hintz, analyst and ex-CFO of Lehman Brothers, questioned publicly at the time: 'How many other hedge funds are holding similar, illiquid, esoteric securities? What are their true prices? What will happen if more blow up?'[24]

This was loudly reported around the world with alarm, but it wasn't clear what the immediate effect on the financial system would be. For those watching closely, it soon became clearer. The key is found not with an American mortgage giant or a high-risk investment bank, but with the relatively unknown German bank, IKB.

On 20 July 2007, IKB announced happily that it had had a successful year. It was confident with its earnings forecast. It publicly dismissed rumours of a credit downgrade. Looking back, it is like a master class in pride coming before a fall. A mere ten days later, on 30 July, the bank was forced to admit that its earnings were 'significantly lower' than forecast. The German banking sector produced a rescue package worth €9 billion over the weekend in an attempt to protect itself and its national reputation. IKB's losses had been sustained by two off-balance-sheet SIVs, called Rhineland and Rhinebridge, which had been set up to buy long-term MBSs, funded by short-term wholesale borrowing. These SIVs, like most, were linked by a credit line to the bank that owned them, so while they were off the balance sheet for accounting purposes, the bank was liable to make good its borrowing if it lost money. The credit lines were invoked. IKB didn't have enough funds to bail them out. The bank was set for collapse. Much to the relief of all concerned, in the immediate term the situation was hurriedly resolved. Germany's government and banking sector rallied round, bailout money was provided, and calamity postponed.

To an outside observer, this looked like the collapse of one small German bank. In comparison to Bear Stearns running into trouble, IKB's difficulties seem a smaller part of the tipping point. But the ramifications of the two were immense.

If you look at the combined effect of the Bear Stearns hedge fund and IKB collapse, the prognosis is fatal. It clearly showed, at least to those who were looking, that AAA ratings were meaningless, that off-balance-sheet debts were still the responsibility of the bank when things went wrong, and that the confidence of investors had turned.

In September 2007, before being bought by RBS, ABN Amro for example had over $100 billion of credit lines to off-balance-sheet vehicles, more than any other bank in Europe. Many of the losses on these vehicles will never be recovered by the UK taxpayer.

So these early collapses were clear warnings of what was to come. From then onwards, banks increasingly realised that the risks they thought they had passed on to the off-balance-sheet 'shadow banking system' were in fact still with them. Off-balance-sheet vehicles were brought back onto banks' balance sheets, and the value of AAA debt across the financial system was brought into question. Reassessing their balance sheets in this light, it became clear that the banks had a lot of the bad debt, and not nearly as much capital as they thought. As banks realised how exposed they were to bad debt, they became unwilling to lend to anyone else, because no one knew who held what bad debt. Everyone was in the same position. The breakdown in lending of the credit crunch began.

Despite this realisation at the heart of the sector, the finance machine bulldozed on. Astonishingly, the RBS acquisition of ABN Amro was completed, and signed off by the FSA and the government. Many in the markets continued to assert this was a short-term liquidity problem. In part, this was because many of the AAA debts were insured, so holders of the debt expected to be compensated if they defaulted. It took time to understand that a very small number of companies had cornered the market for writing such insurance, so that when all the claims came at once they could not possibly cover them.

So the crisis continued to work its way through the system: next to go down was American Home Mortgage, one of the largest independent mortgage lenders in the US. Meanwhile, during testimony to the US Congress, Ben Bernanke, head of the Federal Reserve, admitted this crisis could cost America between $50 and $100 billion.

And then focus switched sharply back to Europe. On 9 August, BNP Paribas announced it was having to freeze three of its funds because it was simply unable to value them. The announcement sent the London stock market tumbling. The biggest faller was RBS, which despite all these warnings was still pursuing its takeover strategy, with support from the then government and the FSA.

The crisis was about to hit home. On Thursday 13 September, Robert Peston announced the biggest scoop of his career: Northern Rock had been forced to approach the Bank of England in its capacity as lender of last resort. As one of the biggest mortgage lenders in the UK, Northern Rock had struggled to find others willing to lend to it, which triggered a short-term cash flow crisis. With Peston's broadcast, the subprime crisis moved from a problem for the investment banking sector to a threat to the lives of savers up and down Britain. Overnight, millions of savers removed their funds on the internet. By Friday morning, the run on the bank started in earnest. In the leafy suburbs of Surrey 250 people queued to retrieve their savings, while in Golders Green the police were on hand to control the crowds. Even in the City, the Moorgate branch had a queue, and City workers circulated photos taken in their lunch break. The share price tumbled by 32 per cent in a day.[25] The first retail run on a bank in the UK for 150 years, Northern Rock became a global emblem of the crisis.

After a weekend of national panic, the government finally attempted to reassure people that their deposits were safe. By Tuesday 18 September, with a promise that retail deposits would be protected, the crisis passed and calm was restored. The debate turned to what to do with the stricken bank. For five months the government dithered, searching in vain for a private sector solution. Eventually it announced the decision to nationalise the bank on 17 February 2008. The collapse exposed the lack of a failure mechanism for banks and preparation for any financial storm in the Brown-led government. In a whirlwind of confusion, the government rejected the proposal to wind down the bank, the action now in place for future bank failures. Instead they took on the liability for the taxpayer. Less tangible but still important was the brief dent in confidence that the British public suffered. For that one weekend, the financial crisis made itself felt in the homes of people across Britain, leaving a bitter foretaste of what was to come.

The financial crisis retreated to the upper echelons of the investment banking world, where losses continued to accumulate. Huge losses were announced by almost all major banking groups as the value of assets were written down. The Bank of England and the US Federal Reserve cut interest rates in an attempt to stimulate the economy, while Citigroup, Bank of America, and JPMorgan Chase attempted to restore confidence to the market with a proposed superfund to act as a vehicle for troubled funds to wind down operations orderly without a firesale of assets. It never took off. Nothing stemmed the tide of loss. At the end of November, Freddie Mac announced the sale of $6 billion of its shares to cover its losses, only to be trumped by Fannie Mae about a week later selling $7 billion.

Then came another blow: Bear Stearns announced its first ever quarterly loss on 9 January 2008. Throughout February, it continued trading, confident of its prospects. But it finally collapsed on Friday 14 March, when its hedge fund clients panicked en masse and withdrew their assets. Even on the evening before its collapse, most Bear Stearns employees had no idea of the severity of the crisis. As with most business failures, though, while the debts were the substantive cause of the collapse, the immediate trigger was simply that it ran out of cash. Armed with the promise from the Federal Reserve of whatever liquidity was required, JPMorgan stepped in and bought the bank. Employees with their life savings in Bear Stearns shares lost everything. It was in effect a government bailout with JPMorgan as the middleman. While the shock to confidence rippled through the financial world, the US government had acted to keep the system afloat.

Losses carried on rising throughout April, and confidence sank ever lower. In one week in late March and early April, one fifth of mortgage products were withdrawn in the UK.

August 2008 became the month of warnings. HSBC announced that conditions in financial markets were at their toughest 'for several decades' after suffering a 28 per cent fall in half-year profits. And UK confidence fell sharply when Alistair Darling told *The Guardian* newspaper that the crisis was the worst for sixty years. His frank pessimism earned him the wrath of his boss, Gordon Brown, but was backed up by the OECD report of early September that first predicted recession in the UK. And then, on 7 September, Fannie Mae and Freddie Mac, which guaranteed half of America's mortgage debt, valued at $85 trillion, were bailed out. The Bear Stearns impact was nothing compared to this. These mortgage lenders were iconic, government-sponsored institutions. They were part of America's psyche. And they were bust.

When you look at 2007 and 2008 like this with hind-sight, it is surprising the balance didn't tip before it did. The pattern set out so clearly by the early collapse of the Bear Stearns and IKB funds was repeated across the financial world, as more and more pieces of the puzzle fell into place. The original observers of Bear Stearns and IKB watched the truth gradually dawn on the financial sector. But while the pattern was the same, no one knew if or when the whole system would fall.

By September 2008, though, people were primed for panic. All that was needed was a trigger. The US government's decision to take a stand and let Lehman Brothers fail provided that trigger.

Lehman Brothers was no ordinary bank. Not only was it the fourth-largest Wall Street investment bank, but its power drew on over 150 years of history. In a country that notoriously loves its lineage, the bank proudly traced its origins back to 1844 when a German immigrant founded a dry goods shop in Montgomery, Alabama.[26] With over $600 billion of assets at the time of its downfall, it had fingers in every pie on offer in the global financial market. It has been estimated that it was counterparty to $5 trillion of CDS contracts.[27] If any bank was going to be too big to fail, Lehman was it.

In the week before its collapse, Lehman posted losses for the previous three months of $3.9 billion. Confidence tumbled, and like IKB, Bear Stearns and Northern Rock before it, its funding dried up. The vultures began to circle, with Bank of America, Barclays, and the Korea Development Bank looking to buy. But even the most feasible emergency takeover bid, from Barclays, stalled late in the weekend.

On Sunday 15 September 2008, Lehman Brothers filed for bankruptcy.

There are a handful of recent events that everyone remembers where they were when they heard about them, like the death of Princess Diana or the attack on the twin towers. This was the financial equivalent.

To the outside world, watching the sudden shift in the fortunes of finance was like seeing a flock of birds, until now settled calmly on the ground, suddenly, without warning, take off in flight. The amounts of money were so huge, the names so renowned, and the human pictures of despair so striking that it gripped the media and the public in equal measure. In the UK, we watched from a distance as the great American legend crumbled. The press immediately went into overdrive. The *Sunday Times* reported the newly prestigious Dr Doom, Roubini, warning: 'It's clear we are one step away from a financial meltdown.'[28] It was hard to believe what you were reading. The *Daily Mail* captured the mood: 'It is almost impossible to comprehend how Lehman, a giant investment bank founded in the 1850s, that survived the Wall Street Crash of 1929 and the ensuing Great Depression, could have evaporated almost overnight.'[29]

After that, we entered freefall and there was no going back. Capital markets completely froze. As the Nobel Prize-winning economist Paul Krugman commented: 'Letting Lehman fail basically brought the entire world capital market down.'[30] On the same day that Lehman filed for bankruptcy, Merrill Lynch had to be rescued in a buyout by Bank of

America. The insurance giant AIG, which had provided insurance to so many bondholders, was rescued days later in an $85 billion intervention by the US government.

In the UK, on 17 September, Lloyds was pressured into a takeover of HBOS amid fears of its collapse. Less than a month later, both RBS and Lloyds came to the government cap in hand for a bailout worth £37 billion.

Why did the crisis take so long to play out? This is one of the most fascinating parts of the recent crash. No bank had enough liquidity to last them a whole year. They all managed to borrow after the problems became apparent in the middle of 2007. Likewise, although it took time to reassess the value of assets whose ratings had been proved worthless, this process was already well underway in the middle of 2007. The myriad forces at work under the surface, which determined when the collective confidence of the financial world tipped over the edge, have their roots in human behaviour. And that is why it is so important we learn the lessons. Because the human behaviour behind the crash will ensure it happens again, unless we act to manage it.

The same factors that kept the majority ridiculing the fools in the corner earlier in the boom were still in play in 2007. The backfire effect, for example, shows how slow people are to take on board facts that alter their world view. But this was not the only human force at work among the finance hordes. To get to grips with human behaviour in 2007, we need to go back to group behaviour. As early as the fifth century BC, Plato noticed the phenomenon of men being swept away by the forces of a crowd, somehow greater than and separate from the individuals themselves: 'The rocks and the whole place re-echo, and re-double the noise of their boos and applause. Can a young man be unmoved by all this? He gets carried away and soon finds himself behaving like the crowd and becoming one of them.'[31] Charles Mackay wrote *Extraordinary Popular Delusions and the Madness of*

Crowds in 1841 about the South Sea and other bubbles. In the twentieth century, group psychology became the focus of academic study.

Within a growing field of social psychology, the field of criminal psychology honed in on how the sense of personal responsibility is diminished in a group, because responsibility is shared by the group as a whole. This symptom of group behaviour is called the 'bystander effect'.

The Bystander Effect

The name was coined by psychologists in the years after the rape and murder of Kitty Genovese in New York on 13 March 1964. Winston Moseley, the man convicted of the crime, admitted in court that he stabbed Kitty 17 times before sexually assaulting her and leaving her to die. He attacked her as she walked from a car park in Queens to her apartment, in a residential area. Her screams and cries for help were heard around the neighbourhood, but despite this, no one so much as called the police. No one intervened. The entire neighbourhood were bystanders to the crime.

The inertia of Kitty's neighbours sparked horror and disgust around America. Everyone asked the same question: why did no one help? Psychologists in particular seized on it. Against a background of news reports and commentators pointing vehemently to the moral decay and dehumanisation of the modern age, psychologists sought to delve deeper and identify what it is in us that would let us stand by a crime and say nothing. The result was the bystander effect.

We all know that when we see something happening that we know is wrong, we are thrown into conflict. The reasons to intervene are morally strong – our human tendency to empathise sparks our natural desire to stop the harm we see being done. We know it is wrong, and we ought to do something to stop it. But fear often holds us back. We face rational fear of the ensuing consequences: that we might be blamed or punished. Then there are the irrational fears, like our instinctive desire to avoid embarrassment. There is a classic conflict between the pros and cons of acting, with both the rational and irrational arguments making their full force felt.

In the wake of Kitty's murder and the ensuing experiments, psychologists found the now famous result that, as discomforting as it is to admit, if there are more people witnessing an event, fewer people will intervene. It is not a question of 'moral decay', nor that the people watching are psychopaths who lack normal levels of engagement. If you witness something alone, you know that the only source of help is from you. The responsibility and the blame for inaction lie with you. This knowledge may still be outweighed by the arguments not to intervene, but it is a powerful incentive to act. If, on the other hand, you know that you are one of many witnesses, the responsibility and the blame of inaction are diffused. Not only that, but inaction becomes increasingly easy to rationalise away: someone else has probably done something already, so to intervene now will only confuse the situation.[32]

The classic study into the bystander effect was conducted by John Darley and Bibb Latané in 1968. Darley and Latané's crucial insight was to observe the inverse relationship between intervention and the number of bystanders. Importantly, they found that those who did not intervene were largely undecided. They were not indifferent, but were in a constant state of conflict even as they did not act until it was too late.

Forty years on, leaving criminal psychology for behavioural finance, and there is evidence of exactly the same principle at work in the finance sector. We know that the witnesses to the irresponsibility in finance were many. The impending crisis was widely reported in the financial press, countless numbers of people wrote papers informing their peers. A growing number of people knew something was wrong. But the collective body of the finance world did not act.

The feeling that responsibility and blame would be spread out has been validated. Since the crash, despite the best attempts of the press, we know in our heart of hearts we cannot blame individual, run-of-the-mill bankers. Can we ask a young analyst at a boutique investment firm to take full responsibility for not taking a stand and forcing the financial world to listen? Of course not. Responsibility and blame is spread out across the sector as a whole, so that no one individual can really be called to account. Those who designed the system and promoted the flawed ideology may have been the equivalent of the perpetrators of the crime, but the whole finance sector, with safety in numbers, were the silent neighbours.

Indeed, in the public debate around the crash, responsibility has also been dispersed. Not enough distinction is made between different parts of the City: between the thousands of small, highly competitive firms that work to build entrepreneurial companies, and the large, implicitly and explicitly state-backed institutions, which provide utility services, are systemically important, and require safe stewardship.

But just as in the psychology experiments, the bystanders were not calmly watching the events of 2007 and 2008. The majority were worried, unsure of what to do, fearful of embarrassment and, more importantly, of losing their jobs. Our research found that, as for teenagers, the strength of peer pressure in the City shouldn't be underestimated. In a world based on networks, failure to conform is a dangerous, and often costly, exercise. The social norms of the City perpetuated this exclusive atmosphere. No fund manager wants to miss out on the best deal, the best investment. If everyone is in on something, you don't want to be the one who misses out. The downside of this is a groupthink mentality. It is no surprise that Stephen King extended his conformist argument to its main conclusion: 'People behave in herds… If you try and regulate when you see a bubble forming, the vast majority of the sector will say "it's not a bubble, don't interfere".'[33]

As with any social group, there were leaders who had the strongest role in shaping accepted views. Indeed studies in investment patterns have shown that the majority will follow these key leaders. As Joel Stern is said to have put it, 'if you want to know where a herd of cattle is heading, you need not interview every steer in the whole herd, just the lead steer'.

In the banking world, right up until the crash, the lead steers were giving a very clear message that it was business as usual. We were told that John Mack, the CEO of Morgan Stanley, went on a tour of Europe in early 2007 and brought together the brightest designers of complex structured products he could find. His stark instruction to them was to 'dial it up'. The result? As one fund manager put it to us, it is like telling Al Qaeda operatives 'I want more bodies'.[34] No wonder his juniors were taking on huge amounts of risk. When the key players in the market are issuing instructions and comments like these, of course peer pressure perpetuated a business as usual approach.

Hand in hand with this was the danger that large sections of the workforce had no memory of work life before the boom. Adair Turner pinpointed this as part of the problem in 2007 and 2008: 'At the end of a boom there are fewer people who have seen a crash and therefore more who think "it" can't go wrong.'[35] The history of economics has little place in modern economics courses, but even if it did, historical understanding is nowhere near as powerful as personal experience. And the majority of the workforce had no experience of a crash to draw on. So, as a group, there was little impetus to challenge: the world view that shaped the majority of the herd didn't know what a crash looked like. Why, and how, would they challenge the boom? They may have been nervous and fearful, but they didn't know what exactly they were fearful of. As long as you don't have an object for your fear, it is hard to act on it. Instead, it stays a nagging, nebulous worry without real power. When crystallised in the fall of Lehman, unspoken fear found its outlet and exploded across the sector. Put more prosaically, when a large downside risk has been ignored, at the moment the risk is uncovered, all valuations will be shocked, downwards.

Just as the bystanders of Kitty's murder didn't take responsibility and intervene, so too was it hard for those wrapped up in the system to know exactly what could be done. When Lehman fell, the time for inactive internal conflict was over.

The herd tendency of groups helps explain this behaviour. In the boom years, the herd instinct urged on more and more reckless behaviour. A former Morgan Stanley banker explained with hindsight: 'The herd instinct was just amazing. Everyone was looking for yield. You could do almost anything you could dream of and persuade people to buy it.'[36] But when Bear Stearns and IKB faced bailouts in the summer of 2007, individuals on the edge of the herd were startled. Gradually throughout 2007 and 2008, more people noticed, but the bystander effect, the backfire effect, and the dynamics of group psychology kept widespread panic at bay. As Ron Brater, another Morgan Stanley man, described it: 'In banks you have this kind of mentality, this groupthink, and people just keep going with what they know, and they don't want to listen to bad news.'[37] Finally, with the fall of Lehman, the crisis took that one fatal step too far, and triggered panic.

But why was Lehman so different? The backfire effect, the bystander effect, peer pressure, and herd behaviour all explain why the delay lasted as long as it did, but they don't explain why the fall of Lehman in particular had such a spectacular effect.

To answer that question it is useful to think of the financial sector as a complex adaptive system. A growing field of research into complex adaptive systems brings together psychology, anthropology, maths, economics, and neuroscience to study group behaviour. Groups of people are complex because of the almost infinite variations on behaviour; adaptive, because we respond to experience, so history matters; and a system because the actions of the group have feedback, so the group acts in a recognisable or systemic way. Within the system, decision rules in turn develop with characteristics distinct from those of the individuals involved.

The world of politics is another complex adaptive system. The sum of individual behaviour, while complex and unpredictable, is shaped by experience and history, and fits into recognisable and repeated patterns. Leadership matters, of course, but there is a group dynamic that persists outside any individual's control. The peer pressure, herd behaviour, and bystander effect that we noticed earlier can all be recognised within this system.

The patterns of complex adaptive systems lean heavily on the mathematical field of chaos theory. Made infamous by its finding that a butterfly flapping its wings in Tokyo can cause a hurricane in Florida, chaos theory is the study of dynamic systems that are unpredictable yet follow repeated patterns. These so-called chaotic patterns are highly sensitive to initial conditions, or history. Their unpredictable nature comes not from random shocks but from an unfolding of the internal dynamics of the system. After the fact, chaotic patterns can look inevitable, even though they are almost impossible to predict in advance.

It is illuminating to think of finance as a system in this way because it draws together the human behaviour ideas we have already covered with key structural features. Using this model in a brilliant analysis of the crisis, Andrew Haldane identifies four key mechanisms at work within the system: connectivity, feedback, uncertainty and innovation.[38]

It is clear that in the last two decades, the scale and inter-connectivity of the finance sector increased dramatically. This has had countless consequences, but one of them is that something which starts as a local problem is now far more likely to become a global one. The conscious interdependence of institutions within this framework meant that as risk became understood in 2007 and 2008, individual banks rationally attempted to bank up their liquidity. But because of that same interdependence, this in fact increased the difficulties facing each institution. At the same time, the uncertainty that dogged the sector began to reach unparalleled heights as everyone realised that, thanks to the dramatic innovations of the last ten years, the level of counterparty risk simply could not be calculated. All of this resulted in a system that, although hugely more complex, was in fact far less diverse. This systemic analysis supports the understanding of human behaviour, in which social norms and group dynamics dominate the working environment.

The result was a dense, interconnected world of finance balanced on a knife-edge. Up to a point, all these different properties help to absorb and disperse shocks. But after a certain point, they simply increased the shock and magnified its effects. Hence the dramatic tipping point.

The authorities, too, are not separate from but part of the system; their expected reaction informs behaviour, while the authorities' behaviour is itself informed by the rest of the system. George Soros pointed out: 'In the past, whenever the financial system came close to a breakdown, the authorities rode to the rescue and prevented it from going over the brink. That is what I expected in 2008 but that is not what happened.'[39] Thinking back to the Kitty Genovese case, Greenspan's approach to mopping up after crises is a bit like the police charging in, telling everyone to stay calm and to let them handle it. Finance had for a long time been lulled into a false sense of security by the interventions of central banks. As a group, they had been encouraged to believe that they would be rescued. Charlie Bean, then Deputy Governor of the Bank of England, has spoken out honestly about expectation within the Bank: 'We knew [elements] were unsustainable and worried that the unwinding might be disorderly, though I don't think anyone could have guessed the course that events would actually take.'[40] By design, the failure removed the assumption that the authorities would intervene to prop up a failed bank. That shock to so many well-informed individuals tipped the balance.

However you look at it, the collapse of Lehman came as a direct shock. But the reason it came as a shock was not because it was some external event that intruded into the system. Rather, it was a shock because the dynamics of the system led everyone involved to expect something else. The 'shock' was in fact the natural byproduct of the internal dynamics of the system. And this same system was structured in such a way that once it tipped, the cascade was violent. The herd mentality rapidly worked to undo any confidence that remained in the system. The fear that spread across the financial sector pushed people to merge into the crowd rushing to escape the market. It triggered a self-perpetuating vicious circle.

Chapter 3

THE DANGERS OF
BUSINESS AS USUAL

In the worst days of the crash, as the lights went out over Wall Street, Seamus Smith, the head of American Express's European division, was in New York on business. Smith was a man of routine. He always stayed at the Millennium Hilton, five minutes away from Wall Street. As a keen marathon runner, he would rise early and train at the hotel gym. Situated on the fifth floor with a goldfish-bowl view of the city, the gym is a quiet place from which the so-called Masters of the Universe can ponder their creation.

But this day was different. As Smith was changing in the locker room, a muscular Wall Streeter next to him suddenly broke down in tears, sobbing loudly into his BlackBerry. Public displays of vulnerability are virtually unheard of in finance, so Smith was unsure how to respond.

'Are you alright?' he asked hesitantly.

There was no response.

'Do you need help?'

This worked. Between great gasping sobs, the man pieced together a reply.

'I've... lost... everything.'

The broken banker had been caught up in a grand Wall Street tradition. Eighty years before the BlackBerry, the instrument of torture was the ticker tape: a telegraphic machine which punched out stock market data onto a thin strip of paper. By that fatal week in October 1929 when the New York stock market crashed and ultimately lost 89 per cent of its value, the volume of trading was so large that the ticker tape could not cope. Once the markets had closed brokers would sit in agonised suspense while the machines caught up with their last transactions. The delay allowed for the occasional pocket of hope.

Digital technology now allows market movements to be tracked second by second, but the human impact was the same. As we saw in the last chapter, the maddening complexity of globalised finance meant it took well over a year from the turn of the housing market until everyone's exposure to everyone else had been worked out.

And then, as now, people thought they had lost everything. As trillions were wiped from bank assets around the world the markets tipped from irrational exuberance to hysteria. Traders screamed sell, but there was no longer any credit with which to buy. Lines on stock index charts formed themselves into jagged cliffs as financial assets plummeted in value. In New York, grown men sobbed in gyms. The CEO of Lehman, Dick 'Gorilla' Fuld was allegedly punched out cold by an ex-employee while he exercised on the treadmill. In the City of London, bankers bought guns, ready to bed down in bunkers if civil society collapsed.[41] No one was old enough to remember the last Wall Street Crash, but plenty could recall the CNN pictures of food riots during the East Asian financial crisis in 1997. At the time they had told themselves 'it couldn't happen here'. But now they asked: what if it could?

There's a happy ending to this story. In 2010, Seamus Smith was staying at his favourite hotel, exercising at the same gym, at the same time in the morning. The same Wall Street hunk appeared. Gone were the tears, the swagger was back. His only comment?

'Thank God that's all over.'

At the tipping point, the bankers were finally afraid. Their world view – that rock-solid belief in the invincibility of the system – was fatally undermined. Many reports from that time stress the emotional trauma of the crisis. As we saw in Chapter 2, Alan Greenspan, who had provided banking with its own philosophy, was 'shocked' and 'distressed' by the paradoxically suicidal self-interest which was exposed by the crash. As far as the public is concerned, that other paradox 'light-touch regulation' was also shattered.

After the crash, in a period of relative calm, for many in finance the trauma is forgotten. We have witnessed a mass act of mental brushing under the carpet, what Freud called sublimation. Although the consequences of the banking collapse are all around us, these consequences are at one remove from finance. Overseas, the banking crisis has rolled over into a sovereign debt crisis; at home people struggle with falling real incomes and tight credit as a consequence of deleveraging. But while the government has stepped in to pick up the pieces, many in the City carry on with business as usual. New polling undertaken for this book found that over 60 per cent of financial sector workers said that their colleagues would behave no differently if the crisis happened again today.

What is most shocking to an outside observer is that it is hard to see evidence of changed behaviour as a result of the personal trauma people went through. There is what one trader poetically described as a 'haunted' look behind people's eyes.[42] Another said that the crash had been 'ingrained' in people's minds.[43]

These appear to be the exceptions that prove the rule. Few at the top of finance express any sense of personal responsibility, however small. The reaction is generally one of two: 'they either say "blame the directors" or they say "thank god I didn't have anything to do with it and still have a job".'[44] There has been no deep introspection or personal accountability.

Sir Fred Goodwin went so far as to refuse to allow his Chief Economist to attend a parliamentary Select Committee, until the Chair of the Committee was forced to call and explain that if he chose not to attend he would be summoned, with the full force of the police in reserve.

This reticence in facing up to facts is unfortunate. If we fail to associate unwelcome behavioural outcomes with our own decision-making and blame them instead on others – on culture, society, 'the system', or government – then behaviour is unlikely to change. Cognitive behavioural therapy has proven that by consciously changing our habits of thought we can influence the emotional responses which drive dysfunctional behaviour. The Alcoholics Anonymous programme, which employs many of the methods of CBT, encourages members first to accept personal responsibility for their drinking.[45] By contrast, those who do not accept personal responsibility rarely change their behaviour.

The manager of a charity which provides the public with free financial and legal advice told us that in recent years she has seen a significant rise in the number of clients approaching them for advice on debt. The most serious cases – where the debtor is facing legal action – are characterised by the debtor's complete failure to accept that they have a problem. All too often a debtor is only made aware of how much they owe when the bailiffs arrive to take away the family television, after months of compulsively ignoring a barrage of paperwork from banks and credit card companies:

> People come into us with huge bags of unopened letters, and they seem visibly relieved when they hand them over to their caseworker, because they think that now it's our problem. Our aim is to empower people to deal with the problem themselves; we can't be expected to haul our clients along to the post office every week with their chequebooks. They'll disappear off our radar for a few months and then one day, once the bailiffs are back they turn up in the office again with another bag of unopened letters.

The charity manager argued that the easy credit which hooked so many households during the boom years has led to a marked increase in poor financial decision-making. Cases where the charity's clients are behind on their mortgage payments while continuing to pay for a seventy-pound monthly Sky subscription are alarmingly common.

'All the balls are in the air and then something happens.' For people on very low incomes, living on credit means they can enjoy a higher income lifestyle with broadband internet and satellite television, and it eases the pain of rent inflation. The trouble is people do not anticipate something going wrong in the future. If they are made redundant, become too ill to work or are otherwise deprived of a regular income, then all the balls come crashing down. As a pattern of behaviour this unites the people at the wealth extremes of our society. Northern Rock and HBOS were also living on credit, making up the gap between the deposits they took and the loans they issued by borrowing from the wholesale money markets. The strategy allowed them to grow and prosper for a while. Then something happened, something no one had planned for: house prices fell and access to credit became tight.

But despite the scale of the crash that tore through the fabric of the financial system, there has been no widespread acceptance that universal access to credit was a problem. It is already happening again. Adverts have sprung up across the media offering credit to those who would normally find it hard to obtain. Credit is once more being offered to those who are least likely to be able to pay the money back. Take the widespread advert for the Granite credit card in July 2011, dangerously branded to imply the world you build using the Granite card is built on similarly sure foundations to the card's solid name. It proudly claims to be 'The card for people with poor credit'.

It's Not Me, Guv

Senior policymakers at the time of the crash have also failed to acknowledge any mistakes. Former Prime Minister Gordon Brown and his close associate Ed Balls, refuse to admit that government spending was unsustainably high, despite the UK having one of the largest deficits in the developed world as we entered the crisis, and being left with the largest budget deficit in peacetime history. Similarly, when Gordon Brown admitted to mistakes in the design of the regulatory structure in an off-the-cuff remark, he quickly back-pedalled and claimed that he had been misinterpreted.

Some in the City have begun to recognise the need for change. Marcus Agius, Chairman of Barclays, wrote a public letter to the Financial Times in September 2010, co-signed by senior executives from nearly all the major City firms, including Lloyds, JPMorgan, Goldman Sachs and Deutsche Bank, as well as leading law firms, insurance companies and the London Stock Exchange. In the letter, Agius publicly admitted excesses in the sector and called for an 'enlightened culture' in their organisations: 'Ultimately, it is the responsibility of the leaders of financial institutions – not their regulators, shareholders or other stakeholders – to create, oversee and imbue their organisations with an enlightened culture based on professionalism and integrity.'[46]

This is a welcome first step. But shortly afterwards, in January 2011, Bob Diamond, the new CEO of Barclays, was called to testify in front of the Treasury Select Committee in the House of Commons. Under persistent questioning, he said of the public: 'I think they recognise that there was a period of remorse and apology for banks. I think that period needs to be over.'[47] The public would beg to differ.

Barclays's behaviour since the crisis has demonstrated a failure to understand the errors made across the financial system in the-run up to the crash. It emerged that, in September 2009, Barclays had sold $12.3 billion of underperforming credit to a new Cayman Islands company, Protium. The forty-five investment bankers who had managed the assets at Barclays staffed the 'new' company, which was almost entirely financed with a ten-year loan from Barclays itself.[48] According to reports in the press, emails showed the Finance Director of Barclays, Chris Lucas, explaining to the US Securities and Exchange Commmission that they were effectively being held to ransom by their employees:

> Barclays could not offer the management team – at that time Barclays employees – an attractive long-term career path. There was, therefore, a very significant risk that the team would leave, with the result that Barclays would no longer have the expertise necessary to manage these assets effectively.

Protium ran for only nineteen months before Barclays unravelled it at great cost to the shareholders. With an inital charge of £532 million, one of Bob Diamond's first announcements as CEO of Barclays was to begin to try and extract Barclays from the complicated agreement with the fund. Despite this all coming to light, and the great cost to shareholders, there have been no resignations of those involved in the scandal, and no apologies.

Of course such behaviour is not restricted to one organisation.

The buy-to-let market, where landlords buy a property in order to rent it out, has picked up from where it left off with barely a minute's silence to mark the crisis. As a formal concept, buy-to-let only began in 1996, when a change in the tenancy laws made it safer to be a landlord, giving banks the confidence to grant buy-to-let mortgages. It took off in spectacular fashion. In 1998, these mortgages made up just 0.4

per cent of all mortgages granted. By 2006 that had become 11.1 per cent, and the trend is increasing.[49] With interest rates at a long-term low level and property prices booming, it was extremely profitable. But there are winners and losers in every game, and the losers were the first-time buyers for whom house prices kept rising, pushed up by these buy-to-let businessmen. Senior figures in the industry told *Channel 4 News* unequivocally that 'it was buy-to-let that kept house prices artificially high'.[50]

You would think that, with the credit crunch and burst of the housing bubble, this practice would have fallen by the wayside as one of the casualties of the recession. Headlines like 'The day when buy-to-let died'[51] were scattered across the papers as Bradford & Bingley, one of the biggest buy-to-let mortgage lenders, went down. It turns out rumours of its death were greatly exaggerated. One buy-to-let landlady writing in the *Sunday Times* cited her own experience during the crash: 'Despite the credit crunch, I have just managed to remortgage with a loan only 0.5 per cent more expensive than the previous one.'[52] An index tracking the percentage of mortgages that are buy-to-let has been rising on trend since the mortgage was invented in 1996, with barely an impact to reflect the recession.

The explosion of a buy-to-let market based on the expectation of permanently rising house prices belongs to the insidious get-rich-quick-with-a-minimum-of-effort craving at the heart of economic bubbles. Policy debate around buy-to-let has been stifled since the crash in the belief that everything is behind us. But the figures show that the market is simply picking up from where it left off as if the crisis never happened.

Then there are the uncomfortable, tell-tale signs of isolated bubbles simmering away in the margins of the financial world. Take one extraordinary example: there is now a booming market in financial victimhood. Banks are offering to purchase claims from investors who lost their money in Bernie Madoff's notorious Ponzi scheme. The buyers offer the claimants a fraction per dollar that they are owed. Last year, this was under 30 cents, now it is about 75. Kenneth Krys, a bankruptcy specialist, told the *Wall Street Journal*: 'It's like a circus out there, a feeding frenzy... There's people buying and paying quite extraordinary prices.'[53] To make it even more bizarre, UBS and RBS are among those bidding for these claims. Like other banks, they are seeking to benefit from the payouts. But at the same time, they are actually being sued by the trustee of the Madoff estate along with other ex-investors in Madoff's scheme who withdrew just before its collapse. So as they fight these claims, they are seeking to avoid paying money to claimants, who they in turn are offering to insure.

Perhaps the best example of people trying to behave as if the crisis never happened is in the sensitive subject of remuneration.

One of the great skills of management is knowing how to incentivise people to work hard. But it is a fine art – incentivise one thing, like personal level of profit, too strongly and you will incentivise behaviour that is damaging in the long term. The bonus system, in all its secretive, discretionary glory, did just that: incentivised high-earning risk for short-term gain with no eye on the future. The huge payouts, which very few people will ever put a figure on, encouraged the wrong behaviour for years and we have just seen the catastrophic result. Yet after a pause, past behaviour is returning.

In 2009 bonuses were low. Most in the City took the attitude that they were lucky to have their jobs.

The return to high bonuses began with the then government's decision in 2009 to agree a £10m pay package to secure the new head of RBS. Stephen Hester is a highly qualified and impressive individual, but should have been offered the job for a fraction of the pay, and would probably have taken it. Under questioning in Parliament, Bob Diamond could not deny that he would have taken the job for no pay at all.

By 2010 vast bonuses were back. One trader at BarCap boasted to a journalist in a bar on bonus day: 'Even if a guy is really lazy and has done shit all year, he'll still get a £600,000 bonus... Most traders got two, three, four, five and even six million. Some people are annoyed because they don't think they got enough this year.'[54]

In the banks rescued by the then government, cash bonuses for 2010 were capped at £2,000. But despite the massive injection of taxpayers' cash, bonuses for 2011 were explicitly to be set at 'market rates'.

In 2011, painstaking negotiation from the new government secured a deal with the banks in which bonuses would be lower, taxes higher, and lending to small businesses increased.

With ultra-low official interest rates, and high margins on lending, banks are able to rebuild profits, supported by policy and the taxpayer. Given their need to replenish capital, and to hold a more responsible level of capital in future, such profit should be reinvested to support the capital base of the businesses, not paid out to staff.

Banks cite a clear collective action problem. In a highly competitive, mobile, labour market, and in an industry where the direct contribution of an employee to the bottom line can be clearly seen, any bank not paying up fears losing its staff. This argument, while widespread, is flawed. Taken to its extreme, banks would pay staff all of their return to the company, which is absurd. Individuals cannot make profit without the supporting infrastructure of a bank's capital, back office, and brand. Productivity is a team concept.

The Committee of European Banking Supervisors has made some inroads into reforming pay. Effective since the start of 2011, between two-fifths and three-fifths of bonuses should be deferred for three to five years, and half must be paid in shares not cash.

This is welcome progress because the right performance-related pay can be an incredibly effective way to incentivise and motivate a workforce. But the wrong incentives can be very harmful. Given the scale of the crisis that we have witnessed, the potential role that incentives may have played in it and the ongoing anger of shareholders, we might reasonably expect that this would be one of the key aspects for banks to look at. But here, as with many aspects of the City, there is widespread evidence of business-as-usual.

When we asked a group of senior figures in the finance world about post-crash behaviour, they could not have been clearer: 'Nothing's changed, absolutely nothing.'[55]

Because the bailouts have had their effect, and the crisis appears to have passed, the sector seems to think it can make as few adjustments as necessary and move on. We see this most clearly at the top, but it was also the message coming from almost everyone we spoke to: they want to be left in peace to get on with their jobs. The new polling undertaken for this book confirms the anecdotal evidence.

As we have seen, psychology shows us that when a severe disruption happens, unless people take personal responsibility, they are unlikely to change behaviour.

This element of human nature has been compounded by perverse incentives in the financial system that encourage business as usual, known as moral hazard.

I'm Alright, Guv

Moral hazard occurs because if someone is protected from a risk, they will behave more recklessly than if they were fully exposed. The term was coined by the insurance industry, which faced the conundrum that if it insured people against risks, it would encourage people to behave more dangerously.

When insured for the theft of your bicycle, you are more likely to leave it unlocked.

Whether you like it or not, moral hazard is a crucial concept in finance. We see it around us all the time. Sometimes it is useful, sometimes not. You wouldn't go on a high-rise assault course in Thetford Forest unless you were protected from falling by a safety harness. Equally, if a child knows its parents will always take its side over anyone else's, they will misbehave much more with everyone else – every babysitter's nightmare. If you are protected from a risk, you will change your behaviour.

Back in the world of Wall Street, the golden age of moral hazard in banking lasted for Alan Greenspan's uninterrupted eighteen-year tenure at the Federal Reserve. He implicitly reassured the market that he would intervene to stabilise when the going got rough – as he did in the 1987 stock market crash, the recession in the early nineties, when LTCM collapsed in 1998, after the Asian crash, at the end of the dot-com bubble, and in response to the September 11th attacks. After each shock, he cut interest rates to stabilise the economy and encourage recovery. For three UK-based economists watching in 2001, the boom resembled 'not so much "irrational exuberance" as exaggerated faith in the stabilising power of Mr Greenspan and the Fed'.[56] As these economists delved into the bowels of the US and UK investment markets, they found that investors seemed to expect the Fed to intervene to prevent failure but to stand aside to let growth burgeon. With that in the back of their minds, the market was 'lulled into a false sense of security' that their world would never be left to fail.

And then came the collapse of Lehman Brothers. Part of the idea behind the US not bailing out Lehman Brothers was the realisation that 'moral hazard' had built up in the system. By rescuing the bank, a message would be sent to the sector that it could carry on its business even more secure in the knowledge that there was a safety net. Ultimately, Lehman was allowed to fail and US Treasury Secretary Hank Paulson briefly boasted a 'badge of honour' for having the courage to let it go down.[57] That was the idea. Except that as the crisis spread, it became very clear that this decision was the wrong one. The bailing out of the banks became necessary to prevent the system from collapse, and an international rescue strategy was implemented.

The rescue was clearly necessary, but had dire consequences for moral hazard. In a perverse way it confirmed what the banking elite had always secretly believed: they were now infallible. Martin Wolf, one of the world's leading financial journalists, observed in the aftermath of the crisis: 'The financial sector that is emerging from the crisis is even more riddled with moral hazard than the one that went into it.'[58] A survey in 2009 asked investors, fund managers, asset owners and others in the financial world if they agreed with Wolf's statement. Over 90 per cent of respondents answered yes.[59] The results are not surprising. Underpinned by the knowledge that when push came to shove the banks were deemed too important to fail, swathes of the City are acting as if the events of 2007 and 2008 simply haven't happened. One trader laughingly told us: 'Being too big to fail is the best of all worlds for banks... They're all thinking you might as well get your cock in the custard completely.'[60]

Moral hazard compounds a uniquely human ability to believe what we want to believe. This observation from psychology and sociology can be useful – indeed necessary. The American political scientist Larry Bartels points to the way in which political beliefs can filter the perception of economic reality. At the end of the Reagan administration, US voters were asked whether they thought inflation had fallen – which it had, by nearly 10 per cent. Only 8 per cent of those who identified as strong Democrats agreed. By contrast, 47 per cent of Republicans said they thought it had fallen. At the end of Clinton's presidency the study was repeated. The results, of course, were reversed. Republicans were scathing and Democrats upbeat about the administration's economic management.[61] Belief encourages us to act, create, to live life to the full. When you marry, you believe that it will last. If you did not, you wouldn't get married in the first place. You need that belief to allow you to marry. When you give money to charity, you need to believe it will go towards the new well in a parched African village, not a box of paperclips for the company office in Reading. If you believed otherwise you would not give. Now, we all want to believe that recovery is inevitable – the alternative is grim. We have to believe to be able to get on with our lives. In that vein, it is understandable that banks work on the assumption they would be bailed out.

Changing that assumption is crucial to the long-term safety of our financial system. The recent introduction of macro-prudential regulation and 'living wills' point in the right direction. They are important for slowing a boom, and dealing in an orderly way with a bust. But alone they are by no means enough.

The mechanisms put in place to deal with a bank failure must be credible and expected to work, otherwise banks' management will know that in the inevitably difficult circumstances of a crisis, they cannot be used. Further, to reduce moral hazard for management as well as shareholders, the consequences of the failure of a bank should be severe. Spelt out in advance, the downside cost of failure for bank management will help make incentives more balanced, reduce moral hazard, and ultimately reduce the chances of such a failure in the first place.

This is crucial for the future.

Journalists write of the 'Financial Crisis of 2007–08', attempting to seal these events safely into the history books. Dick Fuld, Joe Cassano and Sir Fred Goodwin have already assumed the aspect of historical characters, joining the likes of John Law or Irving Fisher, the American economist who declared that stocks had reached 'a permanently high plateau' three days before the Wall Street Crash – instructive personifications of vice and folly in the long annals of financial misadventure.

But this crisis is not yet over.

In the UK, the crucial goal is to ensure creditors trust the ability of our banks and our government to come good on her debts, while promoting balanced sustainable growth.

Meanwhile on our borders in the eurozone, the banking crisis has rolled into a highly contagious sovereign debt crisis. While governments could stand behind over-indebted banks when they collapsed, there is no higher authority to stand behind over-indebted governments, save for other governments. In the eurozone the problem is compounded by the need to co-ordinate disparate democratic governments. Only the democratic governments are the institutions with the legitimacy to spend taxpayers' money. Yet we have seen how complex the dynamics of group behaviour are.

As the crisis has moved from banks to governments in the eurozone, so too has the question of moral hazard. Monetary union was supposed to curb the fiscal delinquency of southern European states like Greece, which has spent a total of fifty years since gaining independence in 1832 either in default or rescheduling its debt. The rules set out in the Maastricht Treaty were based on the principle that governments should always find it less painful to make difficult and unpopular spending decisions than risk defaulting on their debts. But as many a financial regulator could testify, unless such rules are anchored in institutions strong enough to enforce them, they will be changed when the crunch comes. In the absence of legal challenge, some countries borrowed to excess. Financial markets allowed them to do so in the expectation that Germany would never permit a default from within the eurozone.

And so, when faced with the damaging economic consequences of a default, Greece has been presented with lower
borrowing costs and more time to repay; it will also receive
funds from the rest of the EU to recapitalise its banks and
stimulate growth. Moral hazard applies just as much to
countries as to banks. This is what led David Mackie, the
head of JPMorgan Chase's European economics research, to
remark: 'Given all that has happened, one might be forgiven
for asking what would be the consequence of any further
under-performance in Greece...' It is critical in the midst of
this crisis that the lessons from the crash are learned: that the
fool in the corner that no one wants to listen to might have
a point; that behaviour is not always rational; that herding,
loss aversion, and leadership matter. While this makes the
resolution of the problems more complex, at least there is one
saving grace: that history provides a guide as these patterns
have been repeated. It is this historical guide to which we
turn next.

Chapter 4

FOREVER BLOWING BUBBLES

I acknowledge I have made great mistakes. I made them because I am only human, and all men are liable to err. But I declare that none of these acts proceeded from malice or dishonesty, and that nothing of that character will be discovered in the whole course of my conduct. John Law, letter to the Duke of Orleans, 1720

I apologised in full, and am happy to do so again, at the public meeting of our shareholders back in November. I too would echo [Lord] Stevenson's and Tom's comments that there is a profound and unqualified apology for all of the distress that has been caused. Sir Fred Goodwin, to the Treasury Select Committee, 2009

John Law was the Fred Goodwin of his day. Like Sir Fred, Law was an ambitious self-made man who rose to a position of immense financial power. Like Sir Fred, he embraced the Protestant work ethic of his native Scotland, even while dodging around the strict sexual morality which was supposed to accompany it. Like Sir Fred, he would become a poster boy for the greatest financial disaster of his generation. Unlike Sir Fred, however, he received no reward for his part in bringing it about.

Sir Fred Goodwin began his career in financial services as an accountant. Law's origins were less respectable, though no less relevant. Having tired of his father's well-to-do banking firm in Fife, he headed south, where, in the murky taverns and cobbled back-alleys of 1690s London, he became a professional gambler. Law enjoyed playing for high stakes but his gambler's impulsiveness got the better of him, and in 1694 a nasty incident involving a woman, a duel and a conviction for manslaughter, required him to leave the country. The following years were spent shuttling between continental Europe's major financial centres: Brussels, Amsterdam and Paris, where the card-sharp gambler turned financial speculator.

It was at this point that Law took an interest in economic theory. Then, as now, the great issue of the day was government debt. Governments wanted to spend – on war and colonies in the New World – but holes in the public finances limited their room for manoeuvre. Law's big idea was consolidation. Not just of the debt, but the entire economy. His scheme had two parts. The first was to enable government to take control of the money supply, replacing gold and silver, the prices of which were ruled by the markets, with something more stable. Law suggested that a central bank should be created, something along the lines of the new Bank of England which had been founded the year he left England. In return for deposits of gold and silver, it would issue paper money. As more people deposited at the state-owned central bank, government debt would diminish. The next trick was to give people an incentive to exchange their cold, hard metal for paper, by passing a law requiring people to pay their taxes in central banknotes – much more easily achieved in an absolute monarchy, where the King didn't have to consult parliament first.

This idea would now be regarded as conventional, though at that time it was novel. But this was only the first part of the plan. The second element involved creating a state-controlled investment opportunity so incredibly profitable that the public would be mad not to risk their cash on it.

Law first approached the Scottish government with his scheme, but was scuppered by the Act of Union with England in 1707. France, on the other hand, was open to new ideas. As the economists Rogoff and Reinhart found in their wide-ranging study of the history of government debt, when it came to fiscal policy eighteenth-century France was the basket case of Europe, having defaulted on its debts four times between 1648 and 1715.[62] By the time Law turned up in Paris with his unlikely-sounding proposals, the French Crown was tottering on the edge of bankruptcy. In the French Regent, Philippe Duke of Orleans, Law found an avid audience.

This is an important parallel. Politicians with a desire to spend more than they can afford are often attracted towards powerful financiers. After all, the business of bankers is debt, so surely they know better than anyone how to deal with it? In the United States, Clinton instated Robert Rubin, the former co-Chairman of Goldman Sachs, as Secretary to the Treasury. When running two expensive wars and a vast budget deficit, George W. Bush turned to the CEO of Goldman Sachs, Hank Paulson. In Britain, Fred Goodwin became a key ally of Gordon Brown on matters relating to the City. In 1999, Goodwin – then Group Deputy Chief Executive at RBS – chaired a Treasury task-force on credit unions. According to *The Times*: 'His involvement ensured that he had cordial relations with everyone at the top of the Treasury, and he enjoyed praise from ministers and the benefits of being seen to promote Mr Brown's agenda.'[63]

In 2004 Brown ensured Fred Goodwin was knighted, and in 2006 Goodwin became a member of Brown's International Business Advisory Council, guaranteeing him further access to the Treasury and Chancellor.

Back in eighteenth-century Paris, John Law's powers of persuasion worked their magic on the Duke of Orleans and in 1716 he was given a position equivalent to Chief Finance Minister. A French central bank was established exactly according to Law's scheme and a year later a new government-backed trading company, the Compagnie d'Occident, was floated on the stock market. The Compagnie was granted a monopoly over trade with France's new American colony, Louisiana. Shares were issued at 500 livres apiece and John Law was to own a majority stake. Frenchmen and foreigners were then strongly encouraged to purchase shares with banknotes issued by the new central bank.

So far so good. The next stage involved driving those share prices up. Not only would this ramp up demand for the paper money with which to buy them but, as the majority shareholder, it would, by coincidence, massively increase Law's personal worth. The Compagnie therefore embarked on a huge spree of acquisitions, merging with the East India and China Companies to form the Mississippi Company in 1719, purchasing future profits from the Royal Mint and acquiring a monopoly right to collect taxes for the French Crown. Imagine BP, Microsoft and the UK Department of Health merging into a single company and you have some idea of what drove French investors wild. The public clamoured for a piece of the action and the share price soared, peaking at 20,000 livres by late 1719 – forty times the original value. Law's near-contemporary, the Scottish philosopher David Hume, wrote that at the height of Mississippi mania a man with a hunchback on the Rue Quincampoix – the Parisian street where shares were traded – made a small fortune by renting out his back as a portable makeshift desk for frenzied speculators to deal over. Law became one of the richest men in Europe.

There was just one problem. Where was all the money coming from? The Mississippi Company had not yet turned a profit from the trade with Louisiana. Law had paid for all the acquisitions simply by issuing new shares. These in turn were funded with a reckless increase in the money supply. The French central bank, which Law controlled, was ordered to print more banknotes, allowing investors to borrow to buy more shares in the belief that they would keep rising in value. Law had effectively turned the entire French economy into a gigantic Ponzi scheme. Something had to give, and in December 1719, it did. Law had gambled wrongly on the true market value of his super-corporation and the share price started to tank. At the same time, the new glut of paper money bloating the system caused inflation to rocket. By May 1720, most people had converted their paper banknotes back into the more trusted gold and silver. The currency crashed. Thousands who had tied up their wealth in Mississippi shares were ruined and the French monarchy's fiscal crisis rolled on for the rest of the century, directly contributing to the Revolution in 1789. Law was disgraced, the Duke of Orleans stripped him of his titles and property and he was forced once again to leave the country. He died in obscurity in Venice in 1729.

What went wrong? Why did the Mississippi Company's share price suddenly collapse? It turns out the root cause of John Law's problems is something we're rather familiar with. Answering that question brings us back to Sir Fred Goodwin.

Beneath the creaking edifice of Collaterised Debt Obligations, Credit Default Swaps and Special Purpose Vehicles which modern finance constructed around itself, there has to be something capable of injecting long-term profits into the system – an economic fundamental. What RBS and the Mississippi Company shareholders had in common was their belief in a good news story – a dream called a 'phantastic' object by psychoanalysts. Sustaining the rise and rise of the Mississippi Company share price was a belief in the stupendous wealth supposedly locked up in Louisiana: gold, beaver hides, fisheries and agriculture. The modern-day equivalent was a belief that new technology had enabled the creation of high-yield, ultra-low-risk bonds by lending to the subprime mortgage market. Niall Ferguson said of the latter episode: 'As a business model [it] worked beautifully – as long as interest rates stayed low, as long as people kept their jobs, and as long as real estate prices continued to rise.'

The trouble is that both the riches of Louisiana and near risk-free returns on subprime mortgages turned out to be little more than clever marketing strategies. The settling of Louisiana in the port town of New Orleans – so named to flatter Law's patron the Duke – was an unmitigated disaster. Instead of lush meadows teeming with beavers and gold, the colonists found stagnant, crocodile-infested swamps and lethal clouds of malarial mosquitoes. Eighty per cent of the settlers died in the first year. Three centuries later, excessive lending to Americans with poor or non-existent credit histories turned out to be a similarly faulty business model. The rate of default after twelve months on American subprime loans rose from 14.6 per cent for loans made in 2005, to 20.5 per cent for loans made the following year, and 21.9 per cent for loans made in 2007.[64]

This same pattern has occurred time and time again throughout history: belief in a dream; a new innovation that transforms business and even entire economies; followed by a rapidly inflating bubble and then a tipping point at which the bubble bursts; then huge losses.

Bubbles have been as short-lived as a few months. Or, as with the bubble leading to the economic crash, they can last for years, its unsustainable nature hidden by outside effects such as imported deflation and the inherent need in investors and the markets to believe in that game-changing innovation.

What makes this happen over and over again? What does a bubble look like? Can we spot them and, if we can, why do we keep being stung by them?

Anatomy of a Bubble

Bubbles begin with what the economist Hyman Minsky referred to as a displacement,[65] a change in economic circumstances which creates new and potentially profitable opportunities. The more exciting the innovation, the more alluring the dream. So the most famous bubbles have followed radical changes like the rise of the railways, or the arrival of the internet. In the case of John Law and the Mississippi Bubble, it was the settling of Louisiana, which it was hoped would change the economic fundamentals of the French economy.

The second stage of Minsky's bubbles framework is expansion. Expansion occurs as prices begin to rise in the game-changing business or sector. Initially the rises may be small and in line with the inevitably uncertain improvements in the fundamentals of the market. So the share price of a company will rise in line with realistic expectations of the new opportunity they have. As the price begins to rise, more people begin to notice, leading to the next stage, euphoria.

Under euphoria trading really begins to take off. Prices begin to climb, often fuelled by financial innovation and cheap credit. In the South Sea Bubble in 1719, credit, extended by the company itself, effectively allowed investors to effectively borrow the money to buy shares in the company. As the price skyrocketed, they were able to sell their shares for a profit before their next instalment was due, then recycle their profits to do it again and again. In the Wall Street Crash of 1929, financial innovations such as broker loans and margin trading accounts allowed investors to buy shares without having their full value to invest.

The euphoria stage often features a feedback loop, which sets in as expectations of the size of profits rise, leading to a demand for the asset rising as well. This in turn leads to a rise in the demand for credit, which when met, simply fuels the rising price, beginning the cycle again and actually strengthening confidence. In March 2010, FSA Chairman Adair Turner described how this feedback loop works in commercial property:

> Increased credit extended to commercial real estate devel-
> opers can drive up the price of buildings... Increased asset

prices in turn drive expectations of further price increases which drive demand for credit; but they also improve bank profits, bank capital bases and lending officer confidence, generating favourable assessments of credit risk and an increased supply of credit to meet the extra demand.[66]

Minsky realised that as euphoria kicks in, over-trading begins to occur, with prices heading far higher than the underlying business of a company can justify. The price rises further as outsiders begin to enter the market, attracted by the chance to make quick and easy gains.

In the South Sea Bubble, early investors were the socially well-connected and those with insider knowledge: the aristocracy, MPs and the wealthy. But as prices started to rise, and as cheap and easy credit was extended to all, the type of investor changed. Suddenly maids and servants could enter the market with very little money and make amazing returns that transformed their lives. With shades of the later dot-com bubble, when the mere announcement of an online strategy led to a rapid rise in any company's share price, the *Original Weekly* journal described the impact of the South Sea Bubble: 'Our South Sea equipages increase every day. The City ladies buy South Sea jewels, hire South Sea maids, and take new country South Sea houses; the gentlemen set up South Sea coaches and buy South Sea estates.' Indeed it was said that there were 200 new coaches and chariots in London and as many more being built.[67] In turn this only drew more people into the market, attracted, as throughout history, by the idea that they could get rich quick.

If we think we have learned we are mistaken. Early 2011 saw a new bubble, this time in silver prices. During 2010 silver prices had been increasing slowly. From January prices suddenly shot up, almost doubling in just 14 weeks. With silver prices at an all-time high, antique dealers on Portobello Road in London were approached by scrap metal merchants, and accepted offers to melt down their antiques into silver ingots. Unbelievably, they were worth more in the market as simple ingots than as beautiful antique candelabra and silver service sets.

Then the bubble burst. During May silver prices dropped by 30 per cent. The antique dealers were left with lumps of metal, but had destroyed beautiful and historically important objects in the process.

In most bubbles, by the stage of rapidly rising prices, the fools in the corner have already started to point out the fallacies driving the market: the so-called missing fundamentals. In the dot-com boom it was the fallacy of promises rather than profits in company valuations. In the financial crisis it was the fallacy of ever-rising house prices. Ultimately a bubble cannot be sustained forever. But as we have seen, prices continue to rise in spite of mounting evidence, and those who speak out are ever more marginalised.

The next stage of Minsky's bubbles framework is the tipping point for insiders: distress.

In the distress phase outsiders continue to flood into the market, driven by their friends and associates making what appears to be free and easy money. But some insiders are brought down to earth, and remember the fact that an economy and a market need to have fundamentals.

Time and again, those with a vested interest in the success of the boom continue to bang the drum after the tipping point has been reached. Shortly after Gordon Brown entered the Treasury, he was claiming that he had abolished boom and bust and continued to do so throughout his time as Chancellor. In the House of Commons alone he said it just under thirty times.[68] Like John Law, who continued to talk up his paper economy until the very end, and like Blunt, the lead director of the South Sea Company who kept offering fantastical terms for share offerings, Gordon Brown continued to say he had changed the economy forever. Even today he will not publically admit to his failures. Similarly, Sir Fred completed RBS's ill-fated takeover of ABN Amro in October 2007, after the closure of the money markets and the run on Northern Rock. In 2008 he told shareholders: 'We are happy, we bought what we thought we bought,' while it was being discovered elsewhere that ABN was exposed to $100 billion worth of dubious asset-backed securities including subprime mortgages.

This was when John Law and Sir Fred Goodwin should have known better. As insiders they should have been placed to see the house of cards that their money-making empires were based on, but instead they failed to get out early enough. Goodwin knew about, and should have understood the implications of, the collapse of the German bank IKB after some AAA-rated assets turned out to be worthless. Yet Goodwin actually invested RBS further into the bubble, completing the acquisition of ABN Amro. Just as the Mississippi Company investor sipping spiced coffee in his Paris Salon had no sense of the real picture in Louisiana, so the board of RBS seems to have had no detailed understanding of the business decision it had just approved.

Minsky referred to the final bursting of a bubble as the revulsion phase. As insiders flee the market, taking their profits with them, the price begins to fall, leading to outsiders selling up to minimise their losses. When a large number of people suddenly appreciate a risk they had previously ignored or not known about, the value of the asset in question can fall dramatically. As they start to sell there are no new outsiders coming in to buy. So prices fall swiftly, causing even more investors to run from the market, further depressing prices and leading to a downward spiral. If at the same time cheap credit is withdrawn, the effect can be multiplied as the supply of cash that has enabled outsiders to invest in the market disappears.

This bursting can happen incredibly quickly. As the South Sea Bubble collapsed, investors in businesses across the board saw their profits disappear fast. Holders of Royal Exchange shares lost 76 per cent in just seven days. South Sea stock fell 51 per cent in six days in September. The collapse of the bubble rippled through London. At the coach manufacturers whose books had swelled, orders were suddenly cancelled. One coach builder saw twenty-eight of its forty orders cancelled, while a newspaper correspondent foreshadowed the infamous portrait of the 1929 crash when he stated that 'weekly throughout the streets of London you may see second-hand coaches'.[69]

Like other bubbles, the Japanese asset bubble in the 1980s followed the Minsky framework. After the Second World War, the Japanese people had been encouraged by their government to save their income. This in turn created a large pool of cash for banks to lend, meaning that loans became easier to obtain. Stories abounded of the brilliance of the Japanese working culture, and how the Japanese economy was set to beat the world. The yen increased in value against foreign currencies, so Japanese financial assets became extremely lucrative. This was the displacement: an enticing story of success coupled with easy credit and a change in financial circumstances. As speculators moved into the stock and housing markets, prices continued to rise, leading banks to grant increasingly risky loans. The Japanese market had reached the euphoria stage and over-trading kicked in.

At its peak on 29 December 1989, the Nikkei stock index hit 38,957, closing that day slightly down at 38,916. In the same year, the value of property in Tokyo's premier real estate district reached as high as a million dollars per square metre.

By the new year, the Japanese central bank was the one to trigger the distress phase. The Bank came to the conclusion that the bubble was unsustainable and something had to be done. The solution was to tighten monetary policy by increasing interest rates, so withdrawing the cheap credit that had fuelled the boom. What was meant to induce a gentle deflation of the bubble turned into a giant bust as revulsion set in. The debts that had fuelled speculation and growth defaulted as property and equity prices fell rapidly, leading to a cascade through the banking sector. Many banks and corporations could no longer afford their debts, but were considered too big to fail and given injections of liquidity to bail them out. In reality they simply became too indebted to carry on trading and were reliant on bailouts to survive. The so-called zombie banks were born.

Fifteen years later, in 2004, prime Tokyo real estate had fallen to less than 1 per cent of its peak price. A 9m² property, essentially a small 3m x 3m room, worth $9 million in 1989, was now worth less than $90,000. By March 2009 the Nikkei had dropped by 81 per cent from its 1989 peak to just 7,054.

So if bubbles are as inevitable as they are unpredictable, what can be done? The debate among economists on how to deal with bubbles has been conducted in the context of a crucial speech given in June 1999 by the then Federal Reserve Chairman, Alan Greenspan. Addressing the Congressional Joint Economic Committee, Greenspan laid out his philosophy and thinking on bubbles, which was to define the economic policy landscape for the next decade.

Greenspan argued that that bubbles cannot easily be spotted as they form, and that even if they can be, they cannot be stopped from inflating without causing a substantial contraction of the wider economy.

'Bubbles generally are perceptible only after the fact. To spot a bubble in advance requires a judgment that hundreds of thousands of informed investors have it all wrong,' he told Congress. He argued that you cannot confidently lean against a growing bubble, because investors get asset prices right.

In 2002, at Jackson Hole, he further extended his defence of being unable to slow a bubble when he pointed to a three percentage point rise over the course of 1989 and another three percentage point rise over the course of 1994; neither, he said, saw stock market growth slow. Therefore only a significant and rapid rise in interest rates, which would have a knock-on effect on the rest of the economy, and possibly cause a significant recession, could control a bubble.

The solution, according to Greenspan, 'was to mitigate the fallout when it occurs and, hopefully, ease the transition to the next expansion', an approach known as mopping up. The catastrophic effect of Japan's bubble bursting was not the bubble itself, he explained, but the policy response to it afterwards. Effectively, he was arguing that if only monetary policy had been loosened, just as it was after the dot-com boom, then Japan would not have lost a decade.

Greenspan's explanation of his policy of mopping up demonstrated an unquestioning belief that the price investors are willing to pay is the only valid valuation of an asset. His argument that only a sharp change in interest rates could lean against a growing bubble revealed an ideology that no other tools should actively be used to manage the economy. Both were flawed.

The ideology that the only effective tool was the short-term interest rate grew out of the failure of 1970s regulatory regimes. It relied on the belief that no other tools would have an effect, and that as long as narrow inflation was controlled, everything else would take care of itself. This in turn relied on the assumption that people are rational.

Likewise the belief that the only valid valuation of an asset was the market price for that asset was put forward because other valuations are necessarily less precise and based on subjective judgement. The decades-old principle that a valuation had to be a 'true and fair' reflection of the value of the asset was downgraded. But the market prices of assets do not behave as for other, normal goods. The theory that only the market price matters depends crucially on the validity of the efficient markets hypothesis, which itself requires people always to be fully informed and rational.

This central assumption of perfect rationality runs through the Greenspan doctrine.

But the assumption is wrong, and the unrestrained bubble was of historic proportions.

How policy should respond to a bubble depends crucially on the impact of its bursting on the wider economy. This in turn depends to a large degree on whether the bubble is funded by debt.

When a bubble only affects asset prices, like the silver bubble of 2011, or even the dot-com bubble, then the consequences may be fairly small. But when people borrow against inflated bubble prices, as they did before the financial crisis, then the consequences of the bust can be calamitous.

Such borrowing against overvalued asset prices happens in the euphoria stage of a bubble; when trading takes off and when cheap credit starts to allow more investors into the market. As Adair Turner described it: 'The 2000 boom and credit boom were the same structure. The difference is an equity boom might lead to some misallocation of resources but can be absorbed by the economy, whereas a debt boom causes economic crisis'.[70]

So did the dot-com boom really have the same basic structure as that which led to the crisis in 2008? In effect, yes. In both cases, the essentials set out by Minsky are clear. First was an innovation, which led to a boom in prices. Euphoria kicked in, then we saw over-trading followed by distress, and finally revulsion as people fled the market. In 2000, the collapse of companies like boo.com – a media darling with ambitious plans to launch across Europe and transform the way we purchased clothes – showed the world that profit and loss really did matter. In 2007, the failure of AAA-rated securities was the first reminder to people of exactly the same thing: that fundamentals matter.

What then was the difference? Why did the dot-com bubble disappear gently, while the financial crisis in the UK led to the longest recession since the war?

It's All About Froth

As we have seen, in a bubble the value of an asset like a house or a share increases, often rapidly. As euphoria kicks in, the valuation becomes disconnected from the asset's underlying value. This gap between the real underlying value and the value at the top of a bubble can be called the froth: the profit, on paper, gained by buying at a sensible valuation, and the market price at the right point of the bubble. In theory the bubble can collapse, and if you get out at the right time – which isn't as easy as you might think – then all you'll lose is the froth. Imagine a frothy cappuccino. If you blow the froth off the top then you're still left with the coffee underneath. In reality of course it's not that easy. Blowing the froth off is likely to mean that we slop some of the coffee out as well, leaving some of us with less than we started with.

Now imagine we had borrowed that cup of coffee. What happens then?

In a debt bubble, people borrow against the froth, taking out credit secured on over-valued assets to fuel further specu-lation, which in turn drives the price up further, allowing more borrowing. In a property bubble fuelled by debt, such as the Japanese bubble in the 1980s, you might take out a mortgage on the nominal value you held in one property to purchase another. Then, after the price on that had gone up, take out another mortgage on that property to buy another, or even take out a further mortgage on that property to pay the mortgage on the first. In effect, it's a Ponzi scheme for paying off loans. In the same way a classic Ponzi scheme works, as long as new money keeps coming in to pay fraudulent returns, a debt bubble can appear stable as long as asset prices keep rising. If prices stop rising you are in real trouble.

The problem in a debt bubble is that the boom is on both sides of the balance sheet. Assets and liabilities are both increased. When the bubble bursts, asset values fall, but the debts remain the same.

In the South Sea Bubble this happened when the South Sea Company started allowing investors to buy shares with just a 10 per cent deposit. In the Wall Street Crash, investors were able to use broker loans with little collateral. In the bubble running up to the credit crunch, banks lent against over-inflated property owed by people who had no way to pay the money back, even before the prices of their house crashed. These were all debt bubbles, and the economic consequences of their collapse were devastating.

Now compare some other bubbles. The dot-com bubble saw huge amounts of paper profits wiped out, but few had borrowed against the shares. The railway bubble in the 1840s saw share prices in railway ventures almost double in three years, and although there was a slowdown afterwards, the wider economy did not collapse.

Between 2005 and 2007 there was a bubble in uranium in which investors and then speculators first piled into uranium itself, then into mining companies with links to uranium, and then into mining generally. The price of uranium went from less than $20 per pound in 2005 to nearly $140 in 2007 and fell back to $40 by 2010. Uncannily, J. K. Galbraith predicted this little-known bubble with a throwaway line in his assessment of the Great Crash: 'Instead of radio and investment trusts, uranium mines ... will be the new favourites.'[71] It was a classic bubble, but most people outside of the markets didn't even know about it. Even if the credit crunch hadn't brought it to a premature end, it would have had little chance of spilling over into the rest of the economy.

Likewise, the late 1980s saw a bubble inflate and burst

in classic cars. In 1985, E-type Jaguars were worth around £16,000. Each year prices then rose by half, and by 1989 the cars exchanged hands for over £100,000. In 1990, the bubble burst, and a decade later, the cars were worth only a third of their peak value. Fortunes were spent on restoration that could not be recouped, which while technically economically inefficient, was good for Britain's engineering heritage. Only classic car enthusiasts really noticed.

When Turner compared the 2000 asset boom and the credit crisis, he used the classic economist's phrase: a 'misallocation of resources'. This means money being spent where it will not create the most benefit for the economy. At the end of the twentieth century, for example, telecoms companies were falling over themselves to lay fibre-optic cables to power the internet traffic. They all presumed that internet traffic would continue to increase at the pace it had at the beginning of the boom, and discovered that after the crash this was not the case. Demand simply couldn't survive at that level or at a price to support the cost to lay the cable. As a result companies like WorldCom went bust, leaving millions of miles of unused fibre-optic networks strung not just across America but between continents and around the world. Those resources may have been misallocated at the time, but it's those same 'dark fibre' networks that power Google and many other corporate networks today.

The railway boom also saw a misallocation of resources with too much money going into building too many railway lines, all serving too few customers to be economical. Multiple lines were built between towns. However, after the bubble burst, the infrastructure was left behind, and the bubble meant that the UK railway network was delivered more quickly than it would otherwise have been. Of the 11,000 miles of railway track we use in the UK today, an incredible 6,000 miles of it was first laid between 1844 and 1846. By comparison, the six main lines of France's centrally dictated railway network were begun in 1842 and not finished until 1860.

So even when we get bubbles, they can still be positive, providing us with accelerated investment in a sector. The market may not be perfect at allocating resources, but a positive legacy can remain.

But when the bubble is financed by debt, all too often the result is different. People are left unable to pay their debts, and the losses become concentrated in the financial system. If a debt bubble is big enough, then the losses make the banks undercapitalised or insolvent, leading to a credit crunch as banks either collapse or try to repair their balance sheets. The collapse of such a debt bubble can therefore have a negative impact on the whole economy, much wider than the sector in which the bubble occurred.

So bubbles in themselves aren't always bad. But when they leave behind debts, they can be disastrous.

In the case of the bubble that led to the 2008 financial crash, the asset price rises were very clearly financed by debts. With the cover story of the wall of savings and imported deflation from Asia, and with regulatory controls over debt levels removed, debts were expanded to finance asset purchases almost without limit.

This insight into the difference between equity bubbles and debt bubbles gives us a clue as to how to deal with them. Bubbles are part of human nature. Driven both by rational and irrational impulses, they can no more be eradicated than can singing. Indeed, in recent years, crises seem to be occurring more and more frequently.[72] It is more important than ever that we understand that it is debt that brings down an economy. We will then be better prepared to stop bubbles building up, to control the expansion of the debts that fund them, and to cope more resiliantly with their bursting.

Chapter 5

IRRATIONAL ECONOMISTS

Experience of life tells us that people are imperfect. Sometimes we're rational, sometimes we're well informed. Sometimes we are both. Often we are neither. Neuroscience suggests that anywhere between 10 per cent and 15 per cent of our behaviour is conscious; and not even all this is rational.

Yet for years most of those who studied our economy made the assumption that people were well informed and rational. Huge effort was put into work that extrapolated these assumptions to make sense of the world. The gap between economists' models and the real world was not ignored. It was contemplated to try to make sense of what was going on, and to improve the models. Over time these models were not just used to try to predict the future and understand the economy, but became deeply embedded in the plumbing of how the economy actually worked.

Yet the assumptions on which modern economics was based were eminently false.

Let's consider a game, where you can choose between a certain gain and the chance to gamble for more. If you were offered £450 now, or a gamble with a fifty-fifty chance of winning £1,000, but an equal chance of walking away with nothing, which would you choose?

Despite the fact that, on average, you would win more by gambling, most of us would probably choose the dead cert. We would prefer not to gamble, even though on average we would win more money, because there is still a chance that we might not win anything at all. We like the certainty. We can already think of the new iPad we could buy. Indeed neuroscience shows that our synapses would already be responding as if we have bought the iPad. Why risk throwing that away just because we *might* make £1,000?

New polling undertaken for this book shows that under those circumstances, of those who made a choice, just 8 per cent of Brits would take the risk. Breaking it down further, some groups are more likely to gamble: 19 per cent of 18–24-year-olds would, compared to just 4 per cent of over-60s. Twelve per cent of men would gamble, but only 5 per cent of women.

This risk aversion is widely understood, is intuitive, and can be added into an economists' model.

But what if we turned this game into one where you lose, rather than win, the money. So either you lose £450 for sure, or you gamble, with half a chance you lose £1,000, but half a chance you lose nothing. In this second case, the outcomes are exactly the same as in the first example, except that you are £500 worse off under all circumstances. Nothing else has changed.

Yet intuitively, this gamble starts to look a bit more attractive. Why would you let someone just take the £450 off you, when you could gamble for the chance to lose nothing? Whereas before we could feel the certain gain of £450 in our pocket and start to dream what we would spend it on, now we feel the harsh chill and indignation of losing money.

If you chose this time to gamble to avoid a loss, you would not be alone. People are far more likely to take the risk when faced with a loss, but not put a certain gain at risk. It's intuitive: why not gamble if you are losing anyway? But why risk it if you can profit now with certainty?

New polling backs up the intuition. Of those who made a choice, instead of 8 per cent who will gamble to win, fully 25 per cent will make exactly the same gamble to avoid a loss. Among young men, aged between eighteen and twenty-four, 57 per cent will gamble to avoid loss – more than half.

This polling confirms a crucial insight of behavioural

economics: loss aversion. We find it much harder to stomach a loss than to miss out on the chance of a gain. So even though the relative returns and risks are exactly the same, people are far more likely to gamble to avoid a loss than to make a gain. Ironically given the role of Scotland in the crisis, in this research the area of the UK most likely to do what they can to avoid a loss is Scotland, where 40 per cent will gamble to avoid loss. Maybe all the jokes about Scottish thrift have a basis in reality after all.

Some of the most well known events in finance followed exactly this behaviour. Nick Leeson, faced with huge losses from a gamble gone wrong, gambled yet more in the hope of reversing his losses. Instead he lost even more money and eventually broke Barings Bank. As the man himself said: 'I was determined to win back the losses. And as the spring wore on, I traded harder and harder, risking more and more. I was well down, but increasingly sure that my doubling up and doubling up would pay off.'[73]

The trouble is, this natural human behaviour is actually the reverse of that you should employ if you want to be a successful trader. The most successful traders gamble where they see the chance of a profit, and take their losses when they have to. To behave as most young men would in the previous examples is to be like a rogue trader.

The fact we behave differently when confronted with gains and losses was first recognised in the academic world by the psychologists Daniel Kahneman and Amos Tversky, in their 1979 paper 'Prospect Theory: An Analysis of Decision Under Risk'. It became the most cited paper ever to appear in the journal *Econometrica*.[74]

Yet more than a decade later, Barings, one of Britain's oldest and most respected banks, was brought down by exactly the human behaviour they predicted.

In an interview with the *New York Times*, after being awarded his Nobel Prize, Kahneman explained that to understand the problem that prospect theory tackled you had to go back to Daniel Bernoulli, who in 1738 framed a problem:

> The question that Bernoulli put to himself was 'How do people make risky decisions?' And he analysed really quite a nice problem: a merchant thinking of sending a ship from Amsterdam to St Petersburg at a time of year where there would be a 5 per cent probability of the ship being lost.
>
> Bernoulli evaluated the possible outcomes in terms of their utility. What he said is that the merchant thinks in terms of his states of wealth: How much he will have if the ship gets there, if the ship doesn't get there, if he buys insurance, if he doesn't buy insurance.
>
> And now it turns out that Bernoulli made a mistake; in some sense it was a bewildering error to have made. For Bernoulli, the state of wealth is the total amount you've got, and you will have the same preference whether you start out owning a million dollars, or a half million or two million. But the mistake is that no merchant would think that way, in terms of states of wealth. Like anybody else, he would think in terms of gains and losses.[75]

This was Kahneman and Tversky's most important realisation and led to the framing of loss aversion and its introduction to the economic lexicon.

Yet since the publication of the theory, the economics profession has spent enormous resources constructing theories to explain away this behaviour as entirely rational. Of course there may be some circumstances under which there are rational elements to the explanation. For example, you can argue that once Leeson had lost a fortune, he was already going to lose his job unless his gamble paid off. But to understand this result fully, we need to understand that human behaviour combines elements that are both rational and irrational, as Leeson's own testimony bears out.

The consequence of this finding is that instead of assuming rationality, we should observe behaviour, and learn from empirical observation how people actually behave. For all the theories, it isn't possible rationally to explain why this loss avoidance tendency is so widespread.

The economist Richard Thaler, known for advancing the cause of behavioural economics, probably best described the assumption of rationality when he said that 'conventional economics assumes that people are highly-rational – super-rational – and unemotional. They can calculate like a computer and have no self-control problems'.[76]

Yet human beings are not the rational agents that economic theory expects us to be. Accepting this has deep ramifications for the structure of economic policy, and indeed the economics profession itself. Over a generation we became increasingly obsessed with making the wrong assumptions about human behaviour just so that we could model these wrong assumptions into increasingly complex mathematical models, which curtailed the exercise of judgement. Wiser economists realised their assumptions were false, but argued that there was no better way to organise facts, and that the gap between the model and the reality would tell us something. Yet for decades this excused a failure to put enough resources into empirical observation of how people actually behave, and instead a whole pyramid of economic theory and practice was built on false assumptions. Much of the work was worthless.

It would almost be funny were the consequences not so serious.

These flaws in the standard assumptions of economics are increasingly recognised. A growing academic literature supports the importance of understanding human behaviour. Such insights are beginning to support policy changes.

In an incentive-driven pilot that has paid people to recycle, Windsor and Maidenhead Council has seen an average increase of 35 per cent in the weight of recyclable materials collected. Following their lead, the UK government has now established a Behavioural Insights team to apply these findings across Whitehall. For example, HMRC asked behavioural economists to draft tax letters. When they used their understanding of the importance of social norms, and emphasised in the letter that 90 per cent of people in Exeter had already paid their tax, the letters boosted repayments by an additional 10 per cent compared to other letters, at no extra cost. The innovation will save millions in administration costs, and reduce tax avoidance by £280m. In the same vein, an energy conservation programme provided people with comparisons with their neighbours on their energy use. The programme saw a 2 per cent drop in energy consumption.

These innovations are important, and the early signs are that they work. Basing policy on observations of how people really behave is crucial. But they do not go far enough. So far, such insights have been applied to fairly static areas of policy, like tax collection. They provide as accurate a representation of human behaviour as Newtonian physics does of gravity. It works, but they lack a vital dimension. We need the equivalent of an Einsteinian revolution in economics. However, in wider economic management, we must also recognise that policy, and expectations of policy, themselves have an impact on how the system operates. It is necessary, but not sufficient, to base policy on observations of how people behave now. We must also know as much as we can about how groups of people will react to policy, and take that into account. That is very difficult. It means being realistic about what we do not know about how groups will react. It is almost impossible to foresee the way that the dynamics of a system will unfold. So we must not be afraid of designing policy that can cope with all this uncertainty.

Losing Faith

The explosion of mathematics in economics did not happen by accident. The rapid advance of mathematical techniques and computing power were a seductive draw in a profession that had long struggled to justify itself as a science. This new analytical power coincided with a wider breakdown of traditional social structures of trust. As the Western world was gradually liberated from hierarchical structures based on social position, and automatic respect for traditional institutions of governance was questioned, there was a need for a replacement.

Every institution was required to justify its existence. It was not good enough for an institution to argue that it had built up expertise in exercising judgements over time. The legitimacy of any subjective judgement that was not based on apparently objective fact was increasingly questioned. Whether justified or not, where traditional institutions were broken-down, something had to be put in their place.

Across a broad range of policymaking, traditional roles and structures were questioned, and alternatives looked for. The increasingly mathematical models, built on computing power, gave a powerful impression of objectivity that was seen as an attractive replacement for the subjective traditions that were being questioned.

Subjectivity became tainted by distrust, and objectivity was deified as the solution. If we could all see the inputs and outputs of a process, then there was no need to place our trust in one another: we could place it all in the model. As computer power developed, so mathematical models came to be relied upon more and more as the providers of objective judgements. The problem was that models were only as good as the inevitably flawed assumptions underpinning them. But once we had repudiated our ability to make subjective judgements, it was difficult to question legitimately what had gone wrong.

The sheer extent to which objectivity had gained such a hold on economic policymakers was demonstrated by the reaction to the collapse of LTCM in 1998. This fund was set up by esteemed Nobel Prize-winning economists, who had themselves created a model for working out the value of complex derivatives known as the Black–Scholes model. Based on the standard assumptions of economics, this had become the industry standard over the years since it was published in 1976. Almost every derivatives trader used the Black–Scholes model to value their book.

Mr Scholes set up a hedge fund to make money from his renowned complex risk management models. Scholes joined fellow Nobel laureate Robert Merton and John Meriwether, who had run Salomon Brothers' infamous bond-trading operation until he resigned during a scandal in 1991. The new fund initially prospered. The models told them how to invest the money. Over five years LTCM grew to almost $5 billion in size and produced astonishing, world-beating returns for their clients of over 30 per cent per year.[77]

Yet LTCM made a fundamental mistake. While they relied on their models to tell them where to invest, they forgot that their assumptions weren't an accurate reflection of the real world.

Specifically, they assumed that the price of US and Russian government bonds would be correlated and move together. They made huge returns from observing movements in the prices of the two bond markets, selling US bonds and buying Russian bonds at the right time, and hedging their risks in derivatives. But when the Russian government threatened to default on its debts, the correlations assumed in the model broke down. The prices of the bonds they owned moved in a way their model had told them would happen only once in several billion times the life of the universe.[78]

By August 1998, LTCM had lost 44 per cent of the value of the fund. By September they were bust, and the Federal

Reserve had to organise a bailout. Alan Greenspan called the heads of all the major Wall Street firms together and told them to cancel all of the trades they had made with LTCM. The alternative was that others exposed to LTCM would in turn go bust, and even those that would directly benefit from LTCM going bust would suffer from the ensuing crisis in confidence. So the trades were unwound, and the investors lost everything.

The lesson from this failure was that the models in which so much faith had been placed were built on flawed assumptions. They failed to take into account what happens when a crisis occurs. The models assumed markets worked smoothly, but in a crisis, as when a government cannot pay its debts, markets are not smooth. The models failed to reflect how correlations change; how asset prices can move suddenly; how liquidity can disappear; and what happens when the herd shifts.

A trader worth his stripes, using judgement and intuitive understanding of human behaviour, knows that these things can happen. But a hedge fund comprised of Nobel prize-winners was completely unable to predict it. The gut instinct of traders, with all its dirty and discredited association with subjectivity, should have seemed preferable to the fallible world of the objective output of computer modelling. As Merton pointed out in hindsight, 'only a crazy person would have a mathematical model just running, [and] go off fishing'.

Yet even after the failure of LTCM, the march of the models continued.

A decade later, almost exactly the same mistakes were repeated in the credit crunch. The world of MBSs, CDOs, and CDSs grew rapidly, and relied heavily on powerful computers to model the risk that homeowners would fail to repay their mortgages, or that companies would fail to make good on their bonds.

Astonishingly, the models used to value the new instruments made exactly the same type of mistake as the models that brought down LTCM a decade before.

How did this happen?

LTCM's collapse had brought into sharp focus the problem of assuming that the prices on different bonds would move together. It mattered how much a likely default by the Russian government would affect perceptions of a default in, say, Mexico. Applying the new techniques of quantitative finance and using the rapidly developing computing power had made banks on Wall Street and in the City of London huge amounts of money. The collapse of LTCM had shown the risks. But the attitude remained: that mathematics could understand and so control risks, if only the right formula could be found.

In 2003, a Chinese-American called David Li appeared to have cracked the problem. Li had spent years in Canadian universities as an academic actuary, studying the so-called 'broken heart phenomenon'. Li had studied medical research which showed that after the death of a spouse, the brain of the surviving husband or wife would release chemicals into the blood that weakened the heart. Li looked at hundreds of medical records, and found that the effect was not uncommon, but was widespread. In the year after the death of a husband, the chances of a wife dying doubled. And men, he discovered, suffer even more from broken hearts. In the year after a wife's death, husbands are six times more likely to die. In technical language, there is a strong correlation between the deaths of married couples.

Li's understanding of these models of real behaviour made him rich. From the relative backwater of Toronto's Waterloo University, Li was hired to work for the Canadian Imperial Bank of Commerce. There he applied his formula to the market for life insurance. Because spouses are more likely to die a short time apart, the price of a joint life insurance policy, which pays out more on the death of the first spouse, was overpriced compared to a policy for an individual. Understanding this mispricing allowed Li and his bank to arbitrage the market and make money. Li's bank cornered the market and made a fortune, before his competitors recognised the correlation and changed their prices too.

Having successfully applied his understanding of correlation to life insurance, Li turned his mind to the broader question of correlations of bonds. He faced up to the flaw that had brought down LTCM. How likely is it, he asked, that one company or country defaults on their debts if a different country does so? Li thought that by understanding and pricing the risk that had brought down LTCM, then that risk could be managed.

The goal was worth it. Could Li replicate the vast money-making of LTCM, while also protecting his bank from the risk that sank the hedge fund?

Li followed his approach to life insurance. He worked out the expected probability of defaults on bonds from market prices, and compared the likely default across different bonds. By applying the principle that had worked for life expectancy, he could then work out the impact that default on one bond, by a company or a country, would have on the likely default of another. His model was thought to price CDOs accurately for even the most complicated investment products. Even if an unexpected event happened, like the Russian default, any bank using Li's model should be protected from the knock-on consequences.

Specifically, Li applied the thinking to the new securitised instruments that had grown up over the past decade.

The model was an instant hit. The Canadian Imperial Bank of Commerce became one of the biggest players in the markets for the new securities. David Li was showered with praise on Wall Street, and asked to give presentations to the increasingly large number of mathematicians operating in banks across the financial world. He was poached as Global Head of Derivatives Research at Citigroup, which was to become the biggest bank in the world.

As the market grew, it wasn't just the banks of Wall Street who increasingly relied on the model. A year later, the rating agency Moody's changed the way they evaluated the risk on the new securities. Traditionally, rating agencies had insisted that packaged-up securities included a wide spread of bonds to reduce the risk that they would all go bad together. Instead, in 2004, Moody's changed to Li's formula to work out the risk of loans going bad. The result was that new securities could be issued with packages of very similar bonds – for example subprime mortgages – and still attract the very top rating from Moody's. Just a week later, Moody's competitor Standard & Poor's followed suit.

But there was a mistake in Li's model. The sad irony is that in attempting to solve the problem that brought down LTCM, Li had made exactly the same error: he had assumed that markets would broadly continue to operate as before.

How could such a wildly popular and scrutinised model be mistaken?

When working on the cost of life insurance, Li had relied on real-world information about when husbands and wives died to work out the correlations between different events: in economists' language, the data was exogenous; it was not affected by the model. When he applied the same thinking to defaults on bonds, again he needed data, this time on the likelihood of defaults. But such defaults don't happen often enough to be directly measurable, in the way deaths are. There is no equivalent of the public records office. So Li made an assumption that the risk was accurately reflected in market prices for insuring the risk of such a default. He then based his model on that assumption.

But crucially, this assumption made Li's model circular. The valuations that were the output of his model would be right so long as the market price of a default was an accurate reflection of the actual risk of default. But the more people across the financial markets used the model, the more the model itself defined the price of risk, which was itself the input to the model.

So long as the markets worked as they had in the recent past, the problem would build up, but the model would continue to work. But as we well know, markets do not always work as in the recent past. In addition, the data used in the model was taken only from recent history, just as LTCM had done. LTCM's data stretched back only five years,[79] a period which failed to cover any really big events. In some cases, the data fed into Li's model was even shorter.

Li himself knew his model wasn't perfect. 'The most dangerous part,' he said, 'is when people believe everything coming out of it.'[80]

Yet not only did banks start to believe everything that was coming out of it, but rating agencies and then regulators began to use the model to value these assets. The flawed model became part of the plumbing of the financial system.

By the time the flaw in the model became obvious, the whole financial system had come to rely on its valuations. This time, rather than just requiring the bailout of a hedge fund, the over-reliance on mathematical models had led to a bailout of the whole system.

Of course the flaws in this one model do not show that models can't be useful. Models and mathematics can be an important guide to the expected value of an asset, and the risk of a market position. Likewise, it's not unusual for a model to have flaws. Indeed every model has its flaws, because all models need to make assumptions about the world to make it easy to understand.

The problem was not using a model. It was treating the results of a model based on imperfect assumptions as objective fact. Models can guide subjective human judgement but they cannot replace it.

David Li's model was not the only cause of the crash. But the story is symptomatic of an attempt to find objective answers to questions that must in part be based on subjective judgement. Given the complexity of human behaviour, questions about the future of the economy are necessarily subjective. The appearance of objectivity can be soothing. Yet any appearance of objectivity is itself built on subjective assumptions, and so hides the true nature of a judgement. Surely it is better to accept a judgement as subjective, rather than to try in vain to pretend otherwise?

So how did we come to a position where we made the same mistakes within the same decade? We lost faith in the power of subjective judgement. Like Icarus, we forgot ourselves, flew too close to the sun and saw our models melt when exposed to harsh reality. Objectivity was so compelling that we ignored our instincts and believed that the computers must be right.

Models Built on Sand

While Professor Scholes's and David Li's models went spectacularly wrong, it would be unfair to imply that they were unusual. Their assumptions and modelling were standard practice that had built up over decades. Indeed, much of the economics profession was engulfed, and remains engulfed, in a false paradigm.

Economics has always been a blend of art and science. Trying to understand how our economy works, how jobs are created and how scarce resources are allocated needs an understanding of both mathematics and human behaviour.

For almost 150 years after its birth in the late 1700s under David Hume and Adam Smith, the subject of economics was rooted in human behaviour and morality. Both Hume and

Smith sat as Professors of Moral Philosophy at Edinburgh and Glasgow Universities respectively. During the nineteenth and the first half of the twentieth centuries, economics continued to combine empirical observation of human behaviour with analytical thinking about its consequences. Keynes was famous for highlighting the importance of 'animal spirits', and eloquent in his descriptions of the behaviour of man.

But over the past fifty years in the economics profession, this concern with human behaviour has sadly diminished. While earlier economists had used equations for shorthand, from around the 1950s economists began successfully to use mathematical techniques to come to very elegant conclusions. By making assumptions of rationality, telling and insightful new economic theories were established. In 1954, Kenneth Arrow and Gerald Debreu proved mathematically how fully rational, fully informed people would best maximise their well-being if left to trade in perfectly complete, liquid markets. The free market would always lead to the best outcome for everyone.

It is a crucial finding that not only explains why Adam Smith was right 200 years earlier about the invisible hand, but helps tell us what market failures get in the way of the successful operation of free markets. In addition, the elegance of the mathematical proof of Smith's invisible hand is striking and bold. Most economists will remember when they first understood the result.

It is easy to see why economists started to look at other ways to use similar techniques to repeat the success of Arrow and Debreu. To do this, assumptions were needed to make the problems tractable. Without gross simplifications of individual human behaviour, it is exceptionally hard to model how a group behaves.

Based on these assumptions, conclusions continued to follow. The economists who used the new mathematical techniques were honoured with Nobel Prizes. More techniques were developed. Computing power widened their scope. This was progress!

At the same time, a new theory of rational choice developed. This theory stated that people's preferences and desires could best be measured not by anything internal but by observing choices actually made, and then assuming that the revealed preferences people held were consistent. This theory was based on the philosophical construct, following Bentham, that human decision-making was based on conscious decisions that weighed costs and benefits of actions to maximise utility.

Such assumptions built on the philosophical tradition of the time. In the eighteenth century, philosophy saw decision-making as a binary choice. Rational choice theory, and the assumptions that underpinned it, were based firmly in this Enlightenment conception of rational man. The philosophical insights of the later Wittgenstein, which emphasised instead the uncertainty and unknowability of the mind, came too late to be embedded in the axioms of economics.

In the 1960s, economists including Milton Friedman and Robert Lucas developed the crucial insight that the development of the economy depends to a large degree on what people expect. They made the assumption that rational people would have rational expectations. Once this assumption was made, a number of very strong results followed, such as that the market price for an asset is the best possible predictor of its price in future, because all information is distilled into that price: the so-called efficient market hypothesis, put forward by Eugene Fama in 1970. To model expectations that are anything but rational is harder, so the assumption of rational expectations became standard.

Gradually, economics departments began to change too. Those with a strong grasp of the maths were promoted, while those who relied more on description were sidelined. Only those able to build the most complicated mathematical models were respected. The explosion of financial services from the 1980s onwards also developed the trend, with the opportunity to make huge amounts of money out of the modelling. Increasingly, economists were lured out of underpaid professorships in academia to work in finance. Of course finance wanted the mathematical economists most, so courses were changed to focus on the models and to teach the latest mathematical techniques, and mathematical research prioritised. The mathematical approach reached its zenith in the early twenty-first century, when universities taught postgraduate degrees in economics more to physics gradu-ates than economists. In many of the UK's most prestigious economics faculties, such as the LSE and Cambridge, post-graduate courses based on a richer or more historic account of economics were abandoned.

The result of the mathematical paradigm in economics, and the promotion of mathematical ability over and above a wider understanding of human behaviour, was that people stopped questioning the assumptions. For to question the assumptions behind the mathematics was to undermine the use of the mathematics. And no one wanted to do that, because maths was where the money was. Those who did question the maths were stigmatised as not being up to it.

It is an irony that the first step any economics student had to take to get to grips with all this maths was to learn the Greek alphabet.

The changes in academic economics fed through into the world of policy. The efficient market hypothesis means that no asset can be fundamentally wrongly valued, because the market has already processed all the known information, and the asset will trade at 'fair value'. The theory implies that no one can beat the market – unless they know insider informa-tion that the market does not.

But we know that markets do not operate efficiently: for example house prices move gradually, with a lag, so even if fundamentals change sharply, tomorrow's house prices can be reliably predicted to be fairly close to today's. Likewise, rational choice theory is undermined by the fact that we know people's preferences are not consistent. People can make different choices without changing their preferences, perhaps because of their mood or what those around them are choosing.

Neuroscientific research has confirmed that this axiom of modern economics is wrong. A paper by Camerer, Lowenstein and Pralec in 2003 showed first that most of the brain is concerned with subconscious processing, so most decisions are not choices but are automatic, and second that most behaviour is guided by the 'often unrecognised influence of finely tuned affective (emotion) systems that are localised in particular brain regions and whose basic design humans share with many other animals'. Furthermore, they found that without these subconscious processes, the conscious brain cannot function enough to 'get the job done alone'.

But those who opposed the rationalist school of economics faced a problem. In 1976, Robert Lucas first expressed his critique that has become famous for its eloquence in putting the case for rational expectations. The Lucas critique argues that any observation of behaviour cannot be the basis for policy, because the policy itself will change behaviour. In his words: 'Any change in policy will systematically alter the structure of econometric models.'

So long as people look to the future, the critique has no answer. Policy affects behaviour, so changing policy changes behaviour. So any model must take into account people's expectations. So far so good.

Indeed, as the economics profession increasingly looks to empirical observation of how people behave, it must not drop this vital insight.

Unfortunately, the Lucas critique had two unintended consequences.

First, including expectations makes economic models much more complicated. So the simplifying assumption of rational expectations became much more attractive to make models tractable.

Second, empirical economics was undermined, because any empiricist who could not adequately measure expectations could not predict peoples' response to a policy change. As John Gray said, 'the decoupling of history from economics has led to a pervasive unrealism of the discipline'.[81]

Instead of shining light on the frailties of our understanding, as they should have done, these challenges drove the economics profession into an increasingly navel-gazing, mathematical spiral. So for example, the size of banks' balance sheets were excluded from most economic models, and instead were confidently expected rationally to alter to fit what was happening in the real world. Such confidence was unwise.

There is an answer to the challenge laid down by the Lucas critique. It is to be realistic about the limitations of our knowledge, and humble about how little we can predict of the future. After the economics profession's experience of the past five years, a little humility is no doubt appropriate.

For exactly the sort of human behaviour we observed in the crash meant that anyone who challenged the new orthodoxy was undermined. Economic papers became replete with pages of complex, meaningless algebra, but the same lampooning of outsiders that we saw in the credit boom was exercised on those who questioned the use of complex maths. Rational expectations became the norm, and anyone who questioned the assumption of rationality was accused of being irrational themselves.

This assumption of rationality was applied directly to finance. A common assumption was that, based on the efficient markets hypothesis, the movement of market prices followed a normal distribution. Such an assumption allows you to draw some very strong conclusions. The special property of a normal distribution ensures that once you know the outcome of an event, and you know how much typical events vary from that average, you can work out how confident you are of most events being within a certain distance from that average. The distance is called a 'standard deviation'. The consequence is that if you know a pattern has a normal distribution, you can work out the sorts of results you should expect 95 per cent, or 99 per cent, or 99.9 per cent of the time.

The combination of the efficient markets hypothesis and the normal distribution became intoxicating when applied to financial markets. The calculations they allow you to make help you to feel in control of any risks you might face, because you can put a specific figure on how likely or unlikely a certain outcome might be. Risk officers at investment banks became particularly consumed by a concept known as 'Value at Risk' (or VaR), literally, the value of the bank at risk under a 'worst case scenario'. Mathematical calculations could provide the specific answer to the question: What is the maximum we could expect to lose over the next week? The computer would spit out the solution, something like, 'You can be 95 per cent sure that you won't lose more than £32.4 million'. Being able to put numerical values on risk was remarkably comforting for everyone, from the risk officer of a specific department, to the head of the trading floor, and all the way up to the CEO of the bank.

But these outcomes were based on crucial assumptions that were nearly always wrong. A set of outcomes can only be described as a normal distribution if what you are measuring is the product of random and independent causes. And as we have repeatedly seen, people are not perfectly rational. Even largely rational people behave irrationally in large groups. Events are not independent but dependent on history. But flaws in the model – model uncertainty – as distinct from risk in the underlying reality, is rarely taken into account, so these Value at Risks are presented not as the estimates they really are, but as fact.

There is further, more colloquial yet categorical proof that markets are not efficient: some people do buck the market. Warren Buffett and George Soros are the most powerful advocates. Buffett reportedly went so far as to say, 'I'd be a bum on the street with a tin cup if the markets were always efficient.' Soros pointed out that 'this interpretation of the way financial markets operate is severely distorted. That is why I have not bothered to familiarise myself with efficient market theory'.[82]

Despite this evidence, the financial world still clung to it, as a simplifying way of making their models work. Look at the continued dominance of the model for pricing derivatives derived by Black and Scholes despite the fall of LTCM. The Black–Scholes model doesn't represent reality, and traders would lose money as long as they relied on it.

Empirical observation of how markets move shows how price changes do not follow a normal distribution but have more chance of extreme, outlier events. This may be because of the herding behaviour we have seen so much of. This increased likelihood is called a 'fat tail' as the outside ends of a distribution curve are fatter than normal.

But rather than jettison the model completely, or find a better set of assumptions on which to base their model, people operating in financial markets simply fudged it. Traders would add on an extra cost if someone wanted to bet on an extreme event, just to cover themselves in case it did actually happen. Often traders knew that all of the complexity and sophistication of mathematical financial modelling was wrong, and used their subjective judgement to aim off. Yet ratings agencies and regulators took the model as gospel. Despite the shortcomings of the Black–Scholes model, it is still in use today.

So even though we have shown ourselves able to question the validity of financial models, why did we have a collective bout of amnesia over the last decade? There are two broad reasons why mathematical models gained such a hold: because the rise of computer power made it possible, and because human nature made it desirable.

The Rise of the Machines

For centuries, mankind has tried to manage risk. Fear over the future is part of our survival instinct, whether you hoard food, save money, or arm yourself for defence. We all want a world where there is less uncertainty. We all know that bad things can happen, but if we can understand how likely they are to happen, we start to feel more in control of our own destiny. We feel even more in control if we know that we can buy insurance to compensate for the risk. From this basic human desire arose the insurance market: by creating a market for risk, people could protect themselves against the slings and arrows the world throws at us.

Demand for this kind of protection fuelled the growth of financial markets. If risk could be measured and priced, then you could mitigate the impact when something bad happened. Of course this did not prevent bad things from happening: we still had stock market crashes, or company losses. We all instinctively know that insurers, casinos, and bookmakers still lose out once in a while. Risk management cannot stop destabilising events, but it can reduce their impact. The world therefore became used to the idea that certain risks could be hedged away.

To understand why computers were so beguiling, let us consider something known as 'Monte Carlo simulation'. It's a method used for trying to predict how the world might look in the future, by running lots of different random scenarios. It was invented in the 1940s, by nuclear physicists, but it went on to be applied to many other fields, including financial markets.

As the name suggests, its inventors were inspired by the casino of Monte Carlo, where gamblers would be prey to many different scenarios depending on the probabilities they faced. There are some gambles where we all know the probabilities: the chance of a coin landing either heads or tails, for example. But what if we had to toss 100 coins in a row? And then play a round of poker, followed by Blackjack? The possible future paths grow exponentially and we need help to work our way through the maths. Monte Carlo simulation provided a way to deal with the vast numbers of different scenarios: the computer has the power to see all the different paths simultaneously and then spit out a prediction within seconds.

This kind of power was like a drug to the derivatives industry. Derivatives are all about what might happen in the future, and the future can be complicated. Rather than buying insurance now, you might want to buy it in the future if something else happens: so you want to buy an option on an option, for example. This kind of second derivative was beyond the capabilities of the Black–Scholes model. But computers could figure out what these new kinds of options might cost. Computers could look at what might happen if an earthquake were to hit at the same time as a collapse in the currency, or what might happen in a sequence of events, such as interest rates rising followed by employment falling followed by inflation rising. Computers could price up any kind of derivative a person might happen to want.

Consequently, with the march of the machines, the derivatives market exploded. In the six years to 2006, the global derivatives market quadrupled in size, to a total of around $400 trillion outstanding.[83]

There was now an alphabet soup of products that relied on complex financial models for their pricing. The derivatives available became increasingly complex. And the more complex the products, the more complex were the models needed to price them.

The exponential rise in the size of the derivatives market was not a cause of the financial crisis, it was merely a symptom. It was a signal of problems in the allocation of risk – that we had become so overly reliant on the models, we stopped looking at what assumptions had gone into them. Banks fell in love with what computers could achieve, and like infatuated teenagers pushed the limits. Computers were seen as like us, only better. The modellers were dazzled by their own reflection, enchanted by their innovation – and ultimately doomed to self-destruction.

Computers provided us with a false sense of control. If you can predict a risk, you can hedge it. If you can find a buyer of that risk, you can price it. The internet and advances in telecommunications meant that it became much easier to match up buyers and sellers, facilitating the growth in the derivatives market. So, the argument went, we had moved to a period of greater stability: if everyone knew what the price was at any given point in time, and risks were matched up to those who could bear them, then what could possibly go wrong?

Feeding the System

For the private sector, a reliance on financial models was incredibly convenient. It meant they were left alone to do their own thing. If anyone challenged or questioned a bank, it could point to all its complicated risk models and show that it had everything under control. For those running the banks it was a blessed relief from having to worry about the minutiae of regulation: they had their cleverest people working on the job, leaving them to use their time contemplating the next acquisition.

More than that, there was a hubristic sense that the private sector had won the argument. When Peter Mandelson said in 1998 that he was 'intensely relaxed about people getting filthy rich',[84] that was music to the City's ears. Financiers had long argued that being left alone to create wealth for themselves would lead to greater wealth for all. The celebration of light-touch regulation, without any prudential oversight, by its nature acknowledged that markets knew best.

In winning the argument, the private sector could feel superior. It fed their ego to know that their way of managing risk had won. Why should they even bother to think about the frailties of their models when every part of the system was so accepting of them? Even during the credit crunch, the illiquid assets that were causing so much trouble were valued on a 'mark-to-model' basis, where the accountants would routinely use the banks' own models to value assets.

Perhaps it is understandable that private banks would use models to best try to get a handle on the value of very complex assets. It is easy to see how the apparent certainty of a model valuation makes life easier. And as the models were making a lot of money in the short term, and your pay was linked to short-term results, why ask too many difficult questions?

More surprising is that regulators, too, asked banks to make their own valuations of the assets they held. They did so on the basis that the banks knew best. Since it was held that it was in the banks' interests to know the valuation of their own assets, they could be relied on to do just that.

During the boom, almost no one challenged the belief that the markets had it right. The relative success of allegedly efficient markets during this period appeared to confirm that markets really had entered a new period of stability. Regulators and central bankers subscribed to the growing belief that advances in mathematical pricing of risk and increased globalisation had mitigated the chance of any shocks to the system. As Alan Greenspan said in 2005, 'The application of more sophisticated approaches to measuring and managing risk are key factors underpinning the greater resilience of our largest financial institutions.'[85]

With markets becoming apparently more and more efficient, central bankers, regulators and risk managers dangerously built their ideology blindly around this intellectual consensus. Adair Turner commented in 2009: 'We have had a very fundamental shock to the "efficient market hypothesis" which has been in the DNA of the FSA and securities and banking regulators throughout the world.'[86]

How was it that regulators were caught up in the hubris too?

Once again, in looking for our answer we should discard the assumption that the regulators were perfectly rational omniscient beings, and instead look to how human beings really behave.

Again, psychology gives us a clue. Cognitive capture describes how groups of people can become powerfully drawn to a given worldview, even when each harbours individual doubts.

Economic regulators and indeed large swathes of the academic economics profession followed this capture.

Regulators tend to be less well-paid, less qualified, and less aggressive than the bankers they regulate. They find it harder to query assumptions or stand up to banks acting irresponsibly. Good regulators are poached, and use their understanding of regulation to game the rules. This has led to regulators increasingly hiding behind complex rulebooks, insisting on adherence to detailed, prescribed rules rather than exercising their judgement.

But this standard explanation of low-paid and junior regulators does not tell the whole story. Most regulatory bodies also employ people from finance, often in senior positions. The problem is that the more financiers who become regulators, the more the regulator becomes captured in the prevailing paradigm of finance. The common psychological concept of groupthink then means that it's hard to challenge the dominant thinking.

In the case of the FSA in Britain, such groupthink supported key assumptions which went unquestioned.

The FSA assumed it was right to use banks' own models to work out how risky their investments were. Not only was the obvious conflict of interests ignored, but the other, external measures of risk were not taken into account. Work by Andrew Haldane has shown that in the run-up to the crisis, the risk measures used by regulators did not distinguish at all between banks that later crashed in the crisis, and those banks which survived without direct government support. In contrast, by using simple external measures of risk, like the ratio of the bank's share price to its total lending, the banks that went on to fail showed clear signs of distress in advance, while banks that survived the crisis performed much better.

But a deeper assumption by the regulators, again supported by the dominant groupthink, was that if the market was saying something, it must be right. As Adair Turner has explained, 'an organisation like the FSA has worked on the assumption that it has to define that there is some specific market failure, or else our intervention is not legitimate'.[87] This allowed them to shed responsibility for being pro-active.

The reliance on false assumptions, which allowed people to use models to give apparently objective answers to essentially subjective questions also had a deeper, and still more damaging, impact. By removing the link to humanity, the economics profession also removed the fundamental link between ethics and economics.

For the regulator, if the market was the ultimate arbiter then there was no need for the FSA to stand as a judge. The FSA pushed away any potential discomfort that might come from a subjective judgement, and left it to something objective – the market.

Furthermore, the FSA's own statutory objectives led to a focus on the micro-regulation, rather than the big picture. The FSA's statutory objectives were to promote: market confidence, financial stability, consumer protection, and the reduction of financial crime.[88]

We now know that the first two are the most important, but they are also the most intangible. During the boom, the first two tasks were easy, and the prevailing ideology implied they would always be met. It was far easier to concentrate on consumer protection and financial crime, where you could see tangible, measurable results. It provided the chance to secure some easy victories. More importantly for the FSA, as the newest and therefore most junior UK financial regulator, it was a way to justify their existence. They could point to a track record, with tallies of which consumer protection actions had been taken. If you look at the FSA's website, even now, it takes two clicks to take you to their 'Fines Table', where you can see who has been fined what for financial crime.[89] There is no similarly fast route to finding out what they have done to preserve financial stability over the last year. The page which offers 'Essential Facts and Figures about the Financial Services Authority'[90] contains only references to preventing scams or levels of customer complaints.

By focusing on the micro-level tasks, the FSA was allowed to shy away from putting forward subjective judgements about the big picture. Their objectivity fitted in with the wider world's view of the primacy of objectivity: if something could be measured, modelled, and objectively understood, then it took precedence over intangible and subjective judgement. Again, they trusted what could be objectively proven, rather than trusting the institutions to make their own judgements.

This viewpoint suited the prevailing political climate. Brown's granting of independence to the Bank of England was wrongly seen to mark the end of history in economic policymaking. Everything that had gone before was seen as old-fashioned, subjective and irrational. When he unveiled his plans, he boasted: 'I want to set in place a long-term framework for economic prosperity... I want to break from the boom-bust economics of previous years.'[91] The markets welcomed the change with similar hubris. As Michael Hughes, Head of Research at BZW, told *The Independent* at the time: 'The government has taken an important and long overdue step towards achieving the end of stabilising the economy.'[92]

Powerful computer models were an example of the democratisation of previously hierarchical elites: they could help smash down the 'Old Boys' network' in the City as new talents would be required. For New Labour, creating the tripartite system of regulation was their New World Order. There was a sense that if there was a new way of doing something, then in and of itself, it was the right way of doing it.

Thus it was in the politicians' interest to embrace a world where humanity appeared to have conquered risk through the rise of mathematical models. It validated the Brownite philosophy. Sixty-three consecutive quarters of economic growth seemed to provide the evidence that the philosophy was working, and the tax receipts to boot. Why would anyone question what that growth was built on? Why would anyone question whether efficient markets were working, when stock markets were booming and a wall of money was washing over the globe?

Consequences

The unmasking of this hubris finally came when the previously liquid mortgage-backed securities market suddenly dried up. Who actually knew what these mortgages were worth? There simply wasn't enough information, after they had been sliced and diced and distributed through the system, to know.

Such a collapse in the market had not been factored into the mathematical models. They need prices to work; without them, they had no data to work with. Like a car without petrol, they would not start. The credit crunch began when

BNP Paribas told investors they couldn't take money out of two of its funds owing to a 'complete evaporation of liquidity' in the market.

There was initially a collective bout of incredulity. How could the models have failed? Things that the models had predicted would almost never happen were now happening with frightening regularity. Even as the crisis broke, risk managers used the language of the models to express their incredulity. 'We were seeing things that were 25-standard deviation moves, several days in a row,' said Goldman Sachs CFO David Viniar in August 2007.[93] Most of us would use the phrase 'once in a lifetime', but for those deeply embedded in financial markets, a lifetime would be a poor expression of experience when a model could simulate a multitude of lifetimes at once.

Thus the prevailing consensus of rational expectations, efficient financial markets, and normal distributions began to fall apart. So far there has been little for policymakers to fall back on in its place. Supporters cling to the argument that even if flawed, this paradigm is the best way to look at the world because of the lack of an alternative. Even Alan Greenspan, facing the breakdown of his lifelong ideology that markets are self-regulating, could only admit, 'Yes, I found a flaw.'[94]

All the uncertainty banks thought they had tamed has been exposed. Risk management was a chimera. This was upsetting for those invested in the system.

Indeed the high level of consensus between central bankers, regulators and financiers was itself the cause of potential instability within the system. There must be more challenge of received wisdom, rather than an indolent acceptance of the prevailing ideology.

It is not that we should make policy less rational: far from it. But we must recognise the reality of human behaviour, in markets and in regulators, and design policy with our eyes open to how people behave, and how that behaviour is itself dependent on the system. We must use the power of models, but not be dominated by them.

Wiser financiers have long known that the application of mathematical models to financial markets was not a perfect science. The renowned investment manager, Peter Bernstein, points out that there is 'a persistent tension between those who assert that the best decisions are based on quantification ... and those who base their decisions on more subjective degrees of belief about the uncertain future.'[95]

This dilemma can be solved, but only by understanding the dynamics of how people really behave. By facing up to the reality of unresolvable uncertainty and how individual behaviour shapes our society, we can improve the safety of our financial systems and the way we run our economy. We will turn in later chapters to the need for stronger institutions in which to embed discretionary decisions. And we must understand the impact of personal incentives on individuals if we are to start to unravel the unsustainable system that over-reliance on technology has generated. But next, we turn to the single most important determinant of human behaviour, which did not feature in economists' models at all.

Chapter 6

WOMEN ON TOP

In June 2007, as the first rumblings of the financial crisis could be heard, a subsidiary of the German reinsurance giant Munich Re decided to reward its best sales staff with an 'incentive trip'.[96] The company's one hundred top performers were flown to Budapest where they were treated to a night at the city's famous Gellért thermal baths. Gellért is a lavish Art Nouveau spa complex built in the twilight years of the Austro-Hungarian Empire. That night, for the benefit of the insurance men, the baths had been especially converted into an open-air brothel.

Ornate four-poster beds were arrayed around the pool-side. Twenty prostitutes were hired to work on the company's account. The women were colour-coded with ribbon armbands. Red meant available for flirting, yellow for sex, those with white ribbons were reserved for senior company executives and top salesmen only. With the sort of efficiency for which the German insurance industry is renowned, the women were given a stamp on the arm for every service they performed – to ensure there was no haggling over payment at the end of the night.

This distasteful episode highlights the importance of confronting one of the single biggest determinants of human behaviour: sex. The Munich Re 'incentive trip' could only have occurred in a corporate culture dominated by men, where sexism was normal. The cognitive scientist Steven Pinker writes that 'the sexes are as old as complex life... Differences between men and women affect every aspect of our lives... To ignore gender would be to ignore a major part of the human condition'.[97] Whether we like it or not, in both our professional and our personal lives, sex makes a difference to how we experience the world.

Compared to almost any other skilled profession, the leadership of the financial services industry is overwhelmingly male and the culture of finance steeped in testosterone. Does this matter? How male is too male? And what could we do about it?

There is the view that discussion about women in finance is an irrelevance. That one issue is social policy, the other financial policy. But recent evidence shows that society has a direct incentive, both for the sake of financial stability *and* healthier profits, to see more women in the boardrooms of financial institutions. The unspoken assumption that finance, like war, demands such masculine behaviour, and that gender has no place in discussion about economic policy, does not stand up to an honest assessment of the facts. The dominance by men does not exist because of the inherently masculine nature of finance. Rather the masculine nature of finance exists because of its dominance by men.

So as we move on from the crash and build a stronger, more stable financial system, we must not shy away from acknowledging that more women can play a key role in the solution. Once this has been accepted then the question becomes not whether to change the status quo, but how.

Rare Commodities

Let's start with something that's impossible to dispute. In the upper echelons of the UK finance industry, women are rare.

In 2010 there were a mere two chairwomen and five female CEOs running FTSE 100 companies. Across the index as a whole, 95 per cent of executive directors were male.[98] Over half of FTSE 250 companies have no women on their boards at all.[99] RBS, HBOS, Lloyds, Bradford & Bingley and Northern Rock – the five UK banks which required state aid during the crisis – could muster just ten female directors between them in 2007. On one bank trading floor sampled in 2008, just four of the two hundred and sixty traders were female: 1.5 per cent of the workforce.[100]

Until 1973 women members weren't even allowed onto the floor of the London Stock Exchange. Even then, for the first six months they could only look around and make contacts – they were not permitted to deal. Now, in finance, female employees make up half the workforce, although since 2003, the proportion of women has actually fallen slightly from 52 to 49 per cent.[101] But these are heavily biased towards lower ranks. Half of women are employed in administrative or secretarial roles, compared to only a sixth of men. Of the men who work in the finance sector, three-quarters fall into the three categories of 'managers and senior officials', 'professional occupations', or 'associate professional and technical' compared to less than half of women.[102] A snapshot of RBS in 2009 showed that of every ten staff at clerical level, seven were female. At the next level up five out of ten were. At management level, it was three out of ten. At senior management level it was two. At executive level just one in ten staff were female. There were no women on the board.[103]

An Equality and Human Rights Commission (EHRC) report found a pay gap of 55 per cent between average full-time annual gross earnings for men and women, compared to an average gap of 28 per cent across the whole economy. This is not because banks are breaking the equality laws, but because such a disproportionate number of women are concentrated at the lowest-paid levels of the sector.

Women are not progressing to the top. Lord Davies of Abersoch's report into the lack of women on boards called it a 'leaking pipe' syndrome. The lack of progress cannot be accounted for by the argument that because women only entered finance relatively recently they simply have not yet reached the top, so we just need to wait for the so-called cohort effect to reach its conclusion. Women enter finance but do not advance as far as men. At the current rate, it will take seventy-three years before women are fully represented at board level.

Outside banking, the pattern is repeated at the top of corporate Britain. In 2006, women made up only 12 per cent of listed companies' governing bodies.[104] Six out of ten firms in the FTSE 100 have only one or no women on the board.[105] Even in the civil service fewer than a quarter of the Permanent Secretaries are female.[106] But in finance, the statistics are particularly shocking.

So why do more women not get to the top? After all, finance is an extremely competitive business. If talent is being held back, surely rational companies would promote on merit? As the Chairman of a FTSE 100 company summed it up: 'Why would you deny yourself access to half the world's intellect? It's a no-brainer.'[107]

In part, it is because the culture of the system is judged by criteria that are fundamentally male. As Sandra Curtis, a self-proclaimed veteran of the City, argued to MPs: 'Women do tend to behave differently from men. They are being judged by a set of managerial norms that are primarily reflective of masculine behaviour. I think this is in built into the City.'[108] Dr Ros Altmann, a successful investment banker herself, agreed:

> The criteria by which you are judged for getting higher up an organisation tend to be the ones that are valued by the people at the top... You see at the very top it is this aggressive, sometimes short-termist, certainly highly risk prone rather than risk control which is valued.[109]

How is this manifested in the workplace? As one example, women are generally less confident, or are less happy to assert confidence. In a survey of MBA students, 70 per cent of female respondents rated their performance as equivalent to that of their co-workers whereas 70 per cent of men rate themselves higher.[110] Sharron Gunn from the Institute of Chartered Accountants told the Treasury Select Committee: 'One of the things we have come across is lack of confidence in females… Lack of confidence in terms of moving up the corporate ladder.'[111] We see this happening even before people enter the workplace. The irony is that unqualified confidence is far from a virtue in the finance industry. Brad Barber and Terrance Odean analysed over 66,000 trades from discount broker accounts. The traders who were most confident performed the most trades, but they underperformed the overall market.[112]

Because the status quo is dominated by men, confidence and assertion are deemed normal and necessary to climb the ranks. The predominance of aggressive men at high levels determines these social norms. Put it this way: can you imagine Sir Fred Goodwin ever stopping to think 'Am I good at my job'? Yet people like Sir Fred Goodwin set the tone for what it is to be considered successful.

Success criteria are part of the culture of the system and undoubtedly play an important part. So too does the decision to leave to have children.

Of course having the choice to leave work to raise a family is valuable and important. Indeed in other areas of life, women and men very successfully combine work and family life. But the choice should be a genuine one not predetermined by the system. For the choice to be genuine, it needs to be made by both parents, in a culture in which the decision to have children has less professional impact.

An unintended consequence of giving more support to mothers over recent years has been to strengthen the gender bias in the workplace. Currently, statutory maternity leave lasts for a year while statutory paternity leave lasts for two weeks. This means that a woman makes a temporary choice between her career and her children, but a man cannot.

This imbalance strengthens the cultural bias against

women. Women alone bear the brunt of businesses' cost at their choice to have children. One woman, who has children herself, told us that when a female employee says she is pregnant and will be away for a year, she gets genuinely angry. Strict rules outlawing discrimination do not stop companies simply refusing to employ newly married women in their late twenties, or others they think may be likely soon to have children.

This is a far deeper problem than simply getting women to the top of finance. It has its roots in society's expectations that grow from childhood onwards. We have spoken to women who agree that when they were growing up, they were no less ambitious than their male peers and no less successful academically. But when they thought ahead to their career, they expected that if they wanted to have children they would have to take a career hit while they were relatively young. In contrast, their male friends did not factor in family at all to their career expectations. For them, their trajectory was linear without interference from their personal lives. Among employers, the belief that child-rearing is still an exclusively female sphere survives. In June 2008 Theo Paphitis, a star of the BBC's *Dragon's Den* and one of Britain's most high-profile businessmen, remarked in an interview that pregnant women's brains 'turn to mush', rendering them useless as employees for six months. He also described paternity leave as 'a bit soppy'.[113] There is a deeply embedded assumption that the choice between family and work is one that must be made by women and not by both parents. As long as this attitude persists, there will always be a barrier for women in a career like finance, which traditionally demands extremely long hours and absolute flexibility.

Further evidence of the cultural bias against women comes from comparing pay. Despite a strong legal framework, there is still a discrepancy in the levels of pay between men and women. The Equal Pay Act, which became law under a

Conservative government in 1970, was a first step, and was followed by the Sex Discrimination Act of 1975, which made it illegal to discriminate directly or indirectly on the grounds of sex. These Acts have been bolstered by laws which prevent direct and indirect discrimination, and measures addressing inequality in pay.

In theory legislation ensures that men and women now compete on a level playing field. But as well as the pay gap in average earnings, when it comes to discretionary, performance-related pay – better known as bankers' bonuses – the spirit of the Equal Pay Act is all too easily subverted.

Figures show that the average annual bonus for women was £2,875, less than a fifth of the men's average of £14,554.[114] This is in part reflective of the different roles that women occupy in financial services. But even when you take like for like, there is a discrepancy. The 2009 Chartered Management Institute's annual National Management Salary Survey found that male directors getting bonuses receive 39 per cent in additional payments, while women tend to get only 35 per cent. In fact, overall male directors' pay was on average 18.6 per cent higher than female directors' pay, continuing the gap found at the junior professional level of 18.8 per cent between the two sexes.[115]

One reason for this can be put down to human behaviour: reflexivity. People reward like with like. We naturally value the qualities in others that we prize in ourselves. The idea of men recruiting men or people recruiting in their own image was often cited to the Davies inquiry as a problem in the City,[116] and this tendency can be found across the board. In new polling data commissioned for this book, only 17 per cent of men think that if more women had been in finance, the crisis would have been prevented or its impact lessened. But over double this number of women, 40 per cent of those asked, thought more women would have made a positive difference. Academic evidence suggests that this affects the evaluation of women's performances by their superiors, because most of them, as we have seen, are men. Louise Marie Roth, an American sociologist, has researched this aspect of the discretionary reward system, and concluded that 'perceptions of performance within teams of workers adversely affected women because of universal tendencies to prefer similar others'.[117]

One trader told us that she came in to the office after the weekend of London fashion week; she was making polite small-talk, and was in the middle of describing something she had bought when her boss turned round and shouted, 'Would you just shut the fuck up about fashion?' She was proud of her instinctive response, 'I will when you shut the fuck up about football', until she realised it was bonus day and he was in charge of her reward package. Because the system is so opaque and secretive, she could not tell what effect this did or did not have. Only her instinct told her it had not helped.

Women weren't the only victims of this bias. Farcically, in some cases risk managers had their pay determined by the very traders they were supposed to be supervising. But the gender prejudice involved in the bonus payment formula has been particularly pernicious. Jessica Thompson described how she was at a bonus allocation meeting: 'They crossed the women off the list because they thought they might get pregnant, saying, "The money will be wasted, we won't get the work out of her".'[118]

So what are the practical consequences of a financial system dominated by men?

In investment banking, the highly masculine culture has given rise to a working environment shaped by schoolboy pranks, pseudo-military posturing and an unhealthy dependence on the sex trade. A former Merrill Lynch banker told us how trading divisions have established systems of hazing rituals for new 'recruits': 'You line them up in the morning, bark out the breakfast orders, but don't let them write anything down. If they make a mistake and get the wrong bagel then you throw it back in their face.' At other times the sales team will invite a hapless novice out to dinner. Once the group had racked up a thousand pounds on the bill the new recruit was made to pay. Provided they survive the shock, they will be reimbursed the next morning. In both cases the idea is to gauge how well they cope under pressure. The purpose of other games is less obvious. We were told about suit jacket sleeves being snipped off, unattended desks stuffed with rubbish, and a mobile phone injected with ketchup while the owner went off to fetch some lunch. This last-day-of-term atmosphere might sound fun, but imagine discovering your phone's been turned into a sauce receptacle minutes before an important client is due to ring, or being pelted with paper on a bank trading floor – where a moment's lapse in concentration can result in losses worth hundreds of thousands of pounds. This kind of unprofessionalism wouldn't be tolerated in other high-pressure working environments, like hospitals or law firms, and yet it's openly accepted among the managers of the nation's wealth.

Venetia Thompson, who was fired for gross misconduct when she printed an exposé in the *Spectator* of a year of excess in a top broking firm, put it like this: 'I had stumbled into and was now bolting around the school playground at an East End comprehensive, wearing stilettos, and there was no head teacher on patrol – just dozens of men in their thirties and forties, throwing things at me, all the while trading millions of bonds.'[119] Her schoolboy analogy is apt, but in parts of the financial world that culture has grown unchecked. Women must either dive in headfirst or not at all. As our Merrill Lynch banker put it: 'Short skirts, high heels, tits out – many women on trading floors do this to bring business in. Women can either copy men, or be aggressively feminine, there's no middle ground. They define themselves purely in relation to the men.'

These are not isolated anecdotes. The reports of incessantly masculine banter, the overwhelming male presence and the attitudes of these men to the few women are exhausting. Trading is known as an extreme. One woman who has worked as a trader in the City for over a decade said her colleagues would go to strip clubs about once a week, to the point where they bestowed their own nickname on Stringfellow's – 'Chez Pierre'. These visits are not just for recreational purposes. Kat Banyard of the Fawcett Society appeared before a Treasury Select Committee hearing to testify, on the basis of extensive interviews with female City workers:

> It was becoming frequent for meetings to be held in lap dance clubs… I also had women speak to me and say that prostitution was being used in client deals or in ways to generate business – and that all of this culture created a very hostile environment, as you would expect, for female employees of those firms.[120]

Meanwhile Jessica Thompson, who left a hedge fund job in 2009, has publicly vented her frustration: 'Lap-dancing clubs, been there. Smutty, offensive jokes, heard them all… All night benders in anonymous clubs full of lecherous bankers, done that. Pornographic footage on the mobile, seen it all. Oh, and leering, personal remarks. I doubt there is one I haven't heard.'[121]

Gender stereotypes are diligently adhered to. In a survey of 25–35-year-old women by a female trader, female respondents reported being treated like admin staff. The incidents were minor in themselves but cumulatively show how deep-rooted the sexism still is. If someone called for a male colleague to organise a meeting and a woman answered the phone, they would ask the woman to book something into the male colleague's diary, instantly assuming she was a secretary. Male staff would routinely ask female staff to sort through their receipts for them in order to be processed for expenses. And one described how she was expected to collate and organise responses to events or dinners even though she occupies the same position as her male colleagues. Men, they all added, were very rarely asked to do the same.[122]

Women are not alone in speaking out about the masculine culture of finance. Stuart Fraser, the Chairman of the Policy and Resources Committee for the City of London, a man who has worked in the City since 1963, summarised succinctly: 'A lot of alpha males with testosterone streaming out of their ears.'[123] An experienced banker, codenamed Phillip in the *Daily Telegraph*, explained it this way:

> We're always in the business of wooing [clients] away from other finance houses or schmoozing them into staying with us. They are paying for us to do business for them. If that means taking the guy to a strip joint, so be it... And a lot of it is posturing: rival alpha males ... squaring up to each other.[124]

In the years before the crisis, this 'squaring up' was one of the most destructive consequences of unrestrained male aggression. The people at the top of banks making the key decisions were engaged in very masculine competition. It can be called the 'sexio-economic effect', or to put it more plainly, a 'my bank's bigger than yours' phenomenon. For people lower down in organisations, the social norm was set at the top where there were a handful of men whose names are entering financial folklore: Dick Fuld, the former CEO of Lehman Brothers, who was known as the Gorilla because of his combative attitude and aggression. Or Joe Cassano, head of the financial-products division of AIG in London, nicknamed 'Patient Zero' because of his pivotal role in bringing down AIG. Or Fred Goodwin, possibly the most notorious banker in the UK, who made twenty-seven acquisitions in seven years and completed RBS's acquisition of ABN Amro after the credit crunch had started so as not to lose face by backing out. And why did Sir Fred Goodwin persist with the doomed ABN Amro deal? As one City worker put it: 'It was just a pissing contest with Bob Diamond.'

Why is the masculine domination of finance a problem?

Other professions with deeply ingrained gender disparities often point to special skills or attributes – typically more developed in one sex than another – which their careers happen to reward; like primary school teaching, or sheet metal-working. So might it be that the traits required for a successful career in finance are more widely prevalent in the male population as a whole? More to the point, does it matter for good business?

Testosterone and Risk

We know that higher levels of testosterone fuel aggression and competitive behaviour. We also know that they sedate risk aversion. Studies find there is a correlation between testosterone-dependent risk aversion and career choice: only a third of female US MBA students choose careers in the risky parts of finance like trading, compared to over half of men.[125] In home life, too, research confirms the common-sense notion that women, on average, are more risk averse than men when they make financial decisions.[126] New polling conducted by YouGov for this book backs this up. As we have already seen, on average only 5 per cent of women would rather give up £450 and gamble with a fifty-fifty chance of losing everything or winning £1000. The figure for men is over twice that, with 12 per cent opting to gamble. The only group in which over half of respondents said they would gamble was men between eighteen and twenty-four.

So, the argument runs, men make better bankers for the same reason that they make deadlier soldiers: both professions reward lower levels of risk aversion. For finance this is true in a very material sense. The greater the risk, the higher the payout. The US investment banks which were hit hardest by the crisis comfortably out-performed their rivals throughout the previous decade precisely because they were taking the bigger risks with regard to funding and exposures. This fact alone should caution us against the assumption that he who dares wins.

A gripping new study by two British neuroscientists, John Coates and Joe Herbert, shows that at a deep neurological level the masculine response to risk may well be implicated in boom-bust cycles. They investigated how men and women react physically to life on a trading floor. What they found was that trading decisions are not the dispassionate syntheses of all possible market data imagined by economics textbooks. Instead they are powerfully influenced by excitement, pressure, and levels of testosterone. Their conclusion was that before the crash, we were 'doing what no society ever allows, permitting young males to behave in an unregulated way'.[127]

The research measured the effects of testosterone and cortisol in male traders in the City.[128] Testosterone mediates sexual behaviour and competitive encounters, while cortisol affects responses to a physical challenge or psychological stress. They tracked the levels of these steroids in the saliva of seventeen male traders as they went about their work, on the trading floor with 4 women out of 260 traders. Their findings are illuminating.

We already know that persistently high levels of testosterone increase the appetite for risk and fearlessness in the face of novelty, which of course can mean higher short-term profits.[129] Studies have also found that if levels stay chronically high, we see a pathological reverse: impulsiveness, harmful risk-taking, even euphoria and mania if additional steroids are taken at the same time. Cortisol has almost the opposite effect. If exposure is short and sharp, it can increase motivation and concentration. But if exposure is prolonged, it will increase anxiety and so dampen the appetite for risk.

Levels of testosterone were found to rise when the day's takings were higher, while cortisol increased with risk. The scientists concluded that if the 'acutely elevated' levels of testosterone and cortisol remained high as volatility increased, they could 'shift risk preferences and even affect a trader's ability to engage in rational choice'.[130] More importantly, however, they realised they had discovered a biochemical basis for the split market behaviour we associate with boom and bust cycles. Immense profits at the high point of a bubble create a glut of testosterone which feeds back into the market. With their appetite for risk increased, traders are more likely to borrow to buy and lenders will demand smaller margins; the flood of credit drives asset prices far higher than economic fundamentals can ever justify. Once the bubble bursts, however, the rush of cortisol from the increased risk decreases appetite for risk. This leads financiers to rush to dispense of their riskiest assets, creating a 'one way' market, where asset prices race downwards because no one wants to buy.

All of this suggests, from a scientific perspective, that bubbles could in effect be a more male phenomenon. In conversation, both scientists have been explicit about this. Joe Herbert told the *New York Magazine*: 'Anyone who studied neurobiology would have predicted disaster.' Coates argues that if women made up 50 per cent on the trading floor, we would not see the volatile swings that we do.

John Coates was inspired to explore the effect of these steroids by his time running a trading desk for Deutsche Bank, where he noticed that 'male traders ... were delusional, euphoric, overconfident, had racing thoughts, a diminished need for sleep. The guys had their eyes rolling back in their heads, desperate to get involved in what some genius was up to, and the women just didn't buy into it'.[131]

Personal testimony backs this up. Barbara Stcherbatcheff, author of *Confessions of a City Girl* and a trader in the City, cites her old risk manager, who used to say that in propri-etary trading women were often the best performers not least because they take more precautions before entering trades. As a female trader herself, Stcherbatcheff makes the case succinctly: 'Trading thrives under caution, thoroughness, and the ability to admit you're wrong. Trading is ideal for a woman.'[132]

So even though appetite for risk is a more masculine trait, and even though some areas of finance could not function without risk-taking, the current gender imbalance seems to be contributing to the kind of market manias which cause financial crises. The Coates and Herbert study suggests that too many men on the trading floor are subconsciously increasing the very risks they are supposedly so well-equipped to handle.

So on the grounds of financial stability, there is a powerful argument for more women in finance. But there's an equally pressing business case. Evidence shows that the more female executives boards have, the more successful the companies are. In a piece of research by McKinsey, eighty-nine listed companies with the highest level of gender diversity had operating returns of 11 per cent – double the average of 6 per cent. Stock price growth was also improved sharply: over the period 2005–07 the diverse companies had stock price growth of 64 per cent compared to 47 per cent for the male-dominated firms.[133] Meanwhile, another study found that having at least one female director on the board cut the risk of insolvency by around 20 per cent.[134]

Another report by the Canadian research group, Catalyst, found in 2007 that companies in the *Fortune* 500 index with the highest percentages of women board directors signifi-cantly outperformed those with the lowest percentages. Their return on equity was over 50 per cent higher, their return on sales was over 40 per cent higher, and their return on invested capital was two-thirds higher.[135]

Some suggest attendance at board level also improves once more women are on the board, both because they are more likely to attend and because male directors attend more meetings when women are present.[136] This is underpinned by survey data that shows women being more assertive on corporate governance issues like evaluation of board performance, while boards with both men and women emphasise board accountability and authority more heavily.[137]

Research into top French firms – the CAC 40 – has linked the number of women at management level to share price. The share price of companies like Alcatel-Lucent and Renault, which have mainly male management, decreased more than the average CAC 40 company in 2008. Hermès, on the other hand, with 55 per cent of the management made up of women, was the only large company whose share price rose, by 17 per cent. With banks, BNP Paribas, with 39 per cent of its management made up of women, best resisted the financial crisis and its share price fell by 39 per cent. Compare it with Crédit Agricole, where the figures are 16 per cent and 63 per cent respectively.[138] The sample size of this research was small, and of course simply because there is a correlation does not prove there is a direct causal link. But take it with larger, more thorough studies with the same conclusions and the emerging argument is strongly in favour of increased gender diversity.

So through a combination of the embedded cultural bias and a skewed framework, women are not progressing as they could. The numbers show they are not. The evidence shows that, for the sake of good business, they should. And the reasons why they are not need to be tackled.

Does this mean women should stage a coup and take over finance? No. Indeed, an entirely feminised financial culture would have its own problems, and women in positions of immense corporate power are quite capable of making their own mistakes. But the evidence does make the argument that finance is a man's world look tired.

Instead, the case is for diversity. Any good board needs different perspectives to make the organisation as stable and effective as possible. John Last, HR Director at RBS, explained this: 'It is diversity of thought you want on a board, which diversity itself and gender diversity should give you.'[139] And Kat Banyard at the Fawcett Society backed him up: 'When you have greater diversity and more women on boards you have less groupthink. Women and men lead very different lives at the moment. They bring different experiences with them.'[140] Finance is a world based on diversification. So why is there such reluctance to diversify in a way that could reduce risk?

Since social norms are such an important determinant of behaviour, and people tend to reward people like them, it is clear that significant barriers exist to a meritocracy of sexes in finance. The evidence shows that these barriers not only risk financial stability but also hold back corporate perform-ance. So it is time to accept that finance is not full of men because it requires masculine behaviour, but that finance is dominated by masculine behaviour because it is full of men. That must change.

Chapter 7

REWARDS FOR FAILURE

Fairness is central to the British sense of self. It lies behind the events leading up to the English Civil War in the seventeenth century, the campaign to repeal the Corn Laws in the nineteenth century, and the female suffrage movement in the twentieth. Fairness is about equality of opportunity and protection of human dignity. But it is also about rewarding achievement – paying people according to the value they create and not rewarding them for failure. So it's with some unease that we find that fairness in this sense being driven out of the national game.

In the run-up to the 2010 football World Cup, there were widespread fears within the Football Associaton that the England manager Fabio Capello might abandon the team and transfer to another club. It is impossible to speculate as to why the rumours were taken so seriously, but they were certainly advantageous to Capello's position. The England team had qualified for the tournament in a comfortable position at the top of their group, and FA Chairman, Lord Triesman, was determined to quash any uncertainty. Without properly consulting the full board of the FA, Triesman and a small band of confederates covertly arranged for the removal of a release clause in Capello's £6 million a year contract.

We all know how the England team performed at the subsequent World Cup in South Africa. Following the humiliating ejection from the tournament, several members of the FA board wanted Capello gone. But the removal of the break clause meant the FA could not afford to dispense with his services without incurring huge damages. Having failed risibly in the most important duty of an England coach, he maintains his position as the best-paid manager of a national football team in the world, and the fourth-highest-earning manager overall.

This rankled with our sense of fairness. Capello's leadership resulted in the shattering of national pride. Yet he was rewarded for failure. But unlike the senior management of Britain's high street banks his actions did not result in the destruction of any jobs (with the possible exception of John Terry's), nor was his pension pot made possible by the English taxpayer.

This chapter is about the sustained attack on fairness and trust caused by rewards for failure and the endemic corporate mis-governance that allowed them to become so widespread.

'And Treat Those Two Imposters Just the Same...'

Outside of the evening news, bankers make few appearances on British television. The ongoing popularity of programmes like *Dragon's Den* and *The Apprentice* show we are still fascinated by the drama of the profit motive, but financiers rarely get a look in. The one exception to this is *Deal or No Deal*, a hugely successful game show broadcast six days a week on Channel 4. It was originally developed by the Dutch TV production company Endemol and has been exported around the world. There is even a version airing in Afghanistan.

The basic format of the show is always the same. The game is played with a number of sealed boxes; twenty-two in the UK version. Each box contains a hidden amount of prize money, ranging from a few pennies to hundreds of thousands of pounds. Before an episode begins the boxes are sealed and randomly assigned to contestants. One contestant is then selected to play. The sum in the player's box, which remains unopened until the end of the game, is then owned by them.

The game consists of six rounds in which the player invites a set number of other contestants to unseal their boxes and reveal the contents. These prizes are then eliminated from the list of possible sums which could be in the player's box. At the end of each round, a shadowy figure who supposedly puts up the money for each show, called the Banker, phones the host, Noel Edmonds, on an old-fashioned Bakelite phone and offers to the buy the player's box. The potential value of this box varies depending on which sums have already been revealed. Edmonds conveys the Banker's offer to the player and then poses the question: 'Deal or No Deal?' If the player deals, they win whatever the Banker has promised, their box is unsealed and the game ends. If the answer is 'no deal' then the game continues, either until the player agrees to a deal, or they reach the final round with only two boxes left in play. The Banker offers them one last chance to deal, and if the offer is still refused the player's own box is unsealed and they win whatever sum it contains.

The game works entirely according to chance. Neither the player, the other contestants, the Banker, nor even the host know what is in any of the boxes. In theory the player estimates the value of his or her box based on which sums have already been removed from play, and then makes a decision based on elementary probability. People who aren't familiar with the show often dismiss it, wondering what possible entertainment value could arise from a series of blind guesses. The game 'demands the mental skill and dexterity of a fridge magnet'[141] wrote legendarily acerbic critic A. A. Gill, in a review of *Deal or No Deal*. Yet, as Gill continued, 'it is utterly compelling... Like putting heroin in the TV remote in the middle of the afternoon'.

Much of the appeal of *Deal or No Deal* lies in the adversarial relationship between the player and the Banker. Originally conceived as an impersonal computer, the unseen financier at the end of the phone has over the years risen to become the most important character in the game. Although his identity is never revealed, he regularly interacts with Edmonds and the contestants, taunting them with unreasonable offers, and cackling sadistically down the line when the larger prizes are eliminated.

It's interesting to reflect that this malignly anonymous high-stakes gambler has become the most mainstream representative of the finance industry on UK television. Like the financial system itself, the Banker is invisible, extremely powerful and essential to the workings of the game. But he's also the villain of the piece, a figure whose interests are perceived to be utterly at odds with our own. Fans of the programme report that the most satisfying episodes are often those in which the player manages to 'beat the Banker' by dealing at a much higher price than their box turns out to be worth.

But this insight into the reputation of bankers isn't the only interesting thing about *Deal or No Deal*. It has also been used to provide compelling evidence for a new theory of risk.

The academic study of behavioural economics has long rested on experiments with college students, roped into a series of experiments into how they behave, usually involving coloured marbles or chessboards. Over the years these experiments have yielded many valuable insights into the way people behave in a market environment, often in marked contrast to the unthinking assumptions made by more traditional branches of economics. Some scenarios, however, are harder to simulate than others. Anything involving risk or gambling, for example, suffers from the tight budgetary constraints of a university economics department. How do we know if someone will gamble in the same way if the stakes are £500,000, instead of £5?

Indeed, many people choose both to gamble, and to insure against risk in their lives. The glorious sport of horserac-ing is the second most watched sport in the UK, and the most bet on. Yet those who bet on the horses will also often insure their home against theft, or keep savings in a low-risk bank account.

Deal or No Deal provides a breakthrough in our ability to observe attitudes to risk. Four academics, Thierry Post, Martijn van den Assem, Guido Baltussen and Richard Thaler, saw the programme and its potential for study.[142] *Deal or No Deal* was the perfect laboratory. Quite unwittingly the show's creators, Endemol, had invented a rigorous experiment into the nature of decision-making in a high-risk environment. Not only were some of the amounts of money at stake life-changing, but the show's global popularity meant they also had a large sample to examine. In 2008 the economists set to work. Friends dutifully recorded dozens of episodes, polite phone calls were made to television networks and hundreds of hours of footage were amassed. The economists did without Noel Edmonds's inimitable banter and chose episodes from the German, Dutch and American versions of the show, because they offered the 'purest' form of the game, placing minimum emphasis on the strategic interaction between Banker and player.

For each contestant they collected data on the eliminated and remaining prizes, the Banker's offers and 'Deal or No Deal' decisions at the end of each round. They found that it was possible to categorise some of the contestants into extreme groups of 'winners' and 'losers'. Losers were defined as contestants whose choices had removed the valuable boxes, so the likely prize money was low. Winners were the exact opposite: those who had eliminated the less valuable options, so their likely prize was high. The economists noticed that both winners and losers were found to be significantly less likely to 'deal' and settle for the certain offer than neutrals.

They found that towards the later rounds the contestants' choices were driven largely in response to previous outcomes experienced during the game. Choices were 'path dependent'. Rather than calmly assessing the situation on its merits, as more traditional economic theories predict they should, players were swayed by events. Not only did lucky contestants keep gambling, as they felt 'in luck', unlucky contestants also took higher risks. Following a dramatic event in a previous round, both winners and losers would routinely reject generous offers from the Banker, even if the offer was greater than the average remaining prize – a clear example of irrational risk-seeking behaviour.

Big bets by both winners and losers are a phenomenon found in casinos across the world. Big losers suffer from the 'break-even effect'. This is where unlucky gamblers bet big in the hope they'll make good on their previous losses. The most notorious instance of this effect in the world of finance must be Nick Leeson's unauthorised trading on behalf of Barings Bank in 1995, and is supported by the new polling evidence in Chapter 6. Winners suffer the so-called 'house money effect', also found in casinos, where high rollers continue to gamble even after a big win because they don't think of the recently acquired chips as 'theirs'.

This 'house money effect' helps to explain a genuine puzzle from the crisis. Often finance is attacked for failing to align shareholders' incentives with the incentives of the companies themselves. Many shares are owned by bureaucratic pension funds, or bought by disinterested brokers who do not bother to vote in corporate AGMs. Yet in the crisis, many of the banks that crashed were run by people with vast shareholdings. A 2010 study found evidence that the CEOs who were most invested in their own institutions ended up presiding over the worst-hit banks. Dick Fuld, for instance, owned $1 billion worth of Lehman stock at the end of 2006.[143] Indeed, 30 per cent of all Lehman shares were owned by employees. Share-ownership seems to have had no restraining effect because the shares were treated as 'house money', which they were, in effect, because they had been 'won' rather than purchased.

Some have argued that as the crisis approached, share ownership incentivised bank bosses to double up in the hope of escaping collapse, effectively increasing risk in the face of disaster. At the point of collapse, this explanation may have incentivised banks' management to increase risk. But it does not explain why owner-managers took such extraordinary risks in the first place.

There is an alternative explanation. Even when the chips are down, shareholders always have the option to cash their shares in and walk away. Dick Fuld sold his Lehman stock for a little under $500,000 on the Friday before Lehman filed for bankruptcy. Jimmy Cayne was luckier. In March 2008, the bridge-playing former CEO of Bear Stearns dumped his stake in the bank he'd ruined and made $61 million, to the outrage of fellow shareholders. When the share price was at its peak Cayne was said to be worth a billion, but he was prepared to keep it in the bank until the battle was lost. In a world of such huge numbers, pay is seen as a signal of success as much as being valuable in its own right. They were prepared to gamble with the bank, even though they owned a large part of it.

This observation has important consequences for how pay should be structured. While these observations do not undermine the widespread evidence that share ownership helps boost productivity in companies, we should question the automatic assumption that aligning owners' and share-holders' incentives is sufficient for responsible management. Culture, it seems, matters as much as share ownership.

When Rudyard Kipling wrote: 'If you should meet with triumph and disaster / And treat those two imposters just the same' he didn't mean load up on risk. Yet this is what people do. Our cognitive processes are historical in nature. Gathering together disparate strands of habit, association, pattern and precedent allow us to create models of the world. We can then hold them up to reality, test, amend, adapt and adjust them. But as the study recognised, the experience of sudden gain or loss may create a 'Year Zero' in the mind –

a 'holiday from history' – it can wrench our usual frames of reference out of joint, sideline our hard-won experience, and make us forget that what goes up must come down. As Richard Thaler, one of the four authors of the study, has argued, people 'adapt incompletely' to recent losses or gains.

The psychology literature confirms these observations. Psychoanalysis postulates a 'divided' mind when in search of a dream or 'phantasy', in which emotions of anxiety that get in the way of the dream are 'split off'.

Between the end of the dot-com boom and the financial crisis, the senior management of the 'bulge bracket' and universal banks do indeed seem to have 'split off' emotions of anxiety and doubt about the risks they were taking. Every risk they took was further proof that the world had changed forever. Hope of success has the same physiological impact as actual success, in gaining an adrenaline rush. The result was ever more risk-taking, tumescent balance sheets, and a global market for the willing suspension of disbelief – with a new language to describe the brave new world.

Fear

But what is the best way to correct excessive risk-taking? One of the answers is fear. In the *Deal or No Deal* study both the winners and losers possess an insufficient sense of fear; losers because they have nothing left to lose, and winners because, under the study's definition, they can't lose.

In a landmark study conducted in 1997, a group of neurologists[144] asked their subjects to play a card game. They were given $2,000 and told to choose cards from four decks. If they picked bad cards they would lose money. The decks were stacked. Two of them contained cards which produced more extreme wins and losses, but on average would set players back. The other two contained cards which produced less extreme wins and losses but a more favourable long-term average. Half the subjects in the test had suffered damage to their prefrontal cortex, the part of the brain which governs 'the ability to orchestrate thought and action in accordance with internal goals'.[145] The other subjects were intended to form a representative sample of the population as a whole. Both groups were found to sweat when large-loss cards were first encountered: they both experienced the unconscious symptoms of fear. But compared to the control group, the subjects with prefrontal damage were much more likely to return to the high-risk deck after suffering a loss. As a result they went 'bankrupt' more often.

What this group lacked was the ability to consciously experience fear. They unconsciously felt its effects, but they could not form the crucial emotive link between those effects and the external source of the fear. So they repeatedly took risks that cost them in the long term. The researchers concluded that their prefrontal cortices 'did not store the pain of remembered losses' as well as the control group.

J. K. Galbraith wrote that the 'pain of remembered losses' can restrain a society, as well as individuals, from excessive risk-taking. He characterised post-war financial stability in the United States in terms of a response to the trauma of the Great Crash: 'As a protection against financial illusion or insanity, memory is far better than law. When the memory of the 1929 disaster failed, law and regulation no longer sufficed.'[146]

A paper by three neuro-economists, commenting on the study's economic implications, concluded that 'insufficient fear can produce nonmaximising behaviour when risky options have negative value'.[147] Negative value is a term familiar to poker players. It means a situation in which average losses outweigh average gains when all probable outcomes have been taken into account. Let's say we have a bet. If the next car that drives by is red then I pay you £10, if it's a different colour then you have to pay me £15. That's a situation exhibiting negative value. 'Nonmaximising behaviour' on the other hand is an economists' euphemism for screwing up. Sir Fred Goodwin's leveraged buyout of ABN Amro at the top of the market, completed after the crash began, reeked of negative value.

What was Sir Fred thinking? Like the winners and losers in *Deal or No Deal* he was partly the victim of path-dependent decision-making. To his mind, the pattern of previous RBS acquisitions proved one thing: that acquisitions would make the bank stronger. No matter that this time the world was on the brink of recession, the global credit market had dried up, and ABN Amro was severely compromised by its subprime exposures. But anecdotal evidence from those around him suggests Sir Fred's other problem was that he experienced 'insufficient fear'.

Sir Fred is a prime example of this 'fearless' breed of banker, indicative of the men making it to the very top. Grammar school educated, he was a success at university and later as a trainee accountant. It was in the banking sector that he made his name. Rapidly promoted to the top, within nine years he steered RBS from a small player to a global brand. In doing so he had overseen a period of aggressive expansion externally and an equally aggressive cut in costs, largely through internal staff cuts.

The fact that RBS performed more than twenty-five major acquisitions between 2000 and 2007 shows the gung ho strategy undertaken by Goodwin. This huge appetite for takeovers even led shareholders to call for a stop to big deals in 2006. The promise was kept until 2007, when RBS entered a bidding war with Barclays for ABN Amro.

As David Buik, partner at City firm BGC Partners, has said: 'Fred Goodwin is a megalomaniac. RBS never had a chance to digest anything they bought and so they've never delivered shareholder value. It's a combination of relentless greed and an inability to deliver shareholder value.'

Sir Fred Goodwin was a CEO renowned for his decision-making process, his aggressive management style, and risk-taking. One striking example was his so-called 'five second rule' which meant that all major decisions he made person-ally were dependent on his intuition. At a key board meeting to decide RBS's worldwide marketing strategy, Goodwin was presented with an idea that had been the result of months of careful research. The executive stood up to introduce his idea: to invoke RBS's traditional Scottish heritage in the bank's global marketing strategy, especially in target markets like the USA. As he left his chair and began his speech, Goodwin stopped him after seconds. The Chief Executive stated that he didn't like it and wouldn't be using it for RBS. The pitch was over, a failure, mere sentences in, and after months of work.

After Sir Fred Goodwin's downfall, the stories of his dicta-torial attitude and its trickle-down effect have come tumbling out. The catering staff were threatened with disciplinary action in an email entitled 'Rogue Biscuits' after someone had the audacity to include pink wafers in the Executives' afternoon tea.[148] Staff 'went into panic mode' after a window cleaner fell off a ladder in Goodwin's office and broke a small model aeroplane. The story goes that staff were more worried about Goodwin's broken toy than the hurt window cleaner.[149]

This overarching fear dominated the employees' rela-tionship with Goodwin. 'Most people in the bank were absolutely terrified of him,' said corporate financier Peter de Vink, managing director of Edinburgh Financial & General Holdings. 'He treated anyone who had a different view from his own with contempt.'[150] Given this fierce reputation, it is astonishing what was missed. For all his attempts to control and amalgamate power, at its point of collapse RBS had critical internal flaws and shambolic practices. As a result of the frequent takeovers, the bank was operating over twenty different computer systems, which did not easily interact, so it was impossible easily to get an overall picture of the position of the bank. Despite having over 2500 risk managers, not one considered liquidity risk. The seeds of the bank's collapse were sown in its poor management.

In Bret Easton Ellis's 1991 novel *American Psycho*, the reader is cast adrift amid the murderous delusions of Patrick Bateman – a deranged Wall Street investment banker who may or may not be a serial killer. He's both the predator and victim of an emotionally void Wall Street culture – where reality is made up of surface appearance, and no one perceives beyond the haircut, the handshake and business card. When the novel first appeared it was generally greeted with unfavourable reviews – too few critics understood what it was Easton Ellis was satirising. In the wake of Enron, Bernie Madoff and the global financial crisis, it's now considered a modern classic.

Like all the best satires, the novel grasps an element of truth that even the author may have been unaware of. Since its publication, the psychopathology of the modern business executive has become a popular subject of academic research.

Individual psychopathic traits – inability to empathise, lack of remorse, stimulation-seeking, impulsiveness, and poor behavioural control, among others – are diffused among the population at large. Psychopaths are people with unusually high concentrations of these traits. Studies estimate that 1 per cent of the population might be considered psychopaths in the strict psychiatric sense, but this percentage rises within the corporate world.

In 2006 Dr Paul Babiak and Dr Robert Hare found that of two hundred high-profile executives sampled, 3.5 per cent matched the psychopathic profile. Research from Babiak and Hare among others, suggests that highly functioning 'industrial psychopaths' tend to thrive in transitional organisations. One example of such an organisation might be a company undergoing rapid expansion. The rapidly changing business environment provides the psychopath with the constant stimulation he needs while diverting critical attention away from his personal failings. There is also a clear correlation between psychopathic tendencies and risk appetite. As Holly Andrews of Worcester Business School puts it, 'studies have shown that once focused on a goal, psychopaths are not good at attending to cues that suggest their current course of action is likely to lead to failure'.[151]

None of this is to suggest that the senior British banking executives mentioned in this book are psychopaths, merely that the culture of modern finance is structured in a way which risks mistaking psychopathic behaviour for brilliant business acumen.

Payoffs and Pensions

Imagine a very special episode of *Deal or No Deal*. It follows the standard rules of the game but with one important difference. The contestant knows exactly how much is in his box, and it is a high number. Naturally he will be less risk averse during the game because he is starting out from a stronger position than other players. Even if he gets lucky and one of the Banker's offers exceeds the prize his box contains, will he not be tempted to gamble in the hope of an even higher offer in the next round? This is exactly the situation that the senior executives of failed banks found themselves in; despite the failure we have documented, the leaders of many failed banks still got their deal.

Part of the reason for the observed lack of fear may have been psychological. But it was backed up throughout the financial sector by the way pay was structured. Compensation contracts of senior management created a one-way bet. Sir Fred Goodwin left RBS with a pension pot worth £8.4 million.[152] Given that he had posted the biggest loss in UK corporate history, the deal brought a new meaning to the phrase 'got off Scot-free'. Gordon Pell, head of retail banking at RBS, walked away with £13.5 million in

2010. Adam Applegarth, the former CEO of Northern Rock, was given a £760,000 payoff, a £346,000 pension top-up, and a continued cut-price staff mortgage upon departure. Peter Cummings, the head of corporate lending at HBOS, received a £630,000 payoff and a pension pot worth £6m. In February 2008 he had said of the housing market: 'Some people look as though they are losing their nerve – beginning to panic, even – in today's testing real estate environment. Not us.' Steve Crawshaw, Chief Executive of Bradford & Bingley, retired with a lump sum pension commencement worth £400,000 and a pension worth £105,000 a year.

As with the prefrontal subjects in the card game, these men were incapable of forming a strong enough association between risk and fear. Their pay contracts supported this bias by ensuring they could not lose. As far as their personal finances were concerned, there really was nothing to fear.

These are the most serious examples of a 'rewards for failure' culture within modern retail banking. They were bestowed on men who drove their banks to ruin by directing them to lend more than their deposits could ever justify. But rewards for failure are deeply ingrained. Annual bonuses supposedly motivate performance, yet in a post-crisis world the link between executive pay and shareholder returns is often tangential at best. Barclays CEO John Varley received a 250 per cent increase in his bonus in 2010, in defiance of the fact that the Barclays share price had slipped by 6.7 per cent.

Such behaviour is not limited to banks. Between 1998 and 2010, share prices of the FTSE 100 barely changed overall. Yet Chief Executive pay doubled, and rose from 47 times that of the average employee, to 120 times. Even over 2010, median earnings for FTSE 100 CEOs rose by a third, while average earnings across the economy rose by 2 per cent.[53]

Shareholders, who were happy to wave through risky decisions and dubious incentive structures in the good times, have now started to dissent. In August 2007, 94.5 per cent of RBS shareholders voted in favour of the fatal ABN acquisition. But by the time of a tense post-bailout AGM in April 2009, one RBS shareholder received a roomful of applause for suggesting that the management should be 'in jail'.[154] This kind of AGM has become a familiar scene: a packed auditorium, rebellious mutterings, onstage a row of stony-faced executives sipping mineral water and fiddling with their microphones, impassioned speeches, a rumble of assent, clapping. Pleas from the management: it's time to move on, it was a tiny minority, they've gone, what's done is done, we have to stay competitive, look to the future. Then scattered booing, shaking of heads, a journalist in the corner scribbling fast. At HSBC's 2011 AGM, the scene of a 19 per cent shareholder revolt, a private shareholder argued that if the bank 'aspired to be a company of integrity' it should lead the way in 'closing the escalating disparity between board-room and shopfloor pay'. At the Barclays equivalent in April, another shareholder compared the management to 'Somali pirates' while others, echoing a widespread public sentiment, lambasted 'obscene' bonuses.[155]

But in spite of these grumblings little has changed. Across the FTSE 100 Chief Executives saw their median earnings rise by 30 per cent last year. This was treble the rise in share prices and shot past the average worker's 2 per cent pay award. According to MM&K and Manifest, two consultancies which specialise in corporate governance issues, share prices have, on average, scarcely shifted in real value since 1998. And yet between 1998 and 2010, CEO compensation soared. A large proportion of that growth can be attributed to the rise of share option schemes and bonus payouts, which, as a proportion of total earnings, increased by 70 per cent last year. In banks, where bonuses at the highest level are routinely paid out as a multiple rather than a percentage of annual salary, this culture is particularly pernicious.

Why have banks allowed skewed incentives to be written into legally binding contracts? Rewards for failure springs from two phenomena: the myth of irreplaceable talent and poor corporate governance.

'The Best Talent'

Defenders of excessive executive pay argue that in a globalised labour market pay must be world class in order to attract the 'best talent' from around the world. After all, Steve Jobs is Apple, and Richard Branson is Virgin. How they behave filters through their organisations. So the DNA of the leaders of our banks weighs heavily on the DNA of their businesses. The CEOs of failing banks were able to cling to power for some time, even at the height of the crisis, precisely because of this belief that they were irreplaceable. Fabio Capello made just this arrangement ahead of the 2010 World Cup. Then he managed to negotiate a contact with the FA that made him virtually unsackable, despite his woeful performance. When Andy Hornby, the CEO of HBOS, was dismissed in 2008 he gallantly waived his leaving fee. A few weeks later Hornby was back on the HBOS payroll, commanding a £720,000-a-year fee to advise the bank on the merger with Lloyds.

Hornby had made his name in the retail sector, having started his career with Boston Consulting Group where he focused on consumer goods. This led to him joining ASDA where he later became the Director of Corporate Development and Retail Managing Director, with the responsibility of overseeing 36 stores and 14,000 employees. In common with Adam Applegarth of Northern Rock and RBS Chair Sir Tom McKillop, he had no formal banking qualifications.

Below the top layer of the board, even the pool of top traders seems relatively small. The FSA now requires banks to detail how many employees of 'significant influence' they have; these are employees whose decisions are regularly taken into account by the board, or whose actions result in material risk to the bank's bottom line. In RBS's 2010 annual report, they reveal that they have around 300 such staff – just 0.2 per cent of its total employees.[156]

Of course, this measure of significant influence is imperfect, and many senior financiers are talented people. Nevertheless, given what the 'best talent' collectively did to our economy in 2008 we might be forgiven for our scepticism. Rather than being possessors of rare financial genius it is more accurate to say that bank CEOs have inside information on the structure of their firm, know where the bodies are buried and can hold the companies to ransom. Furthermore, there is no evidence to suggest their abilities have risen in a way that would justify the very sharp rise in senior salaries.

As many fund managers have been at pains to emphasise, the best talent of all has tended to migrate towards the hedge fund industry. The crucial managerial difference between banks and hedge funds is that there is no free lunch for hedge fund managers. Fund managers have far more personal liability, not only because they tend to own large stakes in the company but because they only get paid on delivery of profits to their investors. The 'house money effect' is therefore less pronounced. What is more, the role of retail banking in an economy is closer to a utility, which needs careful stewardship, than an innovative, thrusting enterprise. Taxpayers' money is not put at risk to save a hedge fund that fails.

Toothless Boards

A second reason for the rewards for failure springs from poor corporate governance. As Andrew Haldane has argued, shareholders are becoming ever more addicted to short-term profits. This is why the moral indignation of surviving RBS shareholders only carries so much weight. Haldane points to data which indicates today's investors are significantly under-pricing the value of long-term cash flows. He also notes a PwC survey which polled FTSE 100 and 250 executives, 'the majority of which would chose a low return option sooner (£250,000 tomorrow) rather than a high return later (£450,000 in 3 years)', in order to satisfy their investors. Haldane concludes that this short-termism represents 'a market failure'.[157]

A consequence of this market failure has been for shareholders to rubberstamp any compensation package, no matter how indulgent, provided the management agrees to maintain a regular short-term delivery of high returns. But this is a devil's pact. In order to justify his pay a CEO has been obliged to engage in the kind of high-risk, high-yield strategy that generated a steady stream of returns, employing strategies like leveraged acquisitions, investment in mortgage-backed securities or underwriting insurance for events which are conveniently assumed never to happen.

In banking, performance targets remain set in terms of return on equity, not return on assets. But any company can improve return on equity without improving underlying performance by simply gearing up. The incentives to do so in the boom were strong.

Now, as banks reduce their balance sheets, return on equity is sluggish. You might be forgiven for imagining that tighter profit margins would prompt greater shareholder oversight. As Robert Peston has written, if investors come to believe that the only reason for handing over capital is to allow investment bankers 'to generate huge bonuses for themselves – with little left over for dividends – the rational thing for investors to do is to ask for their money back'.[158] But investors are not rational creatures, and supervisory indolence is a hard habit to break.

Recent work in psychology suggests that people have a strong unconscious bias to choose 'the default option'. Below the level of conscious awareness our minds constantly usher us along cognitive shortcuts, allowing us to dodge past sustained thought or difficult decision-making wherever possible. Studies have shown that when a company provides an automatic opt-in to their pension plan, employee enrolment shoots up. Conversely, when an opt-out is the default option, take-up is significantly reduced, in direct contradiction to the employees' long-term self-interest.

Just so in investment culture; shareholders continue to choose the default option of non-interference with their boards' affairs. In January 2011 the Treasury Select Committee forced Bob Diamond to admit that Barclays shareholders would not be offered any specific figures relating to the size or allocation of that year's bonus pool – until after they had been determined by the board. This was a quibble, Diamond insisted. The shareholders had no need of these numbers. All they required to sign off the board's decision was an awareness of the Barclays 'philosophy: which is pay for performance'.[59]

The non-executive directors of financial institutions ought to be part of the solution. Unlike outside shareholders, they should know just how much risk the bank can take, when to call the executives off and how to make the case for doing so. Economist Ruth Lea is a non-executive director at Arbuthnot's Bank, an institution which weathered the credit crisis by imposing strict limits on its ratio of loans to deposits, and unlike Northern Rock refused to fund itself from the wholesale money markets. Lea pointed out that a non-executive will never know as much about the business as a member of the executive management, but Arbuthnot's fostered a culture where all members of the board were intimately involved in the bank's inner workings. The social norm is that questions are welcomed: 'I'm in the bank twice a week – I know what's going on. I can go up to any of the CEOs and say I want to know X.'

Yet all too often in recent history there has been no incentive for board members to challenge the management. Unlike the executives, they are removed enough from the day-to-day operations of the bank to escape unfavourable comment when something goes wrong. Because non-executive directors typically hold several boardroom positions across the economy, when a financial institution blows up they can simply cross it off their CV and find a replacement.

Of the seven executive directors of the RBS board, three have gone to ground, but two continue to sit on boards and two have become 'advisors' to other companies. Sir Fred Goodwin became Group Strategic Advisor to the Edinburgh-based architecture firm RMJM. In March 2011 the firm had to request a cash bailout from its biggest investor. The record of contrition at the other failed banks which were bailed out by the taxpayer is similar, both among executive and non-executive directors. At Bradford & Bingley, six of the eleven-member board continue to sit as non-executive directors at other institutions. At HBOS, all seventeen of the 2007 board still serve on other boards, including the board of Halifax itself. HBOS CEO Andy Hornby went on serve as Chief Executive of the retail pharmacy giant Boots, picking up £2.1 million in his first year, before stepping down in March 2011. Northern Rock does little better. Of its ten-member team, five continue to serve on other boards, while Adam Applegarth, like Sir Fred, hires out his services as an 'advisor', in this case to an American private equity firm. This 'advisor' designation means Applegarth evades the FSA's all too limited ban on working at a regulated financial institution.

Why Should We Care?

If the senior management of a major financial institution do not have good reason to feel at least moderately risk averse, there are serious implications for financial stability. This is the economic concern about rewards for failure. But the implications for financial stability of low risk aversion are not the only reason so many people care about the pension plans of millionaires we have never met.

The crisis transformed the way we talk about the finance industry. Before August 2007 the terms of reference were strictly technical: share-price, merger, dividend, yield, fixed-rate, bond, FTSE 100. For most of us this was just the background chatter of the economy: white noise from the markets. Now not only do more people find they have a view on banks and banking, but these views now carry an explicitly moral dimension.

In the years leading up to the crash, many argued that finance and ethics belonged in separate spheres. When questions of ethical behaviour made an appearance in public life it was usually in relation to issues like abortion, euthanasia, stem cell research and minority rights – intensely emotive issues that cut right to the heart of most people's idea of what it is to be human. Finance by contrast seemed to exist on a non-moral plane. Scrutinising the moral values of markets, and the people who ran them, was said to be irrelevant.

This orthodoxy sprang from Milton Friedman's famous essay penned in the *New York Times* magazine in 1970 entitled 'The social responsibility of business is to increase its profits'. Yet in that essay, Friedman argued that business executives should 'conduct business in accordance with their desires, which generally will be to make as much money as possible while conforming to the basic rules of society'. He defines the 'basic rules of society' to include 'both those embodied in law and those embodied in ethical custom'.[160] Friedman's argument was based in the social norms and customs of the time, in which the recklessness of the recent crash would have been socially unacceptable.

The New Labour government that was 'intensely relaxed about people getting filthy rich' and desperate to shed an historic reputation for economic incompetence, only read the headline and pursued it as orthodoxy with the zeal of a convert. But it was a false orthodoxy, because business and ethics are mutually dependent. As John Kay has written more recently:

> Market economies are always vulnerable to chancers and spivs who sell overpriced goods to ill-informed customers and seem to promise things they do not intend to deliver. If such behaviour becomes a dominant business style, you end up with the economies of Nigeria and Haiti, where rampant opportunism makes it almost prohibitively diffi-cult for honest people to do business.

Returning to the decision by RBS to take over ABN Amro, it is baffling that the deal went through. It was very clearly not in the interests of the bank or its shareholders. But the rewards given to those involved help explain why it was pursued so relentlessly. ABN Amro were advised by Goldman Sachs, UBS, Morgan Stanley, Lehman Brothers, and Rothschild, all of whom earned advisory fees regardless of which bid eventually won the takeover. RBS had its own army of advisors being paid on the deal: Merrill Lynch, Greenhill, Fox-Pitt, Kelton, NIBC, Santander, and Fortis. The main advisors to RBS, Merrill Lynch, are said to have earned around $100 million when the takeover was completed. The man who helped put the deal together from Merrill Lynch was awarded a bonus of $30 million. The underwriters – Goldman Sachs, Merrill Lynch, and UBS – were paid £210 million. Suddenly, it becomes clearer where the momentum for the deal sprung from. The personal and corporate incentives for the deal to go through were enormous, regardless of the health of the deal itself.

Duty and Trust

In his *Theory of Moral Sentiments* the father of capitalism Adam Smith observed, 'How selfish soever man may be supposed, there are evidently some principles in his nature which interest him in the fortune of others, and render their happiness necessary to him, though he derives nothing from it but the pleasure of seeing it.' Smith believed that the basis of all ethical reflection was 'fellow-feeling': our instinctive urge to recreate or mimic another's feelings in ourselves – what we would call empathy. But he was realistic enough about human nature to know that most of us won't be able to empathise with the same degree of sensitivity in every situation. This is where duty comes in. 'Duty', for Smith, is our regard for 'the established rules of behaviour'. It's the social pressure which binds us to a certain standard of conduct, even when we are not really considering the people our actions might affect. Duty, for example, is what stops us from running away from a restaurant without paying, even if the food was bad, the waiter was ignoring us all evening and we are pretty sure we could get away with it.

There is no contradiction between Smith's *Theory of Moral Sentiments* and his later and more famous *Wealth of Nations*. As the crisis has shown, markets need both empathy among individuals and a sense of duty at an institutional level. It is no longer simply enough to be booking big profits at the end of every quarter.

Raghuram Rajan, the economist encountered in Chapter 2, argues it is much harder for financial professionals to consider the social consequences of their actions because those consequences are themselves less visible. Securitisation in particular worked to stifle empathy. Of the subprime mortgage brokers of small town America he asks:

> Should the broker have counseled the debt-ridden home-owners they were working with to cut back on consumption, pay-off credit cards and move to smaller, more affordable home? Perhaps some would have done so had they thought they would see their clients again. Knowing

however, that the mortgages they originated would be packaged and sold, they had little stake in the relationship, other
than the fees…[161]

The work of the financial sector became separated from
reality to the point where the general public underpinning
the system simply became part of the numbers game. Greg
Hands told us about a Belgian colleague of his, whose biggest
client was the Belgian Ministry of Finance:

> He made lots of money out of this client. So much so that
> one day he decided to calculate his profits per Belgian
> taxpayer. It made him happy to figure out that his sales
> profits cost each Belgian taxpayer something like £2.57 each
> – even though the Kingdom's investments in structured
> products would ultimately help the Kingdom towards its
> high profile losses in 1993.

On the question of what Smith called duty, the deepest
outrage with bankers being rewarded for failure in the wake
of the crisis was that they were seen to have neglected theirs.
After being bailed out by the British taxpayer to avert a disaster
of their own making, most of us felt they had an obligation to
return that money, not to pocket it. This, not the politics of
envy, is the true significance of the moral argument surrounding bonuses: strong capitalism is not based on a one-way bet.

In a lecture at the LSE in February 2008 David Willetts
argued that the biggest threat to capitalism was its inherent
tendency to undermine the 'non-market' values upon which
a free-market society depends. These values include trust,
fairness, responsibility and what Willetts terms 'reciprocity', or social obligation. Reciprocity means doing someone
a favour or extracting a commitment in the knowledge
that they will feel obliged to return that favour or honour the commitment in the future. Willetts provides several

examples to demonstrate how an understanding of reciprocity can be used to produce useful outcomes:

> Take for example a problem which affects restaurateurs and the NHS alike – people who make a booking and then do not attend. One tiny change in approach by the telephonist can have a big impact. After the telephonist has given the time and asked the customer/patient to let them know if he cannot attend they should then pause. That gap in the conversation is filled by the customer saying 'OK'. And if that is said there is a much greater chance of feeling bound by a commitment so you phone to let the restaurant or doctor know if you will not be coming.

Willetts argued the best way to enforce the principles of fairness and reciprocity were through civic institutions. These institutions allow us to share information about reputation, the most important form of social currency. Willetts explains:

> In a large society, we cannot count on meeting people again *directly*. This is not to say reciprocity will diminish but we need to have a system which uses reputation. Reputation allows us to enjoy *indirect* reciprocity. If I can punish another person by refusing to help them because they refused to help another person, we can build a virtuous circle. However, this requires that their reputation be known to me, and that their reputation be good.

We know this principle holds from our own experience of canvassing voters. In the run-up to polling day the most important question to ask people at the door is their voting intention. Surveys show that those willing to make a public commitment to vote are much more likely to turn out on the day.

When the Treasury Select Committee questioned Bob Diamond in January 2011, the principle of reciprocity could also be seen in play. The Committee asked Diamond if he was 'grateful to the British taxpayer' for providing Barclays with a guarantee against insolvency, allowing the bank to borrow more cheaply. Diamond refused to provide the 'yes' or 'no' answer the question demanded, instead stressing his gratitude to 'the central banks around the world and to the governments around the world for the actions they took'. Why wouldn't Diamond express his gratitude to the British taxpayer in particular?

Because to do so would have been to enter the realm of reciprocity. Diamond's generalised gratitude to governments around the world did not imply any kind of social obligation because he deliberately avoided reference to a specific society. If, by contrast, he had answered 'yes' to the Committee's question he would have bound himself – not legally but morally – with a duty to return the favour to the British taxpayer. If nothing else this would have been powerful PR in the hands of anyone wishing to unseat Diamond at a later date.

What's strange is that entering into a reciprocal relationship, accepting one's duty towards wider society, can pay big dividends in terms of public profile. The most popular banker in the UK at present is probably Antonio Horta-Osório, the Chief Executive of Lloyds-HBOS. Why? Because he was the first to break ranks and admit his institution's culpability for the mis-selling of payment protection insurance (PPI). He has, more broadly, spoken authentically of the need for more responsible banking.

Recognising the moral significance of the financial crisis is a point of practical importance in other ways. The philosopher John Gray has written that 'Market institutions will be politically legitimate only insofar as they respect and reflect the norms and traditions, including the sense of fairness of the cultures whose needs they exist to serve'. In a poll conducted by the Cobden Centre in 2010, only a third of those surveyed agreed that the government should guarantee a bank's money or intervene in the event of a bank run. Yet such an approach would endanger everyone's livelihoods. When the values of bankers seem so wildly out of kilter with those of wider society then public trust in the financial system is damaged. A YouGov poll conducted the same year found that 54 per cent of those polled trusted banks less than they did before the crisis, 47 per cent were less likely to invest in funds and three times more people were now unsure whether they were making adequate provision for retirement. Ben Page of IPSOS Mori notes that public trust in bankers polls at just 29 per cent. MPs incidentally poll even lower at 14 per cent. What all of this means is that unless financial markets regain the respect of the public by demonstrating that they do feel bound by a sense of social obligation, as Horta Osório has done, then a government's room for manoeuvre will be severely limited in any future crisis.

Loss of public trust can also demoralise employees. After all, they are the ones who have to confront the popular attitude towards their profession on a daily basis: in pubs, at parties and over breakfast in the morning papers. In May 2010 it was reported that Sir Fred Goodwin's successor Stephen Hester had invited RBS employees to post comments reflecting on their jobs on the bank's internal website. One replied: 'I used to be proud to work for this bank after 20-plus years of service. Now I'm embarrassed by whom I work for and tell people I'm an accountant. You get less abuse.' Another said: 'I would love to say I love my job, I love coming to work and I'm proud to tell people I work for RBS – but I would be lying.'

The social stigma radiates beyond RBS: one banker we spoke to bemoaned the loss of social prestige: 'We provide a vital service to society. I would really like banking to be seen as a respectable, useful job, like being a doctor or a teacher. As it is, when I meet people for the first time, I don't tell them what I do.' This breakdown in the relationship between a major section of the economy and wider British society cannot, in the end, be good for business. In *The Social Animal* David Brooks writes: 'Trust reduces friction and lowers transaction costs. People in companies filled with trust move flexibly and cohesively... People in more trusting cultures have wider stock market-participation rates. People in trusting cultures find it easier to organise and operate large corporations. Trust creates wealth.'

Peacocking

Of course profit is not the only value to which bankers subscribed. Money isn't the *only* measure of worth. Success is also about status. As the philosopher Alain de Botton has written: 'We may seek a fortune for no greater reason than to secure the respect and attention of people who would otherwise look straight through us.'[162] The former Head of Derivatives at a global bank pointed out that being the number one financial institution in terms of size or sales didn't necessarily equate to being the most profitable, and yet executives still craved that position at the top of the list in *Bloomberg Businessweek*. A former employee of Merrill Lynch who worked in the mergers and acquisitions department told us how the management required all business presentations to include a league table showing that Merrill was number one, irrespective of the subject at hand. If it turned out the bank did not top the league in any given area, researchers were made to pore through pages of statistics until they invented a definition by which it did.

We can also see this dynamic at work in the notorious ABN Amro acquisition. No fewer than nineteen investment banks advised the competing banks on the deal. 'I cannot recall a deal that has so many advisors,' said Scott Moeller, a professor of mergers and acquisitions at Cass Business School in London and a former banker at Morgan Stanley and Deutsche Bank. 'The most significant issue is bragging rights. It's more important to the bank than the client.'

In retail banking, executives competed on size. At HBOS, for example, Andy Hornby was overwhelmingly concerned with expanding. For a non-financial institution like ASDA, where Hornby had previously been Chief Executive, expansion is constrained by market share of sales. Finance is important of course, but because leverage is so much lower, the liability side of the balance sheet matters much less.

But banks are different. Both sides of the balance sheet matter, as their core business is to take deposits to make loans. Market share matters, but so does the origin of the loans.

The Cobden Centre estimates that for most high street firms, a healthy solvency ratio is around 20 per cent. Anything below that exposes the firm to the risk of bankruptcy. But when six high street banks were surveyed, they found the average solvency ratio was just 0.18 per cent. So while the finance was available, banks had an apparently infinite capacity to borrow and expand market share in their lending.

But in the lending business, market share is not king. It is easy to expand market share by making cheaper loans to less solid borrowers. Easy but not prudent, as Hornby and others like him discovered. In the short term they captured market share and the status that went with it, but they reaped what they sowed.

There is something primal about this fixation with status. The idea of deriving validation from the sheer size of one's financial empire recalls the monarchs of early modern Europe, who would compete among themselves to build the biggest and most splendid palaces, to the dismay of their taxpaying subjects. In Chapter 5 we drew a comparison between Sir Fred Goodwin and John Law, the eighteenth-century Scottish gambler turned economist who became master of Bourbon France's finances. But there also seems to have been something of a Louis XIV complex among the senior management of RBS. They even built a palace. In 2005 RBS built a state-of-the-art £350 million headquarters outside Edinburgh. Sir Fred Goodwin had been intimately involved with the planning process. As the project manager put it he 'has strong opinions... He wanted high-quality finishes, a timeless, understated quality'. His own office overlooked a landscaped woodland area, featuring the stately residence of his nineteenth-century predecessor: John Thompson. The residence may have reflected a glorious past. During the twentieth century it was converted into a mental asylum.[163]

Socially Useless

Perhaps Adair Turner put the case for a moral dimension to the credit crunch most succinctly when in September 2010 he spoke of 'a crisis cooked up in trading rooms where not just a few but many people earned annual bonuses equal to a lifetime's earnings of some of those now suffering the consequences. We cannot go back to business as usual...' Turner was speaking at a Lord Mayor's Banquet in Mansion House, an event where the great and good of the UK financial services industry turn out in black tie to toast their own brilliance. Many shuffled awkwardly in their seats and stared into their soup as Adair Turner delivered his speech.

In August 2009 Turner caused a storm of controversy within the City when he suggested in a magazine interview that some financial activities might be 'socially useless': 'It is hard is to distinguish between valuable financial innovation and non-valuable. Clearly, not all innovation should be treated in the same category as the innovation of either a new pharmaceutical drug or a new retail format. I think that some of it is socially useless activity.'[164]

Turner's language was not used by mistake. His argument was that banks were no longer performing their traditional function – looking after savings and allocating them to the longer-term capital projects which help to generate growth and returns.

Bankers, especially from the investment side, have come to believe that they are entrepreneurs, who can produce economic value from thin air through a combination of ingenuity and sheer willpower. Convinced that they are the ultimate creators of wealth, they no longer regard themselves as stewards of other people's money. In fact they no longer seem to regard other people's money in any meaningful sense as being not theirs. This has led to a general disparagement of the retail side of banking, which is far more like a utility and far less entrepreneurial. Thousands of local bank managers who knew their customers were laid off in recent years, as investment bankers, who now firmly hold the reins of power, sought to streamline their costs.

The inventor James Dyson has written that 'Dyson vacuum cleaners would not exist were it not for Mike Page, my bank manager, who personally lobbied an initially reluctant Lloyds Bank to loan me the £600,000 I needed for tooling – the only way to start out on my own'.[165] No doubt Mr Page feels rewarded that he is able to say that he was the man who gave Dyson his break. And rightly so, because at their very best this is what banks do: put up the money without which a future business success would never get off the ground.

But this is not what the banks became. Rather than tracking down the next Dyson, Gates or Branson they devoted immense intellectual resources to the creation and trade of complex financial products which generated huge pots of money for those who sold them, but which by their nature made the financial system less robust.

In a lecture to the Cass Business School delivered in March 2010, Turner elaborated on the idea of 'socially useless' finance. He pointed out that the combined balance sheet of all UK banks stood at 500 per cent of GDP in 2008. But while mortgage credit had grown from 14 per cent to 79 per cent of GDP over the last fifty years, the amount actually invested in UK housing stock had barely changed. The banks were simply pumping credit into existing properties and driving up their prices.

This is an interesting take on the theme of rewards for failure. Most people support wealth creation. They do not object to the vast sums earned by entrepreneurs like Steve Jobs, or Larry Page and Sergey Brin, the founders and joint-owners of Google. This is because they can see how they are adding value to the real economy we all live and work in. This is not just a crude dichotomy of manufactures versus services. The Google search engine is intangible – essentially it's a mathematical algorithm backed by a huge amount of processing power. Nothing is being 'made', and yet we can all see how it allows for more efficient communication and sourcing of information, which in turn benefits everyone. By contrast, because the products of finance are largely invisible, and some are of questionable worth, people find it much more difficult to regard senior bankers' compensation as 'fair'. The lack of downside risk gives validity to this sense of unfairness.

A leading asset manager explained how new accounting systems based on securitisation have compounded the problem. Old-fashioned retail banks made loans and gradually accumulated their profits as the loan was gradually repaid. The bank and its managers were rewarded over time, determined by outcomes. In the world of securitised lending, pay is determined by expectations rather than outcomes. Loans are made, packaged up and sold on at a fee. The value of the fee the sales person receives is determined by the expected future value of the loans he is selling. But this only makes sense if you believe you can predict the economic future.

In order to establish the value of a ten-year income stream from a US mortgage-backed CDO, for example, you would have to be able to predict the levels of repayments over the next ten years. Of course economic models could make predictions of pinpoint clarity. But the models rested on false assumptions. As Mark Bathgate, an investment manager, put it, 'It's like Toyota saying they know how many cars they'll sell over the next ten years and then booking the profits today.' The result of this accounting system was that bankers were making huge profits in sales fees from products whose value they were unable to establish, some of which turned out to be worthless.

This argument about what constitutes a fair source of income is an old one, and deeply embedded in British culture. In the early nineteenth century, the economist David Ricardo produced a highly influential body of work on the rent income of landowners. Ricardo argued that rent was merely the difference between the value of the most sought-after productive pieces of land and the less fertile land which had nonetheless been brought into cultivation as the population expanded. When the UK population soared during the Industrial Revolution the surplus productivity of the better land was not channeled into extra investment; instead it simply increased the rent landowners charged. Landowners, like bankers, were adding little of value to the 'real economy', they were merely profiting from their fortunate position as occupants of a necessary utility. Then as now, the moral argument could not be politically ignored and Parliament eventually passed the Reform Act of 1832 which opened up the vote beyond the traditional agricultural elite and towards the industrial middle class.

❧

Changing corporate governance so that firms act more responsibly is an important step. But more important still is a different attitude in the regulatory institutions, to which we now turn. Why was it that despite ever more onerous regulation, banks managed to follow every detailed rule, yet still collapse catastrophically? The regulatory institutions, as well as the shareholders, failed. These institutions play a vital role in controlling and taming banks, and ensuring they do not take on unnecessary risk. They were supposed to act as a counterweight to the reward for failure culture to ensure a stable financial system, but failed. A reformed and reinforced structure is needed so that the public can rely on their regulators again.

Chapter 8

RULES, DISCRETION AND THE IMPORTANCE OF INSTITUTIONS

Dictum meum pactum (My word is my bond) Motto of the London Stock Exchange

From the corridors of government to a school assembly, wherever people interact there are rules. Often these rules are explicitly stated and have the full force of law behind them, like speed limits, or the age of consent. Others may be unwritten rules which derive their authority from powerful social obligations – shaking hands, observing a minute's silence, saying thank you, or queuing. Each of these unwritten rules is an incremental expression of our values as a society, of our sense of decency, reciprocity, fair play and what's reasonable. The first kind of course are vital, but when applied unthinkingly and without discretion they can end up fatally undermining the second.

In September 2007 a Wirral supermarket refused to sell alcohol to a 72-year-old man. Tony Ralls was a mild mannered grandfather-of-three, with white hair and a full beard. When an unsmiling checkout assistant demanded he provide proof of age he asked to see the store manager. The manager refused to see the funny side and promptly marched his two bottles of cabernet sauvignon back to the shelf. Mr Ralls abandoned the rest of his shopping on the conveyor belt and left the shop humiliated.

In 2004 Nadhim Zahawi, in a bid to go green, bought himself a scooter. One evening he was riding home to Putney, by way of Lambeth Bridge, when a motorist suddenly pulled out in front of him. There was a collision. Nadhim was thrown off his scooter, hit the road and badly broke his leg. Fortunately, the police were nearby and witnessed the whole incident. An ambulance arrived and the street was soon full of flashing blue lights and the crackle of walkie-talkies. As Nadhim lay grimacing on a stretcher the police helpfully picked up his wrecked scooter and propped it up against the kerb. Moments later an embarrassed eyewitness poked his head round the door to report that a passing traffic warden had just stuck a £100 parking fine on the mangled bike.

We have all come up against this phenomenon: humourless jobsworths on a self-defeating mission to 'make an example' out of everybody. Even if we meekly comply, our trust in authority is silently corroded. When rules are applied indiscriminately, the authority's 'official' standing may be increased – perhaps he gets a performance bonus for every hundredth fine – but his social standing slips and we respect him less. When he delivers the maddening phrase 'I don't make the rules', he reduces himself to an inhuman intermediary between us and the rulebook, an appendage to his clipboard or computer screen. In failing to exercise discretion he has effectively abandoned any responsibility for the rules he is paid to enforce. This can be extremely dangerous. Without an institutional framework which allows people to step into the breach, take responsibility and amend, waive or even rewrite the rules as the unforeseen inevitably occurs, the rules may end up subverting the very values they were designed to protect. For while discretion without rules is tyranny, rules without discretion is mindless bureaucracy.

This is what happened to Britain's financial regulatory institutions in the years before the crisis. Discretion was regarded as outdated while complex rules came to dominate the system. The result was a financial regulator which allowed the British banking sector to implode in almost perfect compliance with its own rulebook, and a central bank legally barred from intervening until the eleventh hour. Official regulation did not just fail our economy, it failed our moral sense too. Thick files of financial regulation crowded out society's unwritten rules of responsibility and ethical behaviour, in effect coming to replace them.

Rules without Discretion

In 1997 Gordon Brown revolutionised the institutions in charge of the UK economy. 'The world has turned upside down. A Labour government is elected and the new Chancellor's first move is to hand over control of macroeconomic policy to the Bank of England,' hailed *The Times* that May. In fact the Bank had only been given operational independence over monetary policy: the ability to set interest rates to meet an inflation target of 2 per cent set by the Treasury. A few weeks later Brown announced that 'responsibility for banking supervision will be transferred, as soon as possible ... from the Bank of England to a new and strengthened Securities and Investments Board'. This Board would shortly become the Financial Services Authority (FSA). The FSA was designed as a financial police force and consumer rights watchdog and tasked with 'promoting orderly, efficient and fair markets'. Brown would remain in control of fiscal policy, to be bound by a 'Golden Rule' devised by his young advisor Ed Balls. The Rule stated that 'over the economic cycle, the government will borrow only to invest and not to fund current spending'; that is, the government would only borrow to fund capital projects like schools and hospitals, not day-to-day outgoings like the public sector payroll.

Together, these three areas constitute the tools we use to manage the economy: fiscal policies of tax and spend, monetary policy set by interest rates and the quantity of money, and financial policy of how we regulate the banks.

Under Brown's new system, the three arms of economic management were split: monetary policy given to the Bank of

England, financial policy to the FSA, and fiscal policy to the Treasury. Of these, monetary policy was tasked with managing economic fluctuations, while fiscal policy and financial policy would be set for the long term. Or so we were told.

This tripartite split was founded on the assumption that the FSA would make a more effective financial regulator than the Bank of England because the Bank's monetary policy objectives were imagined to be incompatible with a regulatory role. What if, for example, it needed to raise interest rates to meet its inflation target but it knew of several institutions that would fail if their borrowing costs went up? This argument had been made as early as 1992 by Balls in a Fabian Society pamphlet entitled 'Euro Monetarism – Why Britain was ensnared and how it could escape', which made the case for central bank independence. Gordon Brown was so impressed with this pamphlet that he offered Balls a job.

Only in a world of dry economic abstraction and arbitrary rules could running monetary policy have been thought to be incompatible with financial stability. As the crisis has unforgettably shown, these two areas of economic management are inextricably linked. Loose monetary policy encourages borrowing as the price of debt – the interest rate – falls. If debt is too cheap, all too often people borrow to buy assets.

When most prices are held down by a combination of cheaper imports and low expectations of future inflation, excess lending finds a home in asset price inflation. Asset prices are unlike the price of most goods, because when asset prices rise, they appear more, not less, attractive. So as we have seen, rising asset prices can swell into a bubble. Eventually it dawns on people that assets are not really worth the market price and the bubble bursts. The assets lose value, but if people have borrowed against them the debts remain, putting financial stability at risk.

As Hyman Minsky, the great theorist of financial crises, pointed out, this is the Greek tragedy of macroeconomics.

A long period of low volatility contains the seeds of its own destruction. The very stability which allows central banks to lower interest rates in the first place gets negated in the bust.

So monetary policy and financial policy are inextricably linked. This is the central insight that motivates different regulation in finance compared to elsewhere in the economy. In finance, the success or failure of private firms has a direct impact on the whole economic system: they can be systemically important. So while burdensome, complex over-regulation was applied across the economy, in finance the critical role of regulating the size of balance sheets, the sustainability of business, and ultimately the level of debt in the economy was neglected. This vital power was removed.

In 1997, the Bank of England was seen to have been discredited as a financial supervisor following the collapse of Barings Bank in 1995. There is a terrible irony here. In a world anxious about banks that are too big to fail, we are quite nostalgic for Nick Leeson. The closure of Barings had no adverse systemic consequences for the UK financial system. Leeson suffered the consequences of his unauthorised trading. The management were punished for inadequate risk management. In a post-crisis world, allowing irresponsible financial institutions to fail safely is now regarded as positive aim of regulatory policy, not a scandal. Even Leeson, who now writes a finance column in an Irish magazine, agrees.

The emasculation of the Bank was part of a wider mistrust in the ability of professionals to make judgements. But regulatory discretion, properly accountable, could have ensured there was no contradiction between monetary and financial policy. That requires us to accept that difficult problems, like regulating finance, do not always have clear-cut solutions and that sometimes professionals must be trusted to negotiate, debate and arrive at a decision over the best course of action. Instead, in a narrow-minded reaction to perceived failures, the traditional role of the Bank of England to regulate the level of debt in the economy was removed. The Bank was turned into a single-purpose inflation-targeting machine, at the very point in history where commercial banks were growing into huge conglomerates with operations in every conceivable financial activity.

In contrast to financial policy, the Bank's Monetary Policy Committee (MPC) was given full discretion within clear parameters to pursue a single target – inflation – with a single policy tool – interest rates. Within this tight definition, the Bank performed exceptionally well. Minutes were published, votes were recorded, the Committee was open and transparent. Over the decade from 1997, inflation did not deviate from target by more than one percentage point on either side. Given the variability in inflation over previous decades, this was a remarkable achievement. It supports the claim that strong institutions, when given clear goals and the discretion to achieve them, can perform very strongly.

But thanks to the very narrowly defined target, the statutory duty to keep inflation on target was fulfilled at the expense of wider economic management. The Bank retained the duty to protect financial stability, and the people to do so, but unlike in monetary policy, it had no powers to act. The Bank could only warn. The FSA had the powers to act, but no duty to listen.

So when the Bank of England warned about the growing debt problem, the FSA did not act. As we saw in Chapter 2, the Bank's Deputy Governor Sir Andrew Large and a handful of others had made the connection between the rise of household debt, chronically over-leveraged financial institutions and government borrowing. They argued how fragile this had made the UK financial system. In May 2006, Mervyn King worried that 'a potentially large social problem, with many households getting into difficulty with their debts, [was] materialising'.[166] The ratio of UK household savings to GDP had been declining throughout the decade. In 2005 it had been 5.6 per cent on average, half that of our European neighbours. By the first quarter of 2008 it was minus 0.7 per cent. At the same time, household lending rose at more than four times the growth of the economy, and became the highest, as a proportion of income, of any G7 country in history. Household credit accounted for 74 per cent of all bank lending, mostly for house purchase. These facts are interconnected. The banks were only able to lend because households were borrowing, households were only borrowing because house prices kept rising, and house prices were only rising because the banks were lending. But with every turn, the 'social problem' King identified was becoming a bigger economic problem as balance sheets expanded and the UK's ability to withstand a reversal in house price rises shrank.

Some raised concerns that the structure was inadequate even earlier. Lord Flight, then a shadow Treasury Minister, challenged the then Governor, Sir Edward George: 'I said: "Consumer debt and house prices have increased too much – aren't you worried?" George looked resigned. He replied that his legal brief was the 2.5 per cent inflation target and "we can't achieve two objectives at once".' Flight was shocked: 'It was astonishing. If there was something he thought had to be done to ensure the stability of the British economy he should have done it or offered the government his resignation.'

Indeed Flight had argued against the tripartite structure as it was set up, foretelling that it meant no one would be in charge when a crisis hit.

George was operating within strict rules set out by Parliament. But the crisis revealed that the narrow focus in these rules did not allow enough discretion to maintain oversight of the system as a whole and with it financial stability.

As Mervyn King later observed after the crash, when charged with a duty to protect financial stability:

The Bank finds itself in a position rather like that of a church whose congregation attends weddings and burials but ignores the sermons in between... It is not entirely clear how the Bank will be able to discharge its new statutory responsibility if we can do no more than issue sermons or organise burials.

By contrast, before 1997 the Bank of England used powers, formal and informal, that have romantically been referred to as 'raising the Governor's eyebrows'. The Governor would keep in close contact with leading bankers. Executives were called into the Governor's office to discuss the viability of their business. The eyebrow metaphor is shorthand for a strong culture of gentlemen's agreements and self-responsibility which was meant to keep an older, more respectable City of merchant banks and bowler hats in check. But all legends have a kernel of truth, as Sajid Javid, a former banker and now MP for Bromsgrove told us.

In 1997, just before the Bank's responsibilities were transferred to the FSA, Javid was working at Chase Manhattan, on the trading side of emerging markets. He recalls the audits from the Bank of England:

> With the Bank you knew that the regulators were reporting to people somewhere who have relationships with banks, with clients, and know the markets. With emerging markets sovereign borrowers, for instance, the Bank of England could be on the phone to the central bank of that country the next day, to check up on you. They might well know them, and have a relationship with them. So when you open up your books to show the risks, you knew they knew what they are looking for.

This unnerving sense that someone, somewhere at the Bank could be on the phone 'to check up on you' if things weren't all they seemed was fatally lost when banking supervision was transferred to the FSA. The soft power of the Bank's vast network of relationships, formal and informal, within the global financial system was a useful disciplinary tool among the firms under its jurisdiction. But because it relied on discretionary judgements, tacit understandings, and institutional prestige it couldn't be codified in a rulebook. In the brave new world, it would have to go.

By contrast Javid and his colleagues preferred it when the auditors from the FSA turned up. They soon discovered that the junior FSA official would tick off their responses to questions like 'Is your position hedged?' without pausing to consider the implications of the answer. The rules only required that a loan be 'hedged' against 'risk'; the auditors did not distinguish between different types of risk, like default risk – the risk that the loan is not repaid – and market risk – where the value of the loan falls in response to market events. This meant traders could spin their position in any way they chose. 'It was great, because you could get them in and out, you could handle them,' said Javid. 'It gave you as a bank much more flexibility on how you manage your risk books.'

An undercapitalised financial system grew up as the rigid rules allowed risky loans to be called capital. The reason the AAA rating was so valued was that such a rating allowed banks to class such loans as capital. But a capital buffer is meant to be a buffer against solvency. AAA loans do not help if the solvency of the bank is under threat. They help even less if they themselves have collapsed in value.

But the role of the AAA rating is crucial to understanding the role of rating agencies. Private agencies were paid fees by the issuers of bonds, in order to classify the bonds. By 2005, for example, half of Moody's income came from structured finance, according to Gillian Tett. The rating agencies' incentives were clear: to please the client with the highest rating possible. And the incentive on the bond issuer was clear: put in the lowest-quality assets consistent with getting the top rating. Rating agencies even published their models so banks could test what structures would get the highest ratings. The three major agencies acted as a herd when the others' models changed. In a candid online conversation in 2007, later dug up by the US House Oversight Committee, a Standard & Poor's employee admitted to a colleague that the model used to rate a mortgage-backed security 'does not capture half the risk'. 'We should not be rating it', agreed his colleague. But, as the first replied, theirs was not to reason why: 'We rate every deal. It could be structured by cows and we would rate it.' This was herd behaviour indeed. Rating agencies were made a crucial part of the financial plumbing. Yet their clear conflicts of interest were made worse by the rules.

In an essay entitled 'Rationalism in Politics', the British philosopher Michael Oakeshott distinguishes between two different types of knowledge: the technical and the practical. Technical knowledge is 'capable of precise formulation' and consists of 'rules, principles, direction and maxims – comprehensively in propositions'. It is the kind of knowledge you might find in an economic forecast, a chess manual, or even a political manifesto. Then there is practical knowledge, which 'exists only in use, and cannot be formulated in rules'. Practical knowledge can 'neither be taught or learned, only imparted or acquired'. To demonstrate the distinction Oakeshott gave the example of a talented chef. When preparing a dish the chef will, to a greater or lesser extent, be following a recipe. This is the technical knowledge. Practical knowledge is whatever it is that makes him a great cook – imagination, intuition and sensitivity. Practical knowledge is the difference between a chess grandmaster and someone who knows the rules but has no feel for the game.

Both kinds of knowledge are vital, but Oakeshott felt modern politics was in danger of excluding the second. Because technical knowledge is self-contained, people think also it is self-sufficient. Politicians came to think that they could solve any problem provided they gathered enough formal information about it first. It's what Friedrich Engels meant when he optimistically wrote of 'replacing the government of persons by the administration of things'. Practical knowledge, by contrast, relies on trial and error, experience, judgement and intuition. This is why acquiring it is a continuous process.

Technical and practical knowledge roughly correspond to what we are referring to as rules and discretion. In a regulatory culture which only permits people to act according to pre-existing rules, the cultivation of practical knowledge is impossible. When a problem arises, regulators will look to the rulebook because they are not allowed to think for themselves; hence the paralysis and indecision over Northern Rock. It never occurred to the people who wrote the rules that a bank might become insolvent and suffer a run. Because financial supervisors had a culture of not making independent judgements, there was no leadership in the crisis.

The run was exacerbated when it became apparent to Northern Rock savers that the Chancellor of the Exchequer had no plan. The journalist Paul Mason recalls the press conference on Monday 17 September 2007, just as the run was in full swing. He told Darling, 'I've been with Northern Rock savers all day and the problem is no one believes you. This may not be rational but it's real.' Mason could see 'from the body language of Darling's aides that they were in completely uncharted territory, for which there was no protocol or playbook'.

The system had been designed to give clarity and an unambiguous rules-based framework so that markets knew exactly where they stood. But the rules-based system could not deal with the unforeseen.

The most common criticism of the FSA's role in the crisis is that, in the words of its CEO Hector Sants, it failed 'to recognise systemic wide risk'. Too focused on the fate of individual institutions, it interfered with banks at the street level without a bird's eye perspective.

While valid, this argument is partial. Yes, there was a failure of analysis, and of technical knowledge – we knew less than we thought we did. But it does not follow that to prevent a future crisis all we have to do is correct our analysis in the light of new facts and design better rules.

To do that would overlook something more fundamental and much harder to grapple with: a problem of institutional culture. After all, the FSA was not completely unaware of the risks lurking in the bowels of the financial system. In its 2007 *Financial Risk Outlook*, it successfully identified many of them, noting of equity markets that 'while volatility remains at recent historic lows, the factors that have contributed to it (such as widely available cheap funding and high risk appetite) could quickly reverse, potentially resulting in a deterioration of global financial market conditions'.

The FSA's real deficiency as an institution is that it had been structured according to a flawed belief based on false assumptions about human behaviour, that financial markets would work in society's interests as long as they did nothing illegal.

The FSA's 'Handbook of Market Conduct' contains a list of principles which the firms under its jurisdiction are asked to observe. Following the crisis, this financial code of honour reads like a hymn to hypocrisy. Firms are told they must conduct their business with 'integrity', 'due skill, care and diligence', that they must organise their affairs 'responsibly and effectively' while maintaining 'adequate financial resources'. But the banks did not follow the FSA's principles. They followed its rulebook, knowing that only a clear breach of the law would result in official sanction. The FSA lacked the discretion to enforce its principles. Without breaking any rules, banks remained undercapitalised, toxic assets were camouflaged in off-balance-sheet 'special purpose vehicles' and outrageous risks were taken using depositors' money as effective collateral. The principles had no teeth.

The obsession with process and box-ticking left no room for discretionary judgement. This is what led Adair Turner in December 2010 to ruefully recall 'the deficiencies in regulatory philosophy', which meant that with respect to RBS 'the FSA simply did not believe our remit included preventing the ABN Amro acquisition – which was highly risky but breached no regulation'.[167]

The FSA spent virtually no time with banks' senior management. To put it in context, the FSA met Northern Rock executives only eight times in the two years before the crash. Of these, two meetings were conducted by phone. Five took place on the same day.[168]

The banks were well aware of this 'philosophy'. They saw that the FSA lacked the will to question the effectiveness of its own rules. They knew that as long as they obeyed the letter of the law they would be safe. So they gamed the rules. The gaming of financial regulation is as old as financial regulation itself. Ever since the bankers of medieval Italy got round the Church's ban on usury by charging risk margins on their loans instead of interest, people in finance have looked for oversights, loopholes and ways of playing the system. The only effective regulatory response is to evolve and adapt the rules in response, but this is only possible with institutional discretion.

Time and again perverse outcomes were produced because no one wanted to rewrite the rules. Northern Rock had been designated a 'high impact bank' even before the run in September 2007. But it was 'not scheduled to have another ... impact assessment until three years after its most recent assessment. Its regulatory period was due to run from January 2006 until January 2009'.[169]

And so the bureaucratic demand of the schedule prevailed over financial stability.

From 2004, the FSA required all deposit takers and insurers to undertake 'stress tests' to assess how easily they could repay their debts in the event of a market shock. During a stress test firms simulate 'extreme but plausible' market events, and then play out the effects on their balance sheets. The idea is that if imagined losses are unacceptable then responsible firms will draw in higher levels of capital, as a cushion against risk. In 2006 the FSA conducted a review of stress-testing across ten major City firms. It concluded: 'Few firms were seeking out scenarios such as those that might require a dividend cut, generate an annual loss or result in shortfalls against capital requirements, while still remaining plausible.' In other words, the firms had designed the tests to provide CEOs and shareholders with the results they wanted, or needed, to hear. No assessment was made of the strength of the system.

What would a fair stress test have looked like at Northern Rock, or RBS in 2006? The FSA did not seek to find out. Rather than administer its own tests it issued a letter to the CEOs meekly requesting that they take account of the findings. Allowing firms to design their own tests using their own risk models was like giving schoolchildren permission to mark their own exam papers. The rules were clearly inadequate, and they were gamed.

A more serious exploitation of the rules occurred in relation to the shadow banking sector. As we have seen, 'shadow banks' are financial institutions which do not take retail deposits and are therefore not regulated. Yet banks control these vehicles without officially owning them and use them to transfer their riskiest assets off-balance-sheet. This allows bank balance sheets to appear healthier than they are, whereas in fact, as we discovered, the banks remain responsible for the risk when things go wrong.

In December 2007 it was reported that twelve of the UK's best-known financial institutions had set up a series of charitable trusts. These trusts were set up to donate to a variety of worthy causes, including the NSPCC. A noble endeavour, you might think. Perhaps, on the eve of the crisis, the banks had finally decided that it was time to give something back. But there was a problem. None of the charities had ever heard of their wealthy sponsors, nor had they received any donations. In fact the trusts were legal fictions. They existed purely to own SPVs on the banks' behalf and had raised £234 billion in investment for their parent financial institutions. Their 'charitable status', while within the rules, was a distasteful exercise in branding. One Treasury Select Committee member suggested it might constitute a form of 'identity theft'. The FSA did nothing.

At the time shadow banking was not well understood, and the newspaper that broke the story suggested the trusts had been set up to avoid paying tax. We now know that shadow banking is one of the most pernicious ways of gaming the rules, a way of concealing liabilities from both the regulators and the market itself, and giving the impression that a bank is stronger than it is in reality.

While obviously immoral, some of this behaviour even bordered on the criminal. In spite of the long arm of the FSA, in the UK the number of successful criminal convictions for financial crime is minimal. Financial negligence leading to the mass destruction of national wealth has gone uncontested. Yet even a small number of high-profile convictions would serve as an important reminder to others of the price of misbehaviour, and such sanctions can underpin a culture of responsibility.

Debt, Where is thy Sting?

Whatever the shortcomings of the FSA, the economic culture in which they had to operate was ultimately dictated by the Treasury, and it was the Treasury which allowed debt to lose its traditional taint of social unacceptability.

For anyone who did want to challenge the insidious debt culture creeping through the marrow of the financial system, there was only one message from the Treasury: debt was not evidence of weakness, it was proof of strength. The fact that we could afford to service our debts showed just how invincible the economy was. When in 2003 Vince Cable asked Brown whether he could explain why no one was 'taking responsibility for the often reckless debt promotion by the leading banks and credit card companies' the Chancellor's reply bordered on the whimsical: 'I suspect that the rest of the hon. Gentleman's party are using their credit cards and injecting spending into the economy at this very moment, so that we can meet our growth target with greater confidence.'

As amusing as the idea of a troop of Lib Dems marching into Debenhams to max out their store cards might be, it is no joke that this is what passed for a serious argument about the levels of debt in our society in the years before the crisis.

This combination of a failure to regulate over-lending, and a rhetorical effort to commend all lending, came to undermine a traditional British value: thrift. It may be old-fashioned, but as we have seen, it has stood the test of time. As early as 1711, Jonathan Swift wrote a pamphlet complaining about the debts left to an incoming Tory government:

> I have often reflected on that mistaken notion of credit, so boasted of by the last ministry... If they call it credit to run ten millions of debt in debt without parliamentary security by which the public is defrauded of almost half, I must think such credit dangerous, illegal, perhaps even treasonable.

It is an irony of the crisis that Scotland, traditionally the thriftiest of the UK's nations, suffered the two greatest banking disasters as the Royal Bank of Scotland and the Bank of Scotland went bust.

The Treasury's approach to private indebtedness reflected its irresponsible approach to public lending. Like the banks, it gamed the rules: in this case its own.

Recall the pre-crisis Treasury's Golden Rule: 'Over the economic cycle, the government will borrow only to invest and not to fund current spending.'[170] The purpose of its own Golden Rule was to 'protect intergenerational fairness' by ensuring that the government would not borrow more than it invested over an economic cycle. This last caveat was made to allow borrowing to rise in a downturn – the so-called automatic stabilisers.

The intention of the Golden Rule was to prevent a short-term incentive to borrow rather than face up to the difficult choices of tax and spend. This incentive was especially strong in a government elected on the basis that it would spend more, but not raise income tax. The crucial caveat that the budget would balance 'over the cycle' gave the Treasury its chance to abide by the letter of the rule while ignoring its spirit. The rule hinged on the definition of 'economic cycle', measured through changing trends in average economic output. As long as the Treasury picked the right years from which to begin and end the cycle, it could calculate an average that made the rule fit. In 2000, the cycle was supposed to have run from 1997–2000. So according to this definition a new cycle would have begun in 2000. But by 2005, when the rule was about to be broken, the cycle was back-dated to 1997 again, pushing the average 'over the cycle' back into surplus. Other sleights of hand included projecting trends into the future and then claiming that these trends would allow the Golden Rule to be met. When the trends turned out to be wrong, new trends across a different timescale could be invented.

The Office for Budget Responsibility now estimates that the economic cycle did indeed begin in 1997, but that it won't end until 2016. According to this definition the Golden Rule was never met, and the average budget deficit by 2016 will be minus 1.3 per cent. This perennial gaming of the Rule and lack of independent oversight meant that according to the Institute for Fiscal Studies 'by the eve of the financial crisis' fiscal drift 'had left the UK with one of the largest structural budget deficits in the developed world'.

In cognitive psychology a *confirmation bias* describes the phenomenon where an individual actively seeks out the evidence supporting a favoured hypothesis, while ignoring any evidence which threatens it. Such a bias is well known within the criminal justice system, which is why there are strict limitations on the kind of questions the police can ask witnesses. By starting with the assumption that bubbles no longer occurred in the British economy, and that the rules would always be met, Brown had built a confirmation bias into the regulatory framework itself. The chances that the authorities would prepare in advance for a crisis, much less predict one, were dramatically reduced. Brown's economic doctrine was exactly the kind of intellectual despotism that a strong institution could have challenged. The Chancellor, who told the British people in one Budget speech after another that there would be 'no return to boom and bust', wanted us all to believe that the good times would last forever.

Rules with Discretion

Britain's most successful and enduring public institutions have tended to strike the right balance between rules and discretion. Think of the Common Law, which relies on a set of uncompromising principles such as *habeas corpus*, but also the discretion of the judge to rule according to precedent.

The earliest stock-brokers were also adept at balancing rules and discretion. In eighteenth-century London shares were publically traded in the coffee-houses around Exchange Alley. Lloyds of London began life as the coffee-house *Lloyd's*, which attracted traders specialising in insurance deals. In such an informal environment, opportunities for fraud were rife and unscrupulous traders could default on debts or refuse to honour contracts without fear of prosecution. (In the aftermath of the South Sea Bubble, the British government tried to dilute the popularity of the stock market by withdrawing all right of legal redress for trades over £5.)

Brokers therefore came up with their own form of enforcement, which relied on reputation. If a particular trader acquired a reputation for dishonest behaviour then he would be barred from the coffee-house. This proved unenforceable, as some of the dodgier dealers proved quite capable of talking their way back in. Consequently, the names of untrustworthy characters would be written up in chalk on a blackboard for all to see. Brokers would then refuse to deal with them. In the words of Adam Smith: 'They who do not keep their Credit will soon be turned out, and, in the Language of Change Alley, be called lame Duck.'

The stock-brokers also established the subscription room system where anyone wanting to trade would first have to pay, ensuring it wasn't in their financial interest to trade dishonestly. Unscrupulous dealers appealed to the courts, who ruled that the stock-brokers had no legal right to exclude them from a public place in this manner. So the brokers set up their own private members' coffee-house, which would become known to history as *The London Stock Exchange*. Every time people tried to exploit or abuse the rules, the system had enough flexibility to alter those rules to ensure that the honest dealers were always one step ahead of the game.

Three centuries later, it is clear that one lesson from the financial crisis is that the balance swung too far from discretion to rules. From the MPC's exclusive focus on narrow inflation measures to the FSA's inability to look at the big picture, a policy of reliance on rules without discretion helped stoke the boom, and was an impediment to rapid action to deal with the bust. Indeed in the limited area discretion was sanctioned – within the MPC's remit to vary interest rates to target inflation – policy was largely successful.

This mistrust of discretion brought with it a culture within the authorities of avoiding the exercise of judgement. Instead, there was a pervasive attempt to find apparently objective solutions, even when this apparent objectivity was false, as it was based on necessarily subjective assumptions. So the rulebook expanded to attempt to cover every eventuality. Even in the latter stages of the boom, as the FSA attempted to move to principles-based regulation, the degree of detailed rules continued to expand.

The FSA was not the only offender. International accounting bodies, which are highly opaque and almost entirely unaccountable, set the rules – called IFRS – by which many of the numbers are calculated. By increasing the scope of so-called mark to market accounting, which values assets without regard to any underlying valuation, and reducing the need for accounts to be a true and fair reflection of the business, they increased volatility of accounts, treated different institutions differently for essentially arbitrary reasons, made the system more cyclical, and limited room for manoeuvre in the crisis. The flawed thinking of international accounting standards bodies must take its share of the blame for the economic misery we have seen.

Of course in some areas of life, following the rules is crucial. Air traffic control is highly rule-based. For decades, air traffic rules have gradually been improved to learn lessons from crashes, and safety has been improved. Likewise, research shows that medical decisions have better outcomes when based on rules, rather than the discretion of the medic. Unlike running the economy, in both cases the rules reflect actual human behaviour and are constantly updated on the basis of past experience. But crucially, unlike in the economy, there is no feedback loop. Pilots do not try to game the air traffic control rules. Our bodies do not change the way they work when the rules of medical practice change. The rules are not an endogenous part of the system.

But those who support detailed rules make another argument. They point out, fairly, that discretionary judgements can only be taken by people, and all people are flawed. Of course discretion is imperfect. So too are bad rules. Hence the need for constrained discretion, held to account, to allow judgement to be exercised in the setting of clear, preferably simple, rules.

For discretion to be exercised legitimately and effectively, the power to make judgements must be embedded in strong institutions. Embedding discretion in institutions has many advantages. Of course, like all people, all institutions are flawed too. They will make mistakes. But a strong institution is one that will respond to its mistakes and learn from them.

A strong institution can set the framework of limits to the discretion, strengthen accountability, support the decision takers, provide continuity, and give weight to the decisions taken. Furthermore, a strong institutional framework allows those exercising public judgements to provide ethical and cultural leadership in their area of duty.

Let us take each of these in turn.

When good public policy requires the exercise of discretion, based on judgements about the most appropriate policy for the general good, the most important consideration is that the decision is the best that can reasonably be made. Setting such discretion within a strong institution helps in the first instance deliver resources and structure to allow decision-makers to consider the objectives, and formulate the best response. That approach also has the benefit of allowing a decision to be seen to be based on appropriate consideration, and thus help legitimise the decision.

Both reaching the right decision and improving the legitimacy of that decision will be further helped by strong accountability. A strong institutional framework that enables transparency and responsiveness to public debate can help embed that accountability.

Given that judgements are necessarily subjective, it is crucial to understand and learn from experience of judgements past. So a strong institutional memory can help support today's decision-makers, and help improve the judgements of the future. Likewise, all decision-makers are human. A strong institution can help develop the leaders of tomorrow.

What's more, the institution can itself give added weight to any decision. Given that judgements necessarily have both a technical and a practical element, the perception of any decision's legitimacy is an important element of the effect it will have. For example, it has been noticed that during the collapse of Northern Rock, people turned not to the FSA but to the Bank of England for leadership, given that institution's long history and weight. Decisions made by respected institutions are more likely therefore to be taken seriously, and ultimately more likely to be effective.

Finally, a strong institution gives a platform for ethical and cultural leadership. We have seen that economic decisions, private and public, cannot be divorced from the cultural and ethical context in which they are made. Even a private decision to set aside moral considerations is itself a decision about ethics. Leaders of public institutions can and should make the moral case for a culture of behaviour for the public good.

The structure of modern banking conspires against ethical business practice. Regulatory institutions have an important role in setting the cultural context in which business operates. Designed properly, strong institutions can provide the space for debate and dissent, for that critical scrutiny of dominant assumptions which we know is the lifeblood of both capitalism and democracy, but which the banks so badly lack. Above all they can help ensure that some of our values as a society are able to permeate the increasingly self-contained culture of finance. As George Cooper, a former banker turned financial analyst, put it to us: 'We need the regulators to save the banks from themselves.'

This of course is not what happened in the run-up to the collapse of 2008.

In Britain the worst offenders were also the system's most highly regulated institutions. Banks borrowed most and took the biggest risks because they had the most valuable collateral: customer deposits backed with an implicit government guarantee. Andrew Haldane points out that over the past two decades the number of different categories of risk used by the regulators has risen from seven to over 200,000. The number of calculations needed to work out the capital a bank is required to hold by the regulator used to be in single figures, but is now over 200 million. Yet this vast rise in regulatory complexity was ineffective. Not only did banks fail, but the regulatory measurements entirely failed to predict which banks were even in trouble. A simple test of the ratio of a bank's share price to its assets, by contrast, was an imperfect but fairly reliable indicator of which banks were in trouble.

The responsibilities which followed from this privileged position of implicit guarantee were not enforced. This is in contrast to the responsible, discretionary, flexible regime of some of our international neighbours. Spain had a simple rule that a bank's lending could not be a simple multiple higher than its capital. In the boom, the multiple was reduced, to ensure banks were as well prepared as possible. Canada, Australia, and even Lebanon all had a similar simple dynamic rule, changed at the discretion of the authorities. In Lebanon, for example, banks had to have at least 30 per cent of their assets in cash. When the central bank saw trouble down the line, they took action. The Governor of Lebanon's central bank, Riad Salameh, made it sound simple: 'I saw the crisis coming and I told the commercial banks in 2007 to get out of all international investments related to the international markets.' Thanks to a system that has been 'tested against wars, against instability, against political assassinations', there is a flexible, risk averse attitude in that country, which meant that the discretionary judgement of the central banker was adhered to. Lebanon weathered the storm remarkably well. Indeed each of these countries had banking systems that coped relatively well with the crash. Such simple counter-cyclical policy is very attractive.

As we saw earlier, there is a delicate relationship between official rules and society's unwritten rules. Discretion helps reduce the tension. Our regulatory tragedy is that that the official rules didn't question the behaviour of the banks because nobody questioned the official rules.

The crisis has shown that it's not good enough to have principles in the abstract if they are swamped by detailed rules. What are needed instead are regulatory institutions which embody those principles, with the clout to enforce them. Think of it like this. Democracy is a principle. Throughout the years it has inspired acts of extraordinary courage in the face of cruel authoritarianism: the Peterloo Massacre, the Battle of Britain, Nelson Mandela's imprisonment, or the events of the Arab Spring. But in the end democracy is of no use to a society unless it has an institutional, practical character as well as a vivid ideological content. Ultimately the word has to refer to an elected representative assembly, or like the names of defunct Communist states, the claim of Democracy won't mean very much at all.

Chapter 9

SO WHAT DO WE DO?

When the so-called masters of the universe discovered they were masters of nothing, we all discovered the frightening truth: they had built a machine they did not understand and could not fix. We are still living with the consequences. The crisis is not yet over. The banking debt crisis has become a sovereign debt crisis, raging in the eurozone. When the banks failed, governments stepped in. When governments fail, only other governments remain. We are yet to see the end of this crisis.

What's at Stake?

Already bailing out the banks and stabilising the system has cost every household in the country the equivalent of over £26,000. The recession that followed was the deepest in peacetime history, and the contraction in credit continues as financial institutions struggle to rebuild their balance sheets in the aftermath of the crash. But this was not the only cost of the crash. The taxpayer's cash was intended to strengthen those balance sheets. The sight of bankers diverting it towards their bonus pools after such failure shattered public trust in the financial system.

For this book, YouGov asked members of the British public in July 2011: 'How much, if at all, do you trust the finance industry to look after your money?' Nearly 70 per cent answered 'not much' or 'not at all'. Only 2 per cent replied 'a great deal'.[171] Yet the financial system is built on trust: that if you save for the future, your thrift will be rewarded.

After the financial crises of the 1930s, several nations

turned against free-market capitalism. They uprooted the liberal institutions necessary to sustain freedom of expression and trade, and transferred their loyalties to an all-powerful state. The result was the Second World War.

Today the democratic tradition is more deeply rooted, but we cannot afford to be complacent. Free-market capitalism can only work effectively if it enjoys public trust. That trust is undermined unless the finance industry – a symbol of capitalism – shows it is founded on trust, mutual respect, and an honourable relationship between debtor and creditor. But in recent times banking has profited in a moral vacuum.

The ramifications of this are making themselves felt. In southern Europe, where whole economies are propped up on rotten stilts of bad debt, respect for the discipline of the market has been ground down. Polls suggest that up to 80 per cent of Greeks rejected the 'austerity measures' voted through by George Papandreou's government in 2011.[172] Large swathes of the population simply do not care about the international bond market's verdict on their government's creditworthiness. Attempts at economic reform are wilfully sabotaged by vested interests hitched to a current of popular feeling. The recurring populist question 'Why should we pay for bankers' mistakes?' is based on a false premise but it is necessary for a leader to answer. In the countries of the former Eastern Bloc, support for capitalism is also in decline. According to a 2009 survey 'the prevailing view in Russia, Ukraine, Lithuania, Slovakia, Bulgaria and Hungary is that people were better off economically under communism'. In Ukraine, Russia, Lithuania and Hungary only half or less of those polled approved of the transition to capitalism.[173] Even in that great citadel of capitalism, the United States, there are rumblings of protest. Ex-Federal Reserve Chairman Paul Volcker has asked for 'some shred of evidence linking financial innovation with a benefit to the economy'. As far as he's concerned, the only socially useful banking invention of the last twenty-five years has been the cashpoint.[174] Meanwhile, factions within the Tea Party movement loudly agitate for a return to the gold standard.

Yet capitalism is the most successful economic system that has ever been tried. Across the fast-growing nations, the expansion of the capitalist market economy has brought billions of people out of grinding poverty. No amount of aid can replace the increased prosperity that such an expansion of commerce and trade can bring. But the system risks being discredited if the spoils of capitalism go to a small few who in turn are supported by the taxpayer.

Central to this task of defending the fruits of capitalism is to restore public trust in the financial system and ensure all have a chance to benefit from those fruits.

Other professions enjoy widespread public trust to perform tasks that are too complicated for most of us to contemplate. Eighty-eight per cent of the public trust doctors to perform the most intricate of operations on our own bodies, but less than 30 per cent trust bankers with our money. We might not comprehend all the complexities of modern medicine but a doctor's job is to ensure we understand the diagnosis and the treatment. Modern banking, by contrast, has all too often exploited the confusing nature of the financial system, as in the mis-selling of payment protection insurance, mortgage endowments, and 'risk free' investments, among other products. An opaque language was employed to bamboozle high-street customer and professional investor alike. It has now been found out.

A leading asset manager described a fellow fund manager with a hugely successful career in the City, who recently moved with his family to Geneva. His friend was not a banker, nor had he caused the crisis. Colleagues asked him why he had chosen to emigrate. Was it lighter regulation, or a more lenient tax regime? No. It was because he didn't want his child growing up in a society where people like him were regarded as little better than paedophiles. This man was probably worth about half a billion pounds to the Treasury.

A survey in Germany found that 22 per cent of people would least like a banker as a friend. To put it in context, this was only 2 per cent behind them wanting a convicted criminal, and 6 per cent behind a prostitute.

There are examples that buck this trend. Handelsbanken, the Swedish bank, has devolved responsibility to branch managers, so that tailored customer service is at the heart of the bank's business model. It boasts top rankings for customer satisfaction and has shown higher profitability than its average competitors. The empowered bank managers use their discretion and judgement to deal with clients that they know, while clients are able to deal with bankers they trust. But organisations like this are few and far between and public confidence in the finance sector is extremely low.

A new culture in banking is needed to ingrain the truth that public trust is as essential to finance as it is to medicine. For those who argue that banks, unlike hospitals, are private businesses, it is clear that the UK banking system cannot exist without taxpayer support. Furthermore, high street banks are utilities which provide an essential service; just like the water companies and railways. They currently benefit from a government insolvency guarantee worth an annual £100 billion in cheaper borrowing costs. The large banks could choose to divest themselves of the responsibilities that a public subsidy implies by breaking themselves up. But as long as they benefit from explicit or implicit taxpayer support, they should be expected to behave in a spirit of gratitude and reciprocity to their subsidisers.

This book has examined the crisis from a human perspective, whether the behaviour of the fools in the corner, who warned of an impending crisis; or the powerfully destructive relationship between debt and asset values built on a flawed modelling culture that would eventually cause a great calamity; or the behaviour of those who shaped the flawed culture that held people to be rational and markets efficient, and thought authorities should not stop the build-up of a bubble, but merely clean up the debris afterwards.

This flawed culture needs to change. Human nature being what it is, that change will not be easy. But a more responsible, ethical, and trustworthy financial industry is vital, and can only be achieved through a change in culture. There have been encouraging steps to implement this shift on other policies at the heart of the government, with a behavioural insight team in the Cabinet Office producing important work on how best to shape policy to understand human behaviour. We need to take these insights and apply them to the financial world.

What, then, can we do to bring this understanding of human behaviour to bear to stop the crash happening again?

Economics Profession

The problems stem from a deep-rooted error in the economics profession. At its root, the assumptions that underpin economic analysis must be more sophisticated, and recognise how people behave. Some at the forefront of the profession have already realised this. But there is a danger that the new strands of behavioural economics do not go far enough. We need also to recognise the dynamics of human behaviour, and how policy and regulation itself is part of a complex adaptive system. So our first recommendation is that the significant resources of the economics profession must do less abstract modelling and do more to understand the dynamics of human behaviour, and that policymakers should take note.

To make this change we should understand how economists behaved as the world moved into the computer age. The economics profession, which was largely funded by the financial industry, harnessed the great silicone beast in pursuit of their models. Simple assumptions were made to explain human behaviour, so complex algorithms based on these simple assumptions could produce numerical results. The fatal flaw was that throughout the economics eco-system, economics students at universities around the world, graduate economists at banks and analysts inside the regula-tory bodies all built models based on the same assumption: that we are all rational human beings and will behave ration-ally. In computing such modelling is known as 'garbage in, garbage out'. Much of the output of economics was garbage. The models delivered a false 'objectivity' that provided false comfort in decision-making. This obsession with 'objectivity' would be fine, if it were not for the flaw in the assumptions.

It is a strength to accept we are all flawed, to accept the frailty of our knowledge, and to protect ourselves from hubris.

Those who defend these flawed assumptions argue that they are the best we can do. In terms of observing the system, this may have some merit. But to insert a flawed model into the system, and then base the system on its output as if gospel, is to undermine the system itself. As Warren Buffett put it, 'observing that markets were 90 per cent efficient, they concluded that markets were always efficient. The difference between the two propositions is night and day'.

The same arguments that determine this broad plea for change in economics apply equally to finance.

The understanding of the realities of the world set out in this book implies a different type of regulation, less based on detailed rules, and more focused on judgements about the big picture. The motivation for such regulation is that the decision of an individual firm may not always be in the best long-term interest of itself or of the system as a whole.

What does this mean in practice?

Reforming Banking Regulation

Given the central role of banks in the economy, there needs to be a new approach to regulation, based not on detailed rules, but on judgement. The UK's flawed tripartite regulatory system is set to be replaced by one that provides such prudential judgement in place of over-prescriptive rules. These changes, which are yet to become law, are vital to the long-term health of our economy.

The crisis has shown that the banks that go wrong tend to do so when they get the big picture wrong. This points towards the need for timely monitoring of the main features of systemically important financial institutions, and a regulator that has enough oversight to be able to implement counter-cyclical policy.

Such regulation should distinguish clearly between banks whose collapse can threaten the system, and the rest of finance that cannot.

Under the proposed approach, responsibility for financial stability will rest with the Bank of England, which will be given power as well as responsibility to protect the system as a whole.

Within the Bank, the Financial Policy Committee (FPC) has been created to join the Monetary Policy Committee in operating a panoramic view of the economy. Individual firms are explicitly excluded from its brief. Responsibility for the prudential viability of individual firms will sit with the Prudential Regulation Authority (PRA) and responsibility for their conduct with the Financial Conduct Authority (FCA). To ensure that valuable crisis experience from the FSA is not lost, the relevant FSA departments will be incorporated into these new bodies.

By combining street-level data from the two Authorities with its own macroeconomic perspective, the FPC will be in a far better position to identify instability as and when it begins to contaminate the system, and to assess the impact of regulatory decisions on the system as a whole. At the same time, the new regulatory bodies created within the Bank will have privileged access to information held by the Bank of

England that would not normally be available to government departments or regulators.

In other words the regulators have knowledge of the Bank's private banking operations and the data it uses to analyse monetary policy. Most importantly of all, they will know which institutions have been receiving discrete injections of cash from the Bank. At the same time, the two bodies monitoring individual firms will relay the raw microeconomic data they gather in their routine contact with the market back to Threadneedle Street. Suspicious patterns emerging on balance sheets, unusual concentrations of risk, a high dependence on particularly volatile financial instruments – this kind of information can only be obtained on a firm-by-firm basis – which is why there will need to be regular exchanges of intelligence up and down the chain of command.

The FPC will enforce its decisions by issuing recommendations and directions to the PRA and FCA. This is where the vital element of discretion will be applied. Rather than following a pre-conceived rulebook, the onus will be on the Committee members to decide how they implement their objective of ensuring UK financial stability. Crucially, this freedom will allow them to reward good behaviour and punish bad. So they could allow banks which can demonstrate they are behaving less riskily to hold lower levels of capital. Unlike the FSA, the FPC will face the tension between financial stability and economic management head-on. There will be debate, discussion and transparency.

Under its new responsibilities, the Bank of England could, for example, introduce a control centre, tracking the financial health of big players in real time. Not only would the authorities then have a clear picture of the state of the system at any moment, but this would force the banks themselves to have full real time management data to hand, which too often they do not.

Such a control centre might track, for example, the ratio of equity to assets, banks' liquidity, and gross exposure to derivative contracts. Just as the Mayor of New York has a screen displaying crime hotspots and statistics in his office, a screen tracking these statistics in real-time in the Bank of England would serve as a strong visual reminder of the state of the system. It would help inform the Bank and the FPC in its deliberations about the up-to-the-minute health of the system.

Crucially, giving the Bank the power to act will allow it to give ethical and practical leadership to the development of a new culture in finance.

It is a concern that proposed EU financial regulation appears to be heading in precisely the opposite direction, attempting ever more complex rules to regulate complex problems. This fundamentally misunderstands that complex, adaptive systems require simple regulation to avoid an ever more spirals of complexity.

Clearly, on a similar basis, the rating agencies and the international accounting bodies need reform in recognition of the role they play in the plumbing of the financial system. They must be more accountable if they are to retain legitimacy.

Likewise within fiscal policy, the Treasury's necessary discretion needs to be embedded in a strong institutional framework. The creation of the independent Office for Budget Responsibility (OBR) has been widely recognised as an important step in separating judgements over the likely future path of the economy and public finances from the political judgements over what policy to pursue as a consequence. The OBR's job is to provide independent and authoritative analysis of the UK's public finances. The government sets itself fiscal objectives, and the OBR makes an independent assessment of its likelihood of meeting them. Its existence will finally put an end to the Treasury's habit of marking its own exam papers.

In George Orwell's *1984*, Winston Smith writes in his diary, 'Freedom is the freedom to say that two plus two make four.' The OBR's purpose is to reinstitute that truth, after a period in which Treasury Ministers insisted the answer was five.

This new framework will strengthen the institutional structures around the three key areas of macroeconomic policy. Narrow inflation targeting will be complemented by the ability of the Bank of England to regulate directly the size of balance sheets. Fiscal policy will be put on a stronger footing to allow judgements to be made against a credible backdrop free from political interference.

Reforming Corporate Governance

But reform of the regulatory rules and the structure of banks alone will not be enough. One consequence of recognising that humans are not always rational is that we must recognise that regulators will fail. Recent experience confirms this, in spades.

So we must put in place systems to ensure that finance can survive regulatory failure. So far, the focus has rightly been on resolution regimes, so-called 'living wills', and the structure of the banking industry.

These are very important. A 'living will' is a battle-plan for bankruptcy. As Sir Andrew Large foresaw, the crisis was exacerbated by the labyrinthine complexity of the failed banks' exposures. There were so many counterparties, occupying positions both on- and off-balance-sheet, that it was impossible for other players to know where the write-downs would fall. Panic rapidly overtook the system and the result was a credit crunch. Resolution regimes attempt to head this problem off in advance by requiring the bank, in co-operation with the regulators, to detail all its exposures and plan for liquidation. It may be a morbid exercise for CEOs, but a healthy corrective to the hubris some of them are prone to.

For living wills to be credible in advance, systemically significant banks need to be able to be wound up in the event of default. It is hard to see how this can be possible for a bank with a balance sheet larger than the UK's annual economy. Indeed, during the crash, banks didn't even know their own positions, and the quality of management information in the biggest nationalised banks was shocking.

That means tackling the structure of the big banks in the UK. Banks should not be able to cross subsidise by taking the capital they hold to protect the deposits of millions of retail savers up and down the country, and use that capital to subsidise their investment banking operations. Banks hold capital for a purpose: to mitigate against losses, so that when things go badly they do not go bust. Banks that hold savings and use those savings to fund loans to businesses and mortgages for homeowners are an important utility in any economy. For the time being, these operations are explicitly or implicitly underwritten by the taxpayer, to ensure millions do not lose their lifetime savings. Running these banks is an act of stewardship, not entrepreneurship. So the capital put aside to support utility operations should be kept within those utility operations. To use that capital to support investment banking amounts to a subsidy. Making this change would not just increase the likelihood of the utilities surviving tough economic times, but also make it easier to protect savers if a bank collapses. The ringfence should be designed to include deposits that are given this protection, and exclude everything else.

Big banks may not like the idea of removing these subsidies from their investment banking operations, but until this happens, they cannot claim to compete in a free market.

The case for smaller banks is strengthened by the fact that the collapse of a large bank has a disproportionately bigger impact on the economy, when rescuing or resolving a bank risks increasing the government's own borrowing costs. Furthermore, there is little evidence recent mergers have improved efficiencies through economies of scale, and so little support for size even on its own grounds. All of this supports the need to reverse the sharp reduction in the number of competitors in the UK banking industry.

But the human analysis of the crash has shown that culture, personal responsibility, and social context are as necessary as the formal rules that surround banks.

These can be changed through leadership, including at the level of the firm. Edmund Burke said that all that is necessary for the triumph of evil is that good men do nothing. Leadership matters in finance as much as in any other area of life, to shape the boundaries of acceptable norms of behaviour. Such cultural boundaries can provide an important bulwark against some of the extremes that we have seen.

The rules of corporate governance can be used to strengthen a culture of responsibility, and shape incentives.

A Public Protagonist

A repeated defence of the current limited liability system is that shareholders can hold management to account and approve their decisions. Yet evidence shows that takeovers rarely add value, and shareholders very rarely vote down management proposals. Even a minor revolt of, say, 10 per cent of shareholders is considered unusually abrasive.

Many have argued for more shareholder activism. But progress has been slow.

Perhaps that's not surprising. Herding behaviour reduces the likelihood that people will stick out from the crowd.

In other areas of life, this problem is addressed by a public protagonist who, on behalf of society, challenges proposals and tests arguments. In the House of Commons we have an

Official Opposition, with a leader paid a Cabinet Minister's salary and given a research budget. Tribunals provide a voice for each side of the argument. In criminal law, public prosecutors make the case. Given the crisis we have just lived through, there is no reason why the public should not also have a representative to improve corporate governance.

To strengthen the effective power of shareholders, a public protagonist would have the authority to convene special shareholder meetings on behalf of the public, and publically test a course of action contemplated by the management. The management would of course remain under their obligation to shareholders, but shareholders would now hear both sides of any argument. Faced with this challenge, and with their monopoly on the supply of information to shareholders broken, a culture of challenge would be strengthened, and the senior executive would consider their options more carefully.

To increase this culture of challenge, a new resolution regime in which bondholders expect to lose out from a bank failure will also ensure bondholders take a more active interest in the banks they fund. After all, those who lend to other companies in trouble expect a call from the bank. The same discipline should apply more to the banks themselves.

Punishment for failure

In the UK no senior banker has been brought to trial for authorising the decisions which brought down their institutions. Regulators' investigations of the crash found that since no rules were broken, no action should be taken.

Even taken at face value this is a dubious assertion.

In December 2010, an FSA investigation into the mismanagement of RBS concluded that although 'bad decisions' were taken, they 'were not the result of a lack of integrity by any individual', nor did they 'identify any instances of fraud or dishonest activity by RBS senior individuals or a failure of governance on the part of the Board'.[175] It later emerged that during the course of the investigation the FSA had not even interviewed the full board of RBS, several of whom claimed, through their lawyers, that they had 'nothing to say' on the subject of their own bank's demise. Those who were interviewed were not asked for their own views on why RBS had failed – as though this was somehow irrelevant to the investigation. Sir Fred Goodwin was only interviewed once. When the Treasury Select Committee got wind of this, the FSA was embarrassed into re-issuing its interview requests, this time with attendance made compulsory. Owing to various legal obstacles the report which resulted from this investigation has yet to see the light of day. At the time of writing it is due to be released in October 2011.

We know that the banks performed inadequate stress tests, and concealed their risks in off-balance-sheet vehicles. Since both were perfectly legal, if irresponsible, this is not where the case for prosecution would lie. A more fruitful area of investigation would be whether the banks knowingly misled investors, regulators and each other as to the true nature of their profits and exposures. Since the courts have ruled that they misled tens of thousands of customers over PPI in their high street branches, it is not inconceivable that a simultaneous deception was going on at a wholesale level, where the rewards were greater.

For the future, to imbue a culture of responsibility and mitigate against rewards for failure, the most important change is to end the immunity which seems to surround the senior management of failed banks. Professional negligence can be prosecuted in other walks of life. The multi-million-pound No Win No Fee industry depends on that fact. If a restaurant gives a customer food poisoning because of the incompetence of the chef then the owner becomes liable, even if he or she is not personally involved with the food preparation. Pleading ignorance is no excuse. A restaurant owner makes it his business to ascertain the quality of the ingredients, and ensure a high standard of food hygiene, in part because he knows he can be prosecuted if he cuts corners and face prison. Likewise election agents face imprisonment for serious breaches of electoral law. Why should financial institutions be treated differently? The failure of big banks poisons the whole economy. It is vital that the senior management of banks bother to find out where their loans come from, and to whom they are sold. The senior management of systemically important financial institutions should be liable for prosecution if their institution becomes insolvent.

As a stronger barrier to more reckless behaviour, acts of extreme negligence should be treated as imprisonable offences. The threat of prison as a result of some of the more egregious acts of greed would help change the culture of finance.

Non-Executive Directors and Sanctions for Failure

The third strand of improving corporate governance is to strengthen boards. Currently, too many boards are weak. Non-executives are rightly at one stage removed, but most spend little time at each company they are supposed to be directing. While the right non-executive board member can undoubtedly bring experience to bear, they are rarely across details of strategy, or able to hold executives effectively to account. Yet as we have seen, the direction of systemically important banks can have critical consequences for our whole economy. The non-executive directors of these large banks should put their full focus on direction and strategy. It is a full-time job. And to deal with rewards for failure, the sanctions for failure should be more significant.

As the crisis unfolded, non-executive directors successfully evaded much of the criticism leveled at the management. There needs to be a more proportionate distribution of responsibility, with boards collectively bearing the repercussions of their failure. Recent research into the psychology of gang culture yields crucial insights. In Glasgow, a new approach to tackling gang-related violence has proven effective. Studies show that one of the most effective ways of changing individual behaviour is to alter the social norms in which choices are made. If a member of a known gang kills someone, the entire gang will be targeted by police. Assigning guilt by association provides groups with a powerful incentive to re-fashion their social norms. As a report explains, 'punishment is replicated in the same way as the delinquent behaviour was – through the social norm of gang membership'. Similarly, if a bank blows up, everyone on the board should be liable, not just the CEO and Chairman. This would act as an incentive for boards to regulate their own behaviour.

Currently the law states that a director cannot be legally barred from sitting on the board of a corporate institution unless that institution has become insolvent. It is ironic that the one type of company which the state effectively guarantees against bankruptcy is a bank. The law should be changed so that any financial institution requiring recourse to public funds to prevent insolvency is *de facto* bankrupt. This will prevent the current situation whereby directors, both executive and non-executive, are permitted to hop from one job to the next in the wake of disaster.

We need non-executive directors (NEDs) to treat their positions less like a pension plan and more like a job. The Walker Review, a government-commissioned report on the state of corporate governance in the UK financial services industry, found that the typical time commitment of an NED at a major British bank was just 25 days a year.[176] Sir David Walker recommended an increased time commitment.

But his recommendation does not go far enough. NEDs should be in the bank several times a month, asking the executive management difficult questions and demanding answers. This requires both time and focus. Take a quick glance at the CVs of many RBS non-executive directors in 2007 and it looks unlikely that they could have had their minds fully on the job. Bob Scott, for example, was Chairman of Yell, a director of both Swiss Reinsurance Company and Jardine Lloyd Thompson, a trustee of the Crimestoppers Trust, and an advisor to Duke Street Capital Private Equity, all the while sitting on the board of Pension Insurance Corporate Holdings. To tackle this, non-executive directors of systemically important banks should spend more time in the banks that they govern, and should only be allowed to hold one directorship. Non-executive directorships of less important public companies should also be capped.

Public companies' remuneration committees are also too often drawn from a small group of people who directly and indirectly end up setting each others' pay. The conflicts of interest are obvious and unacceptable, and should be ended.

These changes would make the task of being a non-executive director more onerous. But this will not lead to a shortage of applications. In other professions, those in a position of trust are held accountable for their actions. If doctors are found guilty of serious malpractice then they are struck off the medical register. Would anyone suggest that this system of punishing professional failure has resulted in the mass exodus of Britain's best medical talent? The boards of systemically important financial institutions are placed in a similar position of social responsibility. If we want them to behave like professionals they must be treated as such. This means negligence, and gross incompetence, must be met with serious sanction.

Co-CEOs

Sir Fred Goodwin's purchase of ABN Amro is now seen as a strategic and tactical mistake; the wrong deal at very much the wrong time. Our proposed Public Protagonist may have given shareholders the opportunity to question and perhaps halt the deal, but it should never have got that far in the first place. In reality, the board should have scrutinised such a deal. Unless the minutes of RBS's board meetings are published, we'll never know how open to challenge Sir Fred's decisions were. But evidence and anecdote seem to suggest that the cult of personality surrounding most bank Chief Executives and the culture of the average boardroom mean that there is little opportunity for non-executives to challenge.

A simple solution to resolve this is to shift the role of the Chief Executive.

When Nadhim Zahawi launched YouGov, it was a partnership. He and Stephan Shakespeare began the business in a shed, and together built it into a company ready to be listed on the stock exchange. The title on their business cards read Co-Chief Executive and there was both a formal and informal recognition that the business was managed by two equals. There was no jostling for position or authority between either of them, but there were at times disagreements and challenges. All of these were played out openly through their joint, glass-walled office.

However, when they first talked to investment banks about their listing, their first unanimous piece of advice was to pick a Chief Executive. 'The City won't like it,' they were told. 'Institutional investors want to know that a company has strong leadership. Without a single Chief Executive, how will they know who to listen to?' was the view in another meeting. They were given an ultimatum: choose one of you or we will find you a new one.

In the end, Zahawi took on the role. But he feels strongly

that the co-CEO approach to management was beneficial to the challenge-friendly culture of both the business and the board. If board members are used to seeing the Co-Chief Executives being challenged by their counterparts, then there is an unspoken authority for others in the business and boardroom to do the same.

YouGov wasn't the only business to be co-founded and come across this problem. Google, the business that was doing things differently, was co-founded by Larry Page and Sergey Brin. But as the business began to head towards flotation it hired Eric Schmidt, a tech industry insider, first as Executive Chairman and then as CEO. While the company's SEC filings stated that Schmidt, Page and Brin ran Google as a triumvirate, it was clear that it was Schmidt who had the legal responsibilities of CEO.

But having co-CEOs is a successful model where it has been allowed to remain. Goldman Sachs has adopted a co-senior partner approach to its corporate governance structure. Even as a public company, it continues to have a number of co-heads of department at board level and retains co-CEOs for its international business.

YouGov is still reaping the benefits of its original co-CEO structure. In 2008, three years after YouGov's flotation, Zahawi was pursuing a £160m acquisition of a US research and polling firm. He was challenged by the board to ensure that the deal made financial sense. Eventually, he aborted it. It may have cost over a million pounds in fees, but Zahawi maintains it is one of the best business decisions the company ever made. The target is now worth a mere fraction of that value. The freedom of the YouGov board to challenge its CEO has its roots in the original co-CEO structure.

For real change in boardroom and organisational culture, the City and its institutional investors need to change their views on the suitability of co-Chief Executives.

Reforming Pay

The culture of an organisation is affected by its leadership, but the wider incentive structure is also crucial. Far from being an expression of robust, globalised competition, the current system of pay incentives cushions senior executives against the effects of poor decision-making and encourages careers in certain parts of finance over others. At its worst it resembles the world of monopolies and cartels which Adam Smith wrote the *Wealth of Nations* in protest against. To foster a culture of more responsible risk management these rewards for failure must be unraveled and managers given something to fear.

In the extreme, a very direct means of re-introducing the concept of personal liability would be to abolish limited liability, but this is not practical.

There has been a valuable debate about paying people in contingent convertible bonds, known as CoCos. These are debt instruments which automatically convert from bonds to shares when a bank's capital ratio sinks beneath a certain level. Because the share price of a bank on the rocks will likely be very low, the value of the CoCo will plummet once it has metamorphosed into equity form. This would mean senior management would see the value of their bonus pool evaporate in the event of a bank failure, and in principle the banks could rely on the bonds for equity capital in a crisis.

Linked to this is the suggestion of shrinking the bonus pool whenever a bank's credit rating is downgraded. This suggestion is valuable, but would also require wholesale reform of the credit ratings agencies themselves. The conflicts of interest in rating agencies would only get worse if personal pay was linked to ratings. It is also untimely. Financial crises may be many years in the making, and the labour market within the financial services industry is notoriously fluid. By the time the bank's credit rating is downgraded, the original architects of its downfall may be long gone. It would be too little, too late.

Using behavioural insights, it is possible to bring loss aversion and the concept of 'house money' to bear. Most people fear loss more than they seek gain. So bonuses should be subject to clawbacks over a long period like 10 years. By actually making the payment, the fear of losing the cash, especially if spent, would kick in. Bankers' families would act as a further constraint on risk seeking behaviour. It would be minimally intrusive but would provide sufficient reassurance to the public that all actions have consequences. In the eighteenth century, stock-brokers who wished to trade on the London Stock Exchange were required to put up a hefty subscription fee. If any brokers was found guilty of financial malpractice their subscription would be seized and distributed to charity. This idea of a clawback should be resurrected.

There is also an opportunity to exploit the widespread status anxiety which characterises the financial services industry. In the years before the crisis, Jamie Dimon, CEO of JPMorgan, took steps to raise the prestige of his risk managers by increasing their pay relative to that of the bank's traders. Previously, in some banks, risk managers' pay had absurdly been set by the very traders whose risks they were paid to manage. In the world of finance where prestige and authority are so closely related to pay, this levelled playing field is an important component of supporting financial stability.

Reforming the Masculine Culture

Sex also matters in the City. We have argued that the evidence shows that existing policy reinforces differences in gender, which impacts negatively on business. So what would a policy that understands and respects human behaviour look like?

Equal Pay

The first area to address is remuneration. Legislation for equal pay is in place, but enforcement requires transparency. Equal pay audits have a positive impact, but fewer than a quarter of organisations have undertaken one. Only 3 per cent of organisations regularly monitor starting salaries by gender.[177]

Pay audits would strengthen the principle of rewards on merit. We have seen how people have a natural tendency to promote and reward those similar to themselves. Where women are largely absent, this leads to a self-reinforcing culture of male dominance that works against meritocracy.

The average salary and bonus in banks should be published for each grade, broken down by gender. Such transparency would itself help break a biased culture. A clearer, published, framework for bonus awards would help ensure the level of each bonus would be more dependent on genuine individual performance.

Parental Leave

Another area in need of reform is parental leave. The current system strengthens the bias against women in the workplace. Removing this bias will require a cultural shift so that it becomes normal for either parent to take time out to look after a baby, and so that career breaks are not limiting on a woman's career.

This argument for more balanced childcare is not to argue for equality for equality's sake. The roles men and women play in having children are conspicuously different; men do not get pregnant, give birth, or breastfeed. But these natural differences in behaviour are exacerbated by cultural stereotypes and reinforced by a law that strengthens the bias against women in the workplace.

So we support the proposal that eighteen weeks of leave will be ring-fenced for mothers around the time of the baby's birth, and two weeks will stay ring-fenced for fathers. The remaining amount of leave can be shared flexibly between either parent, to be structured as the couple chooses.

Women on Boards

These changes aim to get women to the top of finance. Evidence shows that greater diversity at senior levels of the single biggest determinant of behaviour – sex – brings direct improvements in business performance. Yet the male-dominated culture of corporate Britain holds these improvements back.

How can this deadlock best be broken? One of the best ways to make finance more attractive to women is for there to be more women in finance. The Davies Report in 2009 into women on boards showed that to reach a tipping point in terms of behaviour, a board needs 30 per cent of its members to be women.[178]

It is vital not to stifle growth in the economy after the seismic crash we have just survived. In countries like Norway, quotas have increased the percentage of women on boards by almost 30 per cent in nine years.[179] Boards should change to be made up of over 30 per cent women. If this requires boards to expand, as frequently happened in Norway, so be it. We need to tackle these problems without unduly burdening institutions. If the change does not happen on a non-statutory basis, Parliament should be prepared to legislate.

Until this happens, we call for a strong 'comply or explain' policy, where boards are forced to justify being less than 30 per cent female. Australia has used a similar policy since January 2011, and since the changes were announced, women have made up 27 per cent of all new board appointments, in contrast to 5 per cent within the same timeframe in 2009.[180] But we hold the threat of legislation over the industry if progress is not made.

The 30% Club explicitly campaigns for 30 per cent of

boards to be made up of women. They argue that this is not equality for equalities' sake, but is about making companies perform better.'

ↄↄ

In this book we have made ambitious recommendations that follow from our analysis of the crisis. We have made detailed recommendations about corporate governance, the need for more women in the City and Wall Street, the way we use technology to model economies, and the need for regulators willing and able to use discretion to allow finance safely to thrive.

All of these recommendations should support changing the culture to put morality into business decisions, and recognise the ethical context in which we all work.

Only then will we deliver a capitalist system that is fit for the challenges of a globalised world.

EPILOGUE

This book is about human behaviour. We have tried to bring together insights from a wide variety of fields to understand how people actually behave. Our motivation was to try to understand more deeply why the financial crisis of the early twenty-first century happened, and what we need to change to reverse the trend of increasingly frequent financial crises.

In studying behaviour, and applying the lessons to finance, we have been struck by the similarities with other areas of life. Perhaps it should have been obvious that the patterns of behaviour behind the financial crisis also lie behind other scandals. The context was different, of course, and the details equally unpredictable, but the patterns and dynamics were remarkably similar.

Time and again we have seen skewed incentives; optimism bias; short termism; the herding of the crowd; social norms; loss aversion and the tipping point.

In the crisis of MPs' expenses, just as in banking, many people knew of the problem, a few spoke out, but no one wanted to listen. The problem grew and was ignored, as to tackle it would have meant exposing the wrongdoing. People hoped it would carry on as before. Then came the moment of crisis: the tipping point. The depth of the problems was clearly exposed. The vast majority who had followed the herd in their silence now followed the herd in their outrage. Just as in the banking crisis, injustices were done to some who had themselves done no wrong. But the system clearly needed to change. Very strong accountability now ensures discretion is applied responsibly. The rules were changed, and, more successfully than in finance, the social norm is now to claim as little as possible, so the culture has changed too.

The crisis of journalism brought about by the phone-hacking scandal is similar. After years in which only a tiny minority pursued the issue, shocking details of crimes have been brought vividly to life. The herd has tipped from wide-spread silence to widespread condemnation. In its wake the reputation of all journalists – responsible and irresponsible – has suffered. But it is clear to all that the rules must change, and the culture too. Likewise the riots of August 2011, while on a different scale of criminality, demonstrated typical dynamics of human behaviour – herding, green and short-termism – combined with a lack of responsibility.

One thread ties each of these cases together. They follow the relaxation of stricter cultural constraints, and a breakdown of social norms that previously promoted self-responsibility. A similar, widespread culture of amorality led to maximising claims, invading privacy, and irresponsible lending.

By the very nature of human behaviour described in this book, it is impossible to predict where this pattern will strike next. In the economic sphere the crisis of bank default has become a crisis of sovereign default. Where the crisis is most acute, in the eurozone, current policies are clearly not sustainable. The future path will be a product of group dynamics within eurozone governments, political systems, and ultimately populations. The debts owed by eurozone governments to banks, including British banks, are vast, and almost half of our exports are to the eurozone, so we have an acute interest. Throughout history, attempts at currency unions have led to either full fiscal union, or break-up. It is not possible to know how this attempt will play out.

Our conclusions for UK policy are both broad and humble. Broad, in that the whole culture of finance needs to change to learn the full lessons from the crisis. We are emphatically not naively saying that human nature must somehow be changed; rather that the cultural and social context in which people act is a crucial part of the system. Leadership and strong institutions are required.

Just as broadly, it is clear that the economics profession has gone for many decades down an increasingly narrow alley of mathematical precision. That direction must be reversed if we are effectively to use the great advances in technical capability and computing power to understand how economies really work. This has started. But understanding individuals' behaviour is necessary but not sufficient: we also need to understand the dynamics of group behaviour, on which all economies are based.

All people are flawed. All behave at times in irrational ways. So we need to design policy to deal effectively with these inevitable flaws. Hence the focus on strong institutions, on social norms, on stronger governance, on meritocracy, and on better incentives and modesty in rewards.

Do not mistake this for a left-wing critique. Even much of the British left now acknowledges the failure of big-state Fabianism, with its perfect trust in central control over an ever-expanding part of our lives, and perfect distrust of everyone else.

It is essentially conservative to argue that capitalism is based on just rewards, not a one-way bet. That free markets need frameworks not a laissez-faire free-for-all. And that barriers to equal opportunity should be brought down, so that the rewards of capitalism can be fairly shared. Crucially, conservatives instinctively understand that regulators are themselves flawed, and that the law of unintended consequences is unfortunately one of the most powerful laws there is.

In short, this is a case for a stronger framework to ensure a genuinely competitive market can flourish.

Indeed it is a failure of capitalism to allow power to be accumulated, subsidies extracted and competition stymied by private monopolies as much as by the state. A truly free market should promote innovative new entrants and allow market leaders to be challenged. The new government has begun to introduce an understanding of human behaviour into its work. Early results are very impressive: understanding how people behave really does help improve policy. But understanding of these issues is not yet embedded or widespread, and application has been in micro-initiatives. Nudge is not enough. Broader understanding of the dynamics of human behaviour needs to be applied more widely.

Supporters of capitalism must get this right or risk the destructive solutions of the left or far right gaining ground.

The important recent steps to rebuild the UK's economic framework are a crucial move in the right direction, and will reduce the danger of a similar crash. The programme of deficit reduction, the tax on bank balance sheets, the newly independent OBR, and the proposal to embed discretionary power over financial policy in the FPC represent the most significant overhaul of the economic framework in a generation.

The new FPC has yet to act to make financial policy less pro-cyclical. European proposals on financial regulation go in the opposite direction, proposing complex rules to tackle complex systems that apply to the UK despite it being out of the eurozone. To change the culture in finance, we must change the way big banks are governed so shareholders are more active and better informed. We must be modest, though, about the chances of changing culture through shareholders, and so strengthen boards, and strengthen sanctions for those who behave recklessly. More widely, these findings support changes to the education system and other public services to devolve power and let innovation flourish.

None of these changes will tackle the problems Britain faces overnight. Nor will they stop bubbles or crises in future, for bubbles and crises are inevitable.

But they can help reduce the frequency of crises and help to stop the next crisis being so bad.

It is often said that the next really big crisis happens when the last crisis has just receded from the memory of those who lived through it. To push the next crisis back we must learn the lessons of the past. We hope this book adds to the learning of those lessons, and we hope to be around long enough to warn of them for many decades to come.

NOTES

Chapter 2: Fools in the Corner

1   Shakespeare, William, *King Lear*, I.i.l.51
2   *The Times*, 28 January 2006
3   Large, Sir Andrew, 'Financial Stability Oversight, Past and Present', speech, 2004
4   Ibid.
5   IMF Seminar, 7 September 2006
6   Searle, A., 'Group psychology, valuable lessons from our "new-fangled" subject', Psychology Review (1996), 2, 34
7   McNeill, William, *Keeping Together in Time: Dance and Drill in Human History* (London: Harvard University Press, 1995), p.2
8   Interview with Adair Turner, 21 April 2011
9   *Sunday Times*, 29 April 2008
10   *The Times*, 1 January 2010
11   TSC Written Evidence, Bank Crisis, published 17 March 2009
12   *The Independent*, 'Tony Dye: Controversial Fund Manager', 17 March 2008
13   Galbraith, J. K., *The Great Crash 1929* (London: Hamish Hamilton, 1955)
14   Ibid.
15   Testimony of Harry Markopolos before US Senate of Representatives, 4 February 2009
16   Tuckett, David, 'Addressing the Psychology of Financial Markets', IPPR paper, May 2009

Chapter 3: Tipping the Bandwagon

17   Business Insider, 'Why I am an optimist', 29 November 2009

18   Bloomberg, 'Arming Goldman Sachs with Pistols', 3 December 2009l

19   Private Interview

20   Interview with Stephen King

21   *Financial Times*, 13 August 2007

22   S&P/Case-Shiller House Price Index

23   *Financial Times*, 15 August 2007

24   Bloomberg, 21 June 2007

25   Bloomberg Data

26   *Reuters*, 'Factbox: A brief history of Lehman Brothers', 13 September 2008

27   Haldane, Andrew, 'Rethinking the financial network', speech, April 2009

28   *Sunday Times*, 'Lehman Brothers collapse sends shock-wave round world', 16 September 2008

29   *Daily Mail*, 'City Focus: then there were two', 16 September 2008

30   Newsweek, 'Depression Economics', 2 December 2008

31   Plato, *Republic*, p.492

32   Darley, John M. & Latané, Bibb, *Bystander Intervention in Emergencies: Diffusion of Responsibility* (New York: Columbia University Press, 1968)

33   Interview with Stephen King

34   Private Interview

35   Interview with Adair Turner, 21 April 2011

36   Tett, Gillian, *Fool's Gold* (Little Brown, 2009), p.35

37   Ibid.

38   Haldane, Andrew, 'Rethinking the financial network', speech, April 2009

39   *Financial Times*, 'The game-changer', 28 January 2009

40   Bean, Charlie, 'Some Lessons for Monetary Policy
     from the Recent Financial Turmoil', speech, 22
     November 2008

Chapter 4: The Dangers of Business As Usual

41   Private Interview
42   Private Interview
43   Private Interview
44   Private Interview
45   *Psychology Today,* 'Does Alcoholics Anonymous work
     because it's a form of Cognitive Behavioural Therapy?',
     20 July 2010
46   *Financial Times,* 'Financial Leaders pledge excellence
     and integrity', 28 September 2010
         Signed by: Marcus Agius, Chairman, Barclays;
     Sir Winfried Bischoff, Chairman, Lloyds Banking
     Group; Mark Garvin, Chairman, JPMorgan UK;
     Chris Gibson-Smith, Chairman, London Stock
     Exchange; Richard Gnodde, Co-Chief Executive
     Officer, Goldman Sachs; Colin Grassie, Chief
     Executive Officer UK, Deutsche Bank; Stephen
     Green, Group Chairman, HSBC; John Griffith-Jones,
     Managing Partner, KPMG; Sir Philip Hampton,
     Chairman, Royal Bank of Scotland Group; Lord
     Levene of Portsoken, Chairman, Lloyd's of London;
     Harvey McGrath, Chairman, Prudential; Mark Otty,
     Managing Partner, Ernst & Young; Stuart Popham,
     Senior Partner, Clifford Chance; Ian Powell, Managing
     Partner, PricewaterhouseCoopers; Lord Sharman of
     Redlynch, Chairman, Aviva; John Stewart, Chairman,
     Legal and General; Sir David Walker, Senior Advisor,
     Morgan Stanley.
47   TSC Oral Evidence, 11 January 2011, Q535

48 *The Telegraph*, 'US would have shut Barclays' Protium;
    Regulators would have closed arm had the bank not
    done so itself', 6 June 2011
49 Joseph Rowntree Foundation, 'Shaping or Shadowing:
    Understanding and Responding to Housing Market
    Change;, 2007, p.9
50 *Channel 4 News*, 11 October 2010
51 *Daily Mail*, 30 September 2008
52 *Sunday Times*, 'Bye bye, Buy to Let?', 5 October 2008
53 *Wall Street Journal*, 'Madoff Claims Lure Bankers', 17
    June 2011
54 *Daily Mirror*, 16 February 2011
55 Private Interview
56 Miller, Marcus, Weller, Paul & Zhang, Lei, 'Moral Hazard
    and the US Stock Market: Analysing the "Greenspan
    Put"', non-technical summary, p.3
57 Seldon, Anthony & Lodge, Guy, *Brown at 10* (London:
    Biteback Publishing, 2010) p.141
58 *Financial Times*, 'After the storm comes a hard climb',
    14 July 2009
59 AQ research, 11 November 2009
60 Private Interview
61 Brooks, David, *The Social Animal* (London: Random
    House, 2011), p.303

Chapter 5: Forever Blowing Bubbles

62 Reinhart, Carmen M. & Rogoff, Kenneth S., *This Time
    is Different – Eight Centuries of Financial Folly* (New
    York: Princeton University Press, 2009), p.87
63 *The Times*, 20 January 2009
64 Chicago Reserve Bank, 'Economic Perspectives', QII,
    2009, pp.18–37
65 Minsky, Hyman P., *Financial Instability Revisited: the
    Economics of Disaster*, Washington: Board of Governors
    of the Federal Reserve System, 1964

66 Turner, Adair, 'What do banks do, what should they do and what public policies are needed to ensure best results for the real economy?', lecture, CASS Business School, 17 March 2010

67 Balen, Malcolm, *A Very English Deceit* (London: Fourth Estate, 2002)

68 Hansard, House of Commons

69 Ibid.

70 Interview with Adair Turner, 21 April 2011

71 Galbraith, J. K., *The Great Crash 1929* (London: Hamish Hamilton, 1955), p.29

72 Haldane, Andrew, 'Capital Discipline', AEA, 9 January 2011

Chapter 6: Irrational Economists

73 Leeson, Nick, *Rogue Trader* (London: Little Brown, 1996), p.63

74 http://prospect-theory.behaviouralfinance.net/

75 *New York Times*, 'A Conversation with Daniel Kahneman on Profit Loss and the Mysteries of the Mind', 5 November 2002

76 Quoted in: Orrell, David, *Economyths: 10 Ways Economics Gets It Wrong* (Canada: John Wiley and Sons, 2010), p.111

77 Ferguson, Niall, *The Ascent of Money* (London: Penguin Press, 2008)

78 http://www.derivativesstrategy.com/magazine/archive/1999/0499fea1.asp

79 *Economy and Society*, volume 32, number 3, 'Long-Term Capital Management and the sociology of arbitrage', August 2003, pp.349–380

80 *Wired*, 'Recipe for Disaster: the formula that killed Wall Street', 23 February 2009

81 Gray, John, 'The Original Modernisers' in *Gray's Anatomy* (London: Allen Lane, 2009), p.272

82   George Soros, 'Theory of Reflexivity', speech, MIT, 26 April 1994
83   Bank for International Settlements, data, 2006
84   *Financial Times*, 23 October 1998
85   Greenspan, Alan, 'Risk Transfer and Financial Stability', speech, 5 May 2005
86   *Prospect Magazine*, 27 August 2009
87   Ibid.
88   FSA, 'Statutory Objectives', FSMA, 2000
89   FSA, 'Fines Table' (http://www.fsa.gov.uk/Pages/About/Media/Facts/fines/index.shtml)
90   FSA, 'Facts and Figures' (http://www.fsa.gov.uk/Pages/About/Media/Facts/index.shtml)
91   BBC News, 6 May 1997
92   *The Independent*, 7 May 1997
93   *Financial Times*, 13 August 2007
94   'Greenspan Concedes to "Flaw" in His Market Ideology', http://www.bloomberg.com/apps/news?pid=newsarchive&sid=a7is5F_Do6No
95   Bernstein, Peter L., *Against the Gods: The Remarkable Story of Risk* (New York: John Wiley & Sons, 1998)

Chapter 7: Women on Top
96   *The Telegraph*, 'Insurance giant Munich Re admits it used prostitutes to reward staff', 19 May 2011; *The Guardian*, 'Prostitute-filled sex party was reward for German insurance salesmen', 19 May 2011
97   Pinker, Steven, *The Blank Slate: The Modern Denial of Human Nature* (Viking, 2002), p.340
98   Cranfield University, 'Female FTSE Index and Report 2010', p.16
99   Lord Davies, 'Women on Boards', February 2011, p.11
100 Coates, J. M. & Herbert, J., 'Endogenous steroids and financial risk taking on a London trading floor', April 2008

101 NIESR Report 2009, 'Employment and Earnings in the Finance Sector: a Gender Analysis', p.9

102 Ibid., p.17, table 3.7

103 TSC Oral Evidence, 14 October 2009, Q109

104 McKinsey & Company, 'Women Matter: Gender Diversity, a Corporate Performance Driver', 2007

105 Cranfield University, 'Female FTSE Index and Report 2010'

106 Civil service website

107 Cranfield University, 'Female FTSE Index and Report 2010', p.18

108 Ibid., Q78

109 TSC Oral Evidence, Q65, 14 October 2009

110 McKinsey & Company, 'Women Matter: Gender Diversity, a Corporate Performance Driver', 2007, p.8

111 TSC Oral Evidence, Q101, 14 October 2009

112 Brooks, David, *The Social Animal* (London: Random House, 2011), p.219

113 *The Telegraph*, 'Theo Paphitis from the Dragon's Den: Pregnant Women's Brains Turn to Mush', 3 June 2008

114 EHRC, 'Financial Services Inquiry: Sex Discrimination and gender pay gap report of the EHRC', 2009

115 eFinancial Careers, 'The Gender Pay Gap in Financial Services', p.3.

116 Lord Davies, 'Women on Boards', report, February 2011, p.29

117 Roth, Louise Marie, *Selling Women Short: Gender Inequality on Wall Street* (New York: Princeton University Press, 2006)

118 *The Telegraph*, 'Sexism in the City', 15 November 2009

119 Thompson, Venetia, *Gross Misconduct* (London: Simon & Schuster, 2010), p.33

120 *The Guardian*, 14 October 2009

121 *The Telegraph*, 'Sexism in the City', 15 November 2009

122 TSC Written Evidence, September 2009, 76

123 *The Independent*, 'Can women save the economy? At least give us a chance to try', 21 March 2009

124 *The Telegraph*, 'Sexism in the City', 15 November 2009

125 Sapienza, P., Zingales, L. & Maestripieri, D., 'Gender differences in financial risk aversion and career choices are affected by testosterone', PNAS, 2008, p.1

126 Barnes, J. P., Miller, D. C. & Schafer, W. D., 'Gender differences in risk taking: A meta-analysis', Psychological Bulletin 125, 1999, pp.367–383

127 *The Economist*, 'A kinder, gentler finance', 8 April 2010

128 Coates, J. M. & Herbert, J., 'Endogenous steroids and financial risk taking on a London trading floor', April 2008

129 This is in line with other scientific and economic research, e.g. Anna Dreber, economic researcher at Harvard Kennedy School, who found that appetite for risk correlated with testosterone level.

130 Coates, J. M. & Herbert, J., 'Endogenous steroids and financial risk taking on a London trading floor', April 2008

131 *New York Magazine*, 'What if women ran Wall Street?', 21 March 2010

132 www.barbarastcherbatcheff.com, 'Trading – No Job for a Nice Girl?', 19 October 2009

133 McKinsey & Company, 'Women Matter: Gender Diversity, a Corporate Performance Driver', 2008, p.14

134 Wilson, Nick & Altanlar, Ali, 'Director Characteristics, Gender Balance and Insolvency Risk: An Empirical Study', unpublished study, Leeds University Business School, 30 May 2009

135 Catalyst Report, 'The Bottom Line: Corporate Performance and Women's Representation on Boards', October 2007

136 TSC Oral Evidence, Dr Ferreira, 13 October 2009

137 Lord Davies, 'Women on Boards', report, February 2011, p.10

138 Ferrery, Michel, 'CAC 40: Les Enteprises feminisees resistant-elles mieux a la crise boursiere?', 2008

139 TSC Oral Evidence, Mr John Last, 14 October 2009, Q110

140 TSC Oral Evidence, Kat Banyard, 14 October 2009, Q39

Chapter 8: Rewards for Failure

141 *Sunday Times*, 26 February 2006

142 Baltussen, Guido, van den Assen, Martijn, Thaler, Richard & Post, Thierry, '*Deal or No Deal* – Decision Making under Risk in a Large Pay-off Game Show', *American Economic Review*, 98 (1), 2008, pp.38–71

143 Fahlenbrach, Rüdiger & Stulz, René M., 'Bank CEO Incentives and the Credit Crisis', August 2010

144 Bechara, Antoine, Damasio, Hanna, Tranel, Daniel & Damasio, Antonio, 'Deciding Advantageously Before Knowing the Advantageous Strategy', in *Science 'New Series'*, Vol. 275, No 5304, 28 February 1997, pp.1293–5

145 Miller, E. K. & Cohen, J. D., 'An integrative theory of prefrontal cortex function', in the *Annual Review of Neuroscience* (Stanford, 2001), p.167

146 Galbraith, J. K., *The Great Crash 1929* (London: Hamish Hamilton, 1955), p.11

147 Camerer, Colin, Lowenstein, George & Pralec, Drazen, 'Neuroeconomics: How neuroscience can inform economics', *Journal of Economic Literature*, vol. XLIII, March 2005

148 *The Times*, 22 March 2009

149 Ibid.

150 www.ianfraser.org, 'Fred's Downfall: Hubris Followed by Nemesis', 20 October 2008

151 Andrews, Holly, 'Snakes in Suits – Dealing with Psychopaths in the Workplace and the Boardroom', speech, 19 November 2010

152 *Sunday Times*, 20 January 2009, http://business.times-online.co.uk/tol/business/economics/article5549510.ece

153 *Financial Times*, 27 July 2011

154 *The Guardian*, 4 April 2009

155 *The Guardian*, 27 April 2011

156 www.uk.finance.yahoo.com

157 Haldane, Andrew, 'The Short Long', speech, May 2011

158 Peston, Robert, 'Peston's Picks', 11 January 2011

159 TSC Ninth Report, 2010/11, p.81

160 Friedman, Milton, 'The Social Responsibility of Business is to Increase its Profits', *New York Times* magazine, 13 September 1970

161 Rajan, R. G., *Fault Lines* (New York: Princeton University Press, 2010), p.130

162 De Botton, Alain, *Status Anxiety* (London: Hamish Hamilton, 2004)

163 The Independent, 'RBS starts new ear at £350m head office', 13 August 2005

164 *Prospect Magazine*, August 2009

165 Dyson, James, 'Ingenious Britain: Making the UK the leading hi-tech exporter in Europe', March 2010, p.42

Chapter 9: Rules, Discretion and the Importance of Institutions

166 *The Telegraph*, 11 May 2006

167 Turner, Adair, *Financial Times*, 7 December 2010, http://www.ft.com/cms/s/0/a56e3630-023d-11e0-aa40-00144feabdc0.html#axzz1SdU8EJ4E

168 *The Times*, 27 March 2008

169 TSC Fifth Report, 24 January 2008

170 HMT, Budget 2005, p.17

Chapter 10: So What Do We Do?

171 YouGov Survey, 17–18 July 2011

172 *The Guardian*, 29 June 2011

173 Pew Research Centre Report, 'End of Communism Cheered But Now With Reservations', 2 November 2009

174 *Wall Street Journal*, 8 December 2009

175 FSA Statement, 2 December 2010

176 Walker, David, 'A Review of Corporate Governance in UK Banks and Other Financial Industry Entities', 16 July 2009, p.46

177 EHRC, 'Financial Services Inquiry: Sex Discrimination and gender pay gap report of the EHRC', 2009, p.37

178 Ibid., p.8

179 Lord Davies, 'Women on Boards', February 2009, p.26

180 Ibid., p.27

BIBLIOGRAPHY

Reports, Papers, and Speeches

Barnes, J. P., Miller, D.C. and Schafer, W.D., 'Gender differences in risk taking: a meta-analysis', Psychological Bulletin 125, 1999

Bechara, A., Damasio, H., Trnael, D., and Damasio, A., 'Deciding Advantageously Before Knowing the Advantageous Strategy', Science New Series, 28 February 1997

Benabou, R., 'Groupthink: Collective Delusions in Organizations and Markets', NBER Working Paper No. 14764, March 2009

Catalyst, 'The Bottom Line: Corporate Performance and Women's Representation on Boards', October 2007

Coates, J. M. And Herbert, J., 'Endogenous steroids and financial risk taking on a London trading floor', April 2008

Cranfield University, 'Female FTSE Index and Report 2010'

Davies of Abersoch, Lord, 'Women on Boards', February 2011

Dyson, James, 'Ingenious Britain: Making the UK the leading high tech exporter in Europe', March 2010

Equality and Human Rights Commission, 'Financial Services Inquiry: Sex Discrimination and Gender Pay Gap Report of the EHRC', 2009

Ferrery, Michel, 'CAC 40: Les Enteprises feminisees resistant-elles mieus a la crise boursiere?', 2008

Fahlencrach, R. and Stulz, R., 'Bank CEO Incentives and the Credit Crisis', Swiss Finance Institute, Research Paper Series No. 9-27

Haldane, A., 'Rethinking the Financial Network', April 2009

Haldane, A., 'Capital Discipline', AEA, 9 January 2011

Haldane, A., 'The Short Long', May 2011

Lazarus, C., 'Does Alcoholics Anonymous work because it's a form of Cognitive Behavioural Therapy?', Psychology Today, 20 July 2010

Large, A., 'Financial Stability Oversight - Past and Present', LSE, January 2004

Large, A., 'Financial Stability: Managing Liquidity Risk in a Global System', 28 November 2005

NIESR, 'Employment and Earnings in the Finance Sector: a Gender Analysis', 2009

MacKenzie, D., 'Long-Term Capital Management and the Sociology of Arbitrage', Economy and Society, August 2003

McKinsey & Co, 'Women Matter: Gender Diversity, a Corporate Performance Driver', 2008

Miller, E.K. and Cohen, J.D., 'An integrative theory of prefrontal cortex function', Annual Review of Neuroscience (Stanford, 2001)

Miller, M., Weller, P. And Zang, L., 'Moral Hazard and the US Stock Market: Analysing the Greenspan Put', Royal Economic Society Journal, volume 112, 2002

Minsky, H.P., 'Financial Instability Revisited: the Economics of Disaster', Washington: Board of Governors of the Federal Reserve System, 1964

Rajan, R., 'Has Financial Development Made the World Riskier', Kansas City Federal Reserve Annual Symposium, Jackson Hole, Wyoming, August 2005

Roubini, N., 'The U.S. and Global Outlook', IMF Seminar Washington, D.C., 7 September 2006

Searle, A., group Psychology, valuable lessons from our "newfangled" subject', Psychology Review, 1966

Soros, G., 'theory of Reflexivity', MIT, 26 April 1994

Stringham, E., 'The Emergence of the London Stock Exchange as a Self-Policing Club', Journal of Private Enterprise, Vol. 17, No. 2, Spring 2002

Treasury Select Committee, tenth report 2009-2010

Treasury Select Committee, ninth report 2010-2011

Tuckett, D., 'Addressing the Psychology of Financial Markets', IPPR, May 2009

Turner, A., 'What do Banks Do, What should they do and What Public Policies are Needed to Ensure Best Results for the Real Economy?', Cass Business School, 17 March 2010

Turner, A., Mansion House Speech, 21 September 2010

Wilson, N. and Altanlar, A., 'Director Characteristics, Gender Balance and Insolvency Risk: An empirical study', unpublished study, Leeds University Business School, May 2009

Books

Ahamed, L., *Lords of Finance: 1929, The Great Depression, and the Bankers who Broke the World* (Windmill Books, 2010)

Akerlof, G.A. and Shiller, R.J., *Animal Spirits: How Human Psychology Drives the Economy, and Why It Matters for Global Capitalism* (Princeton University Press, 2010)

Aristotle, *Nicomachean Ethics*

Balen, M. *A Very English Deceit* (London: Fourth Estate, 2002)

Bernstein, P., *Against the Gods: The Remarkable Story of Risk* (New York: John wiley and Sons, 1998)

de Botton, A., *Status Anxiety* (London: Hamish Hamilton, 2004)

Brooks, D. *The Social Animal* (London: Random House, 2011)

Chang, H-J., *23 Things They Don't Tell You About Capitalism*, (Allen Lane, 2010)

Chapman, M., *Don't be fooled again* (Harlow: Pearson Education Limited, 2010)

Darley, J. & Latané, B. *Bystander Intervention in Energencies: diffusion of Responsibility* (New York: Columbia University Press, 1968)

Eichengreen, B., *Golden fetters* (OUP, 1996)

Ferguson, N., *The Ascent of Money* (London: Penguin Press, 2008)

Galbraith, J.K., *The Great Crash 1929* (London: Hamish Hamilton, 1955)

Gray, J., *Gray's Anatomy* (London: Allen Lane, 2009)

Harford, T., *Adapt: Why Success Always Starts With Failure* (Little, Brown, 2011)

King, S.D., *Losing Control, The Emerging Threats to Western Prosperity* (Yale, 2011)

Leeson, N. *Rogue Trader* (London: Little Brown, 1996)

Lodge, A. And Seldon, A., *Brown at 10* (London: Biteback Publishing, 2010)

Mason, P., *Meltdown* (Verso, 2009)

McNeill, W. *Keeping Together in Time: Dance and Drill in Human History* (London Harvard University Press, 1995)

Norberg, J. *Financial Fiasco: How America's Infatuation with Home Ownership and Easy Money Created the Economic Crisis* (Cato Institute, 2010)

Parker, D. And Stacey, R., *Chaos, Management and Economics* (London: IEA, 1994)

Peston, R., *Brown's Britain* (London: Short Books, 2005)

Pinker, S., *The Blank Slate: The Modern Denial of Human Nature* (Viking, 2002)

Plato, *Republic*

Rajan, R. G., *Fault Lines: How Hidden Fractures Still Threaten the World Economy* (New York: Princeton University Press, 2010)

Reinhart, C. And Rogoff, K. S., *This Time is Different – Eight Centuries of Financial Folly* (New York: Princeton University Press, 2009)

Roth, L. M., *Selling Women Short: gender Inequality on Wall Street* (New York: Princeton University Press, 2006)

Schelling, T.C., *Micromotives and Macrobehavior: Fels Lectures on Public Policy Analysis* (W.W. Norton, 1978)

Shakespeare, W. *King Lear*

Smith, A., *The Theory of Moral Sentiments* (London: Penguin Classics, 2010)

Sorkin, A.R., *Too Big to Fail: Inside the Battle to Save Wall Street* (Penguin, 2010)

Tett, G., *Fool's Gold*

Thompson, V., *Gross Misconduct* (Simon & Schuster, 2010)

Wight, R., *The Day the Pigs Refused to Be Driven to Market: Advertising and the Consumer Revolution* (Random House, 1974)

Wolmar, C. *Fire and Steam: A New History of the Railways in Britain* (Atlantic Books, 2008)

INDEX